BABY'S
FIRST YEAR

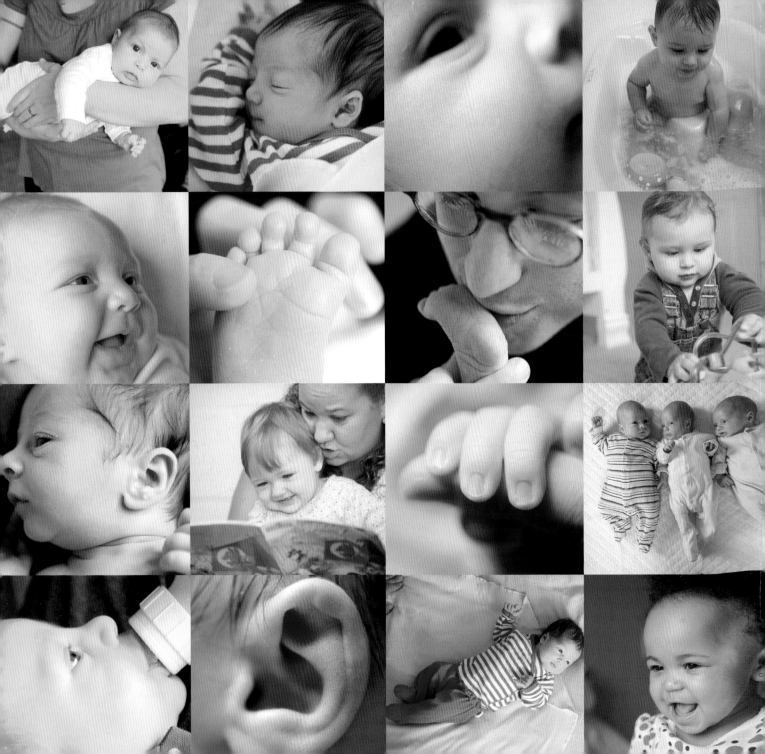

KNACK®

BABY'S
FIRST YEAR

A Complete Illustrated Guide for
Your Child's First Twelve Months

Robin McClure and Vince Iannelli, M.D.

Photographs by Susana Bates

Guilford, Connecticut
An imprint of The Globe Pequot Press

3 0645 11153142

Editor-in-Chief: Maureen Graney
Editor: Imee Curiel
Cover Design: Paul Beatrice, Bret Kerr
Text Design: Paul Beatrice
Layout: Joanna Beyer
Cover photos by Susana Bates
All interior photos by Susana Bates with the exception of p. 40 © Zvonimir Orec/Dreamstime.com, and p. 100 © Eric Isselée/Dreamstime.com

Library of Congress Cataloging-in-Publication Data
McClure, Robin.
  Knack baby's first year : a complete illustrated guide for your child's first twelve months / Robin McClure and Vincent Iannelli ; photographs by Susana Bates.
      p. cm.
  ISBN 978-1-59921-503-7
  1. Infants—Care. 2. Infants—Development. I. Iannelli, Vincent. II. Bates, Susana. III. Title.

HQ774.M438 2009
649'.122—dc22
                                    2009010784

The following manufacturers/names appearing in *Knack Baby's First Year* are trademarks: Cheerios®, Pedialyte®, Band-Aid®, Velcro®, Popsicle®

Printed in China

10 9 8 7 6 5 4 3 2 1

To my beloved husband, Rick, for always telling me that I'm a great mother and loving me as I am; and to my kids, Hunter, Erin, and Connor, for inspiring me every day!

—Robin

For my mother, whom I miss dearly and thought about often during this project. For my father, for whom I am so grateful. And for Thoth.

—Susana

CONTENTS

INTRODUCTION

Most likely you've bought this book while eagerly, and perhaps nervously, anticipating the arrival of a baby. After the news settles in that you're going to be a first-time parent (or perhaps adding to the family), an endless array of questions starts popping into your head over what it is, exactly, that you need to be doing to prepare. That's why parents-to-be are like information sponges—reading books; talking with experienced moms, dads and friends; asking family members about their experiences; and even "test driving" a baby by holding and perhaps feeding one to get a better understanding of what lies ahead. While anyone who has helped raise a baby is quick with advice, usually the specifics are a little vague. It's the useful details you want, and *Baby's First Year* delivers in a photo-rich and no-nonsense format. Congratulations! You're on your way to parenting know-how.

You're expecting: Now what?

Love isn't all you need when raising a baby, although that's a perfect place to start. Babies arrive needing constant care, and whether you are expecting, adopting, becoming a first-time parent, or expanding your family, you need to prepare for baby's arrival.

While soon-to-be parents find it an almost irresistible temptation to purchase precious baby outfits and a fancy crib and changing table that coordinate with a themed nursery, the truth is that your baby won't care about clothes or paint colors. Rather, your wee one will crave attention, comfort, nutrition, and inspiration from his or her greatest fans. While strollers, high chairs, bouncers, toys, bedding and convenience items like diaper holders may be nice to

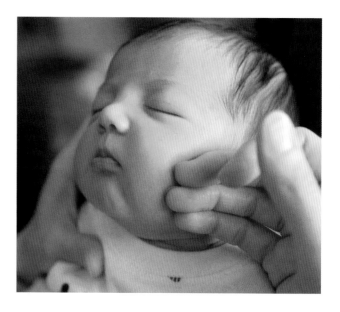

have, they aren't necessities for a newborn. But newborns do require some things, so here is a checklist of essentials to have for when baby comes home.

ZOOM

Just what is a layette anyway? Simply put, it's a newborn's first wardrobe. While those ruffled dresses and infant overalls are adorable, trying to change a newborn's diaper in fancy outfits will undoubtedly teach parents that simple, washable, easy-on-and-off outfits are the rule during the first few months. Resist buying too many items in a single size; you'll be astounded at how quickly baby grows!

What you need for bringing baby home

One going-home-from-the-hospital outfit. Go ahead and dress your newborn in a special outfit for a first picture or keepsake as you take baby home, but be prepared to change baby into comfy clothes after the excitement is over. After all, do newborns really require fancy hats or bonnets, lacy socks, and lace-up shoes?

Seven pairs of socks or several pairs of booties. Look for the types with elastic bands, Velcro wraps, or drawstrings, so that they actually stay on baby's tiny feet!

Four T-shirts. Many parents dress their infant in a T-shirt and diaper when there are no visitors planned and weather permits. Loose T-shirts are best until the umbilical cord stump falls off to avoid irritation and to allow air to help aid with drying.

Four gowns/sleepers. Gowns provide ease in dressing and often include a drawstring at the bottom to keep baby's legs and feet inside for extra warmth.

Seven onesies. These one-piece (hence the name) cotton outfits are considered to be the most practical clothing for newborns. Onesies come in either sleeveless, short-sleeve, or long-sleeve designs and snap at the crotch for ease in changing diapers. Many onesies have matching shorts or long pants as an option for colder weather.

Three coveralls. These are one-piece footed outfits.

Two to four blankets (one of each style minimum). Most parents choose both receiving blankets and swaddling blankets. What's the difference? Swaddling blankets are usually larger in size to make wrapping baby easier while a receiving blanket is used mostly for warmth. A swaddling blanket securely wraps an infant so that movement of limbs is restricted. Newborns may like to be swaddled to give them a greater sense of security in a bound space, like they experienced while in the womb.

Swaddling may help minimize newborns' "startle reflex," in which they jerk and flinch unexpectedly. It also helps to maintain a warm body temperature (although parents need to be careful not to overheat baby). It is only effective for the first few months of a baby's life and not everyone supports the idea behind swaddling, so be sure to check with your baby's pediatrician first.

Cold- or warm-weather attire. Depending on when and where baby is born, you may need a hat, sweater, and bunting (like a baby sleeping bag of sorts) to keep baby warm

outdoors since newborns often don't fit well into jackets. You may also need a hat to protect your baby from the sun.

Fifteen burp cloths. You'll need lots of these! They are readily available in inexpensive packets, or simple white cloth diapers also work well.

Three or more spit bibs. Many babies spit up—a lot—during the first few months, and small bibs can help keep baby dry and comfortable and outfits free of stains.

Baby basics

Stock these essentials ahead of baby's arrival to avoid last-minute scrambles to the store:

Diapers. Since you don't know your newborn's shape and size ahead of time, avoid stocking up on too many diapers. Larger newborns may bypass the smallest size from the get-go, while premature infants may need the teeniest type made. Some newborn diapers feature a cut-out area for the umbilical cord (typically at a higher cost) to avoid irritating the tender area, but parents can also just roll down the waistline and accomplish the same thing. Many hospitals provide a small supply of diapers for new parents to cover the first day or two.

Baby care. Have on hand infant nail clippers, a nasal aspirator, a mercury-free thermometer, and a soft washcloth or sponge, along with baby body wash, lotion, and shampoo.

Pacifier. If you do plan to give your baby a pacifier, buy a couple of varieties and see what your baby prefers.

Bottles and formula (if not breastfeeding). Choose newborn-size bottles, which typically hold about four ounces, and ask your baby's pediatrician which formula he or she recommends. As with pacifiers, your baby may prefer a certain type of nipple.

Infant car seat. A rear-facing car seat should be safely secured in your back seat prior to making the trip to the hospital. A popular choice is an infant carrier, which features a base that stays fastened in the car. The carrier can be snapped into and out of the base in seconds. Infant carriers are usually only for babies under 20 to 30 pounds, so a second car seat may be required before your baby reaches 12 months old. Other parents prefer to get a car seat that adjusts as baby grows, avoiding the need to purchase more than one. Make sure your baby fits securely in his car seat before riding home from the hospital. Of course, you don't need anyone to tell you that it is an absolute no-no to carry a baby in your arms on the trip home.

Baby's bed. While you can use a crib as baby's first bed, many parents elect to use a bassinet or small basket commonly called a "Moses basket" to keep baby in her own room for the first few weeks. Be sure to keep watch of any safety recalls or warnings about baby's bed, and resist using an old

bed without thoroughly checking it out first to make sure it complies with all safety recommendations. Parents expecting twins or multiples can consider crib dividers and other bedding choices to keep newborns close to their siblings while maintaining safety and comfort as priorities.

Changing station. You don't have to have a changing table; many parents who are tight on space utilize a changing pad, while others put a pad down on a bed to get the job done.

Choosing baby's layette and essential items ahead of time will provide you with the peace of mind that you've got everything covered for bringing baby home. Later chapters of *Baby's First Year* discuss gear, clothing, developmental milestones and even entertainment for a growing baby, but a completed essentials checklist means you can shift your focus to learning what to do in terms of actual daily care of your newborn.

Baby care made easy

Baby basics such as feeding, holding, diaper changing, umbilical cord care, dressing, and sleep safety can be a little unnerving . . . but relax! Moms and dads can find comfort that while they may not get it all right the first time (and who does, after all?), caring for a newborn gets easier with practice! The pictures and how-to steps in this book will make the learning curve easier, so that you're saying, "No problem" in no time!

A miraculous transformation lies ahead, from the time you bring home a helpless and often funny-looking newborn who will develop—literally in front of your eyes—into a talking and maybe walking tot over the course of 12 months. In between are magical moments of baby firsts: first laugh, first time to hold up her head, first word, and first kiss. So get set, because ready or not, you're in for the adventure of your life!

BABIES BIG AND SMALL

Babies arrive in all shapes and sizes, ranging from petite to plump

Sonograms let curious parents learn the gender of their baby, but the baby's exact shape and size remain a surprise until birth. Most full-term babies (born between 37 and 40 weeks) weigh somewhere between six and nine pounds. The average length ranges from 19 to 21 inches. But these are just averages. Babies born smaller or lighter or earlier—or by the same token larger or heavier or later—are usually just fine, but may warrant a closer look by the medical team to be sure there are no problems.

Most babies will lose a small amount of weight (5 to 7 percent is considered normal) soon after birth, due to the elimination of excess fluid. If a baby loses too much weight,

Premature or Early Baby

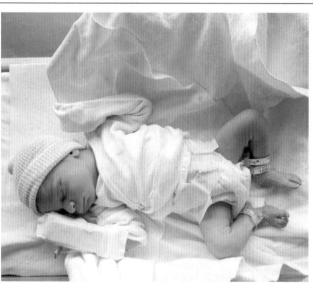

- Babies born before 37 weeks typically debut at a low birth weight. About 1 in every 13 babies is born at less than 5 pounds, 8 ounces.

- A lower birth weight can sometimes be due to a mother's high blood pressure, heart problems, or use of alcohol, cigarettes, or drugs.

- Lower birth weight babies may initially have breathing and feeding issues.

- Premature babies usually receive special medical attention and may spend time in the neonatal intensive care ward until going home.

Petite or Lean

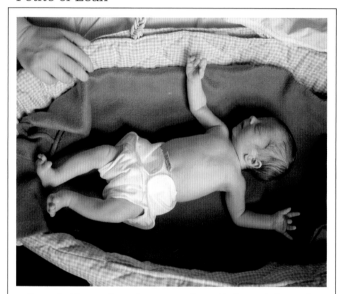

- Some babies are born long and lean—usually the result of genetics of the parents.

- A mother's age, baby's birth order, small parents, gender, and multiples can also impact birth size.

- Since smaller or thin newborns don't have body fat

- found in larger infants, they may have difficulty regulating their body temperature.

- Growth spurts in newborns often occur at seven to ten days and again at six weeks.

however, it could be an indicator of a health concern that requires medical attention. Baby should typically regain birth weight within two weeks.

Weight and size are good indicators of a newborn's health. Your baby's weight and size will be carefully monitored during the first year at checkups. Baby will most likely double his birth weight at three to four months, and triple his birth weight by the time of his first birthday. Baby will also increase his birth length by 50 percent by the end of his first year in most cases.

ZOOM

Most babies receive an Apgar score, which assesses vital signs at one minute and five minutes after birth. This simple scoring process stands for Activity (muscle tone), Pulse (heart rate), Grimace (reflex irritability), Appearance (skin color), and Respiration (breathing), with each quality receiving a rating of 0, 1, or 2. The scores are totaled, with 7 to 10 considered good.

Average-Size Baby

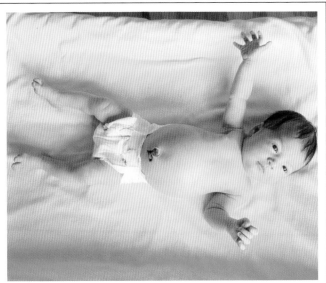

- A baby born right on schedule is most likely to be in the average weight range.

- On-time babies typically have the easiest time feeding, sleeping, and adjusting to life outside the womb.

- Proper nutrition and health of the mom, along with proper weight gain, increase the likelihood of having an average-size baby at birth.

- Being small, average, or large at birth doesn't necessarily relate to future size as a child or adult.

Big Baby

- Babies who are born past their due date may debut at a larger birth weight and with ample body fat.

- Genetics can play a part in birth weight.

- Excessive weight gain by a mother during pregnancy can contribute to baby's size.

- Gestational diabetes is the most common cause of large babies.

- A larger size may mean a more difficult birth.

NEWBORN SKIN

From translucent to red and dry, newborns' skin type varies by gestational age

Immediately after birth, a newborn's skin typically appears as dark red or purplish in color. As baby begins to breathe air, skin tone changes to red and then to a healthy pink. Hands and feet, however, may remain a bluish color for several days or even longer due to a newborn's immature blood circulation.

A newborn's cries can turn a baby's lips, mouth, or even entire face a purple tint, but normal color will return when baby calms down. If the baby's coloring remains a bluish hue, however, the medical team will take a closer look at baby's breathing and heart functions.

Milia

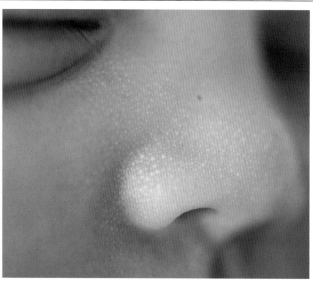

- Milia are tiny white bumps or small cysts, often called "baby acne" (although it is not really a true form of acne).

- Milia are most commonly seen across a newborn's nose, upper cheeks, and chin area.

- Similar white bumps can occasionally be seen on newborn gums and roof of mouth, and are called Epstein's pearls.

- Milia are painless, do not require treatment, and will go away on their own.

Birthmarks

- Newborns may have birthmarks. Most will fade without treatment; others are permanent.

- Salmon patches, nicknamed "stork bites," are the most common birthmark. They usually appear on the nose, forehead, eyelids, or back of head or neck. They usually disappear within the first few months.

- Bruise-like areas on baby's back or bottom, called Mongolian spots, usually disappear in childhood.

- Port wine stains, caused by extra blood vessels under the skin, can sometimes be removed later.

Many babies make their debut with a white, greasy, cheesy coating of substance called vernix over some or all of their body. Vernix is thought to protect baby's skin from dehydration due to constant exposure to amniotic fluid. It may also protect baby's skin during the difficult journey down the birth canal. After birth, it is simply wiped or washed off.

Some babies, especially ones who make an early entrance, are also born with soft, fine prenatal hair called lanugo over much of their bodies. Lanugo insulates the skin, since most babies lack body fat. It is usually shed at full term or shortly after delivery.

Scratches or Marks

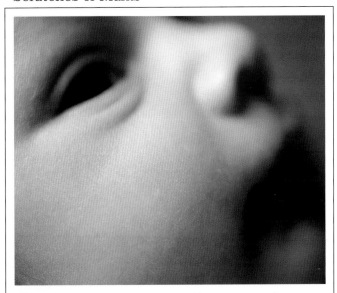

- Parents need to be careful with their own fingernails and jewelry to avoid inadvertently scratching baby's delicate skin.

- Babies sometimes scratch themselves with their fingernails while in the womb.

- If forceps are used in delivery, a baby may have marks or even light scrapes on the face and head areas where the tool was pressed against the skin.

- After a vacuum-assisted birth, temporary scrapes or marks may appear on the top of baby's head.

Dry Skin or Rashes

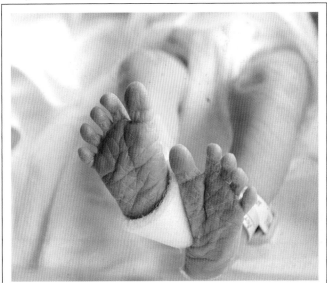

- Babies born late or at term may arrive with dry, cracked skin. Doctors may recommend lotion products to add moisture back and lessen any skin discomfort. Skin may actually peel.

- Most skin conditions will go away without any treatment needed.

- Some babies have red blotches, mottling, or rash-like red bumps when they are born.

- Occasionally, babies are born with blisters (usually on fingers or hand area) from a fetus's suckling while in the womb.

WHAT NEWBORNS LOOK LIKE
Adorable is in the eye of beholder when babies make their debut

Of course your newborn is adorable—what baby isn't? Truth is, after being squeezed through the birth canal, many babies make their entrance looking a little odd, old, and certainly different than the bright-eyed, clear-skinned, and chubby-cheeked cherubs you see in pictures. A newborn's beauty is truly in the eye of the beholder.

Funny-shaped heads and puffy faces with bloated facial features are just for starters. But don't worry! These traits are temporary and will likely go away within a few days, although certain cases may require medication or other treatment.

Regardless of how they were delivered, newborns arrive with disproportionately large heads. A newborn's head is

Newborn Head Shapes

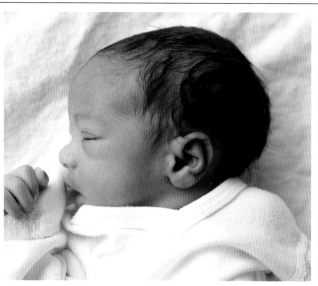

- Pressure while going head-first through the birth canal during childbirth results in many newborns having cone-shaped (oblong) heads. A temporary overlapping of the skull bones is possible.

- Baby's head shape typically returns to normal after a few days.

- Fluid or blood may collect in the scalp area, further altering the head's shape. A small amount of scalp bleeding may occur.

- Babies born in a breech (feet first) position or through cesarean section have normal-shaped heads.

Facial Features

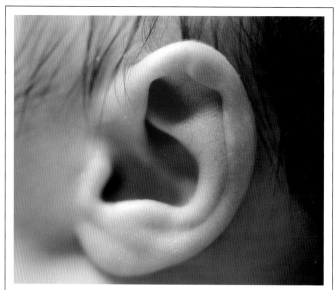

- Since the thick cartilage hasn't yet developed, baby's ears may be temporarily folded or misshapen.

- The stress of childbirth often takes a short-term toll on baby's facial features, with puffy features being common.

- Eyelids may be swollen, and eyes may appear blood-shot with small red specks. The white part may even appear blood-red, a harmless condition that occurs when blood leaks under the covering of the eyeball.

- Nose may seem squished and lips will appear pink.

about one-fourth of the body surface area. Newborns' neck muscles aren't yet strong enough to hold up their heads, which is why parents must pay extra attention to supporting the head and neck areas.

Baby's head circumference is usually measured within the first few hours of birth. While head size may simply be due to genetics, a small or large measurement may warrant further medical review. Baby's head circumference will continue to be measured at well-child checkups throughout the first year.

Baby's Soft Spots

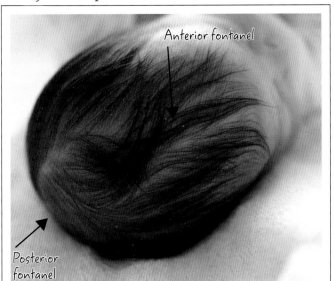

Anterior fontanel

Posterior fontanel

- Fontanels are the two soft spots on your newborn's head. They allow the head to change shape to pass through the birth canal.

- The smaller soft spot is located at the back of the head, is triangular shaped, is difficult to feel, and typically closes by around six weeks of age.

- The larger soft spot is located on the top of the head, is kite-shaped, can be easily felt, and closes by eighteen months.

- No special care is needed.

Positional Molding

Newborns' heads can become flat or lop-sided from spending time on their backs. You can encourage proper head shape by:

- Holding your baby to help relieve pressure.

- Changing body positions and alternating the direction your baby's head faces or repositioning baby's head while in an infant seat.

- Encouraging baby to track movements or sound and providing visual interest.

MULTIPLES

Mother's age, infertility treatments are main reasons multiple-order births are on the rise

The number of multiple births has risen dramatically over the last 25 years. Studies have indicated that twin births have risen by 70 percent since 1980 and the number of births involving three or more babies has quadrupled. Couples who may have opted to delay becoming parents may suddenly find themselves with a ready-made family of multiples. Why?

Heredity and race have traditionally been factors in the development of multiples. A history of multiple births on the woman's side of the family increases her chances of having multiples. Women of African heritage also have a greater chance of giving birth to multiples. More recent trends in women waiting until an older age to become pregnant and

KNACK BABY'S FIRST YEAR

Fraternal Twins

- Fraternal twins are much more common than identical twins, and tend to run in families.

- Fraternal twins come from two separate eggs that are fertilized. The babies may or may not look alike. Multiples conceived through assisted reproduc-

tion treatments are typically fraternal.

- Twins (fraternal or identical) are typically born two to four weeks early.

- Of all multiples, twins normally face the fewest medical problems and complications.

Identical Twins

- Identical twins result from a single fertilized egg, which divides in half and develops two separate but identical babies. Identical twins are thought to develop at random and not due to genetics or age.

- Identical twins are genetically identical, with the same

chromosomes and similar (but not always exact) physical characteristics.

- Identical twins are the same sex, and have the same blood type, hair color, body build, skin, and eye color.

- Fingerprints of identical twins are unique.

the technological advancements in infertility treatments, however, are most responsible for the staggering spike in multiple births.

Women who become pregnant naturally at an older age are more likely to have multiples (some suggest because the body is more likely to release more than one egg during a cycle as a woman's egg supply is diminishing).

Medical advancements and improved health care have enabled babies previously at high risk not only to survive but thrive.

Triplets

- Triplet births are considered high-risk pregnancies, with the babies' newborn weight typically only half that of a single baby.

- Health considerations may include respiratory problems, hearing and vision impairment, heart defects, and developmental delays.

- Triplets are typically born three to six weeks early.

- Any number of babies beyond twins are commonly referenced as "super twins." They may be identical, fraternal, or a combination of both.

YELLOW LIGHT

Pre-term labor is the biggest risk of birthing multiples. A single pregnancy lasts about 40 weeks, but half of all twins are born prematurely (before 37 weeks of gestational age). Higher-order multiple births are even earlier, and as a result, greater health risks may occur. Mothers carrying more than one child will receive extra medical attention during pregnancy and will be checked regularly for fetal growth, placental concerns, and overall health.

Quads, Quints, and More

- Medical advancements have made high multiple pregnancies more successful.

- Multiples are typically delivered around 30 to 32 weeks of age if the pregnancy can be sustained that long.

- Multiple-order pregnancies of four or more have the greatest risk of long-term disabilities.

- Some multiple pregnancies are the result of two fertilized eggs splitting, resulting in two sets of identical twins.

UNIQUE NEWBORN FEATURES

Sonograms don't answer all the questions about newborn features, such as hair color

Babies develop within a really tight space in the womb, so it should come as no surprise that they arrive being more comfortable tucked in a fetal position. It will take some adjustment to learn how to stretch out those arms and legs, but soon enough they'll relish the extra movement. Babies also need time to adjust to sights and sounds, and may react strongly to a phone ringing or the sun shining on their faces. These instinctive survival reflexes will disappear gradually as baby matures. Babies may also literally tremble or shake due to their still-developing nervous systems, especially if they are crying or upset.

Genitals may appear overly large at birth, but it's perfectly

Hair or Bald?

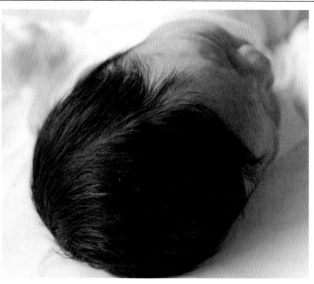

- Some babies are born bald, and stay that way their first year. Others debut with a full head of hair.

- Most newborn hair falls out, and the hair that replaces it may be different in color and texture.

- If you and your partner were born with hair, chances are your baby will be too. Genetics play a key role.

- Babies often rub the hair off the backs of their heads, creating bald spots.

Arms and Legs

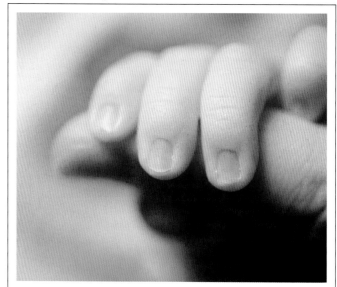

- Hands are usually tightly closed, and can be difficult to pry open.

- Feet may appear to be pigeon-toed (rotating inward). This is due to being curled up, but feet and legs will rotate to a straighter position as baby ages.

- Newborns may appear to be "frog-legged," with legs curving inward.

- Newborns may appear to have flat feet, but arches are there under the extra layer of fat that babies have, and will appear in time.

normal and is due to swelling. A swollen scrotum in boys, labia in girls, and enlarged breasts in either sex may be attributed to the extra fluid in their bodies—which they will lose over the first few days—or to maternal hormones they have in their systems temporarily.

Breathing may also appear to be somewhat irregular, with varied breathing rates and breaths. Many infants also sneeze, hiccup, and even squeak a lot. These are considered normal characteristics of newborns. If in doubt about what's normal, always feel free to ask your pediatrician.

Neck, Chest, and Abdomen

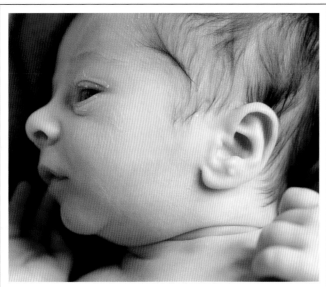

- Newborn necks look short, but only because they get lost in the swelling and folds of skin.

- The chest wall appears thin, and the upper chest will move with each heartbeat.

- The abdomen may appear somewhat rounded or "full" in appearance.

- Parents may notice that the skin over the middle abdominal area may protrude slightly when baby cries or strains. This condition should disappear in a few months.

Instinctive Responses

- Babies are born with survival reflexes and instinctive responses.

- A sucking reflex can be seen by stroking an infant's cheek or putting any object near the mouth.

- A startle response (also called a Moro reflex), is when infants suddenly throw out their arms and legs and then quickly tuck them close to the body. This is usually caused by a loud noise or bright light.

- A strong grasp reflex causes a newborn to tightly close the fingers.

UMBILICAL CORD STUMP

Navel area care involves little more than keeping area clean, dry, and chafe-free

The umbilical cord connects the developing baby to the placenta and serves as baby's lifeline for nutrition and oxygen until delivery. After birth, baby no longer needs his umbilical cord. The doctor or midwife clamps or ties off the jelly-like substance that encases one vein and two arteries, which is then cut, often symbolically by a parent. Because the umbilical cord contains no nerves, the cutting is painless for baby. A nurse may swab the cord with a dye or antiseptic to prevent infection and place a plastic clip on it until the cord area remaining has sealed and dried sufficiently. The umbilical cord stump that remains dries up and eventually falls off, much like a scab on the skin, requiring only basic care. This

Cleaning the Stump

- Opinions vary as to whether the stump area should be cleaned with rubbing alcohol or simply air-dried. Ask your baby's pediatrician for recommended treatment.

- If cleaning with alcohol is recommended, use a cotton swab or small gauze pad dipped in rubbing alcohol to wipe around the base of the stump once or twice a day.

- Some oozing of fluid or traces of blood around the stump area is normal.

- Do not immerse baby in water while the cord stump is still attached because moisture can increase the risk of infection.

Comfy and Dry

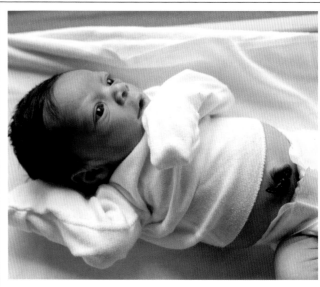

- Keep baby's diaper and clothing away from the umbilical cord area until it has dried.

- Many newborn diaper styles have a notched umbilical cord area to eliminate chafing; if not, simply fold down baby's diaper around the navel.

- Air circulation helps the healing process; if it's warm, let baby just wear a T-shirt and diaper.

- Avoid dressing baby in onesie-style sleepers or gowns until the cord has fallen off.

usually occurs between 10 and 21 days after birth.

Parents today also have the options of either donating their baby's cord blood (at no cost to them, much like donating blood through a blood drive) or privately banking their newborn's umbilical cord blood, for which there is a collection and ongoing storage cost. Stem cells found in the umbilical cord can be used to help treat, repair, and even cure some cancers, blood diseases and inherited disorders. Since this decision must be made prior to childbirth, parents will need to research this choice ahead of time to learn more.

ZOOM

An umbilical hernia, which is a bulge caused by the umbilical cord as it enters baby's abdomen, is not the same thing as an "outie" belly button. Although most umbilical hernias go away on their own, if they don't disappear by the time a child is four or five years old, they are usually surgically repaired. An "outie" is just a variation of a normal belly button.

Stages of Drying

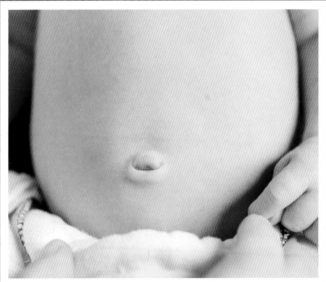

- The umbilical cord stump will change colors as it dries, going from yellow to brown to black.

- The stump may begin to lift on one side. Do not pull it off; it will fall off when dry.

- A slight odor from the area is normal.

- If fleshy granules remain in the navel after the stump has fallen off, ask your child's pediatrician whether any further treatment is recommended.

Signs of Infection

Check with your baby's pediatrician if you notice any of the following signs that your baby's umbilical cord stump area could be infected:

- Pus or bloody discharge appears at the base of the stump area.

- Baby's navel and surrounding area are red or look swollen.

- The area emits a strong, foul odor.

- Your baby develops a fever.

FOR DADS
Dad can quickly get to know and bond with his new baby

The quick pace of a delivery room can often leave a dad struggling to find his place. He usually wants to be helpful, but doesn't want to get in the way. Many dads have the same feelings once their baby is born, which is unfortunate, since dads shouldn't be afraid to share in the experience of their baby's birth.

How can you make sure you have a great experience, don't get overwhelmed, and don't make things more stressful for everyone else around you, especially mom? One sure way is to attend as many doctor visits during your partner's pregnancy as possible. You should also be supportive and helpful, attend birthing classes, visit the

Congratulations, You're a Dad!

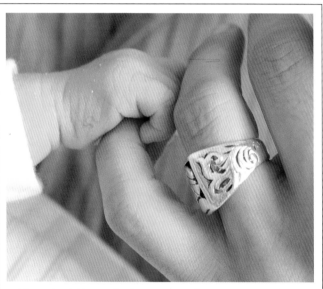

- Mom should breastfeed as soon as possible after the baby is born, but don't worry, you'll have plenty of time to hold your baby.

- Be prepared for the unexpected. Read or learn about situations that may arise, such as baby needing to go

- to the NICU (neonatal intensive care unit).

- It may take some time for it to kick in that you're a dad, but the feeling can be overwhelming when it hits.

Your New Baby

- Learn some basic baby care before you leave the hospital, such as how to swaddle, burp, and change your baby.

- Your baby isn't as delicate as you think, but his head and neck still need careful support.

- Many surprising things you will notice, such as peeling skin, hiccups, and gas, are normal at this age.

- Be sure your home is well babyproofed before you bring your baby home.

hospital where your baby will be born, and help create a birth plan.

While you may want to leave some things to mom, there are other things on which you can take the lead. Baby-proofing the house is a good example, including installing smoke alarms and carbon monoxide detectors, setting the water heater to 120 degrees Fahrenheit, and installing your baby's crib and car seat correctly.

Bonding with Your Baby

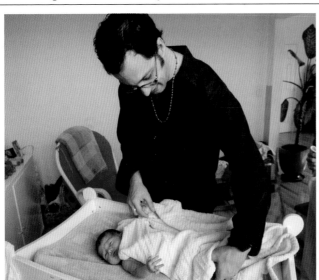

- Giving your baby a bath and spending time doing other day-to-day baby care are great ways to bond with your new baby.

- Your baby can see your face when you hold him close, but can't yet focus on things much farther away.

- Read, sing, or simply talk to your baby to encourage bonding.

- Ask for help if you don't feel comfortable holding, carrying, or picking up your baby.

Finding your Role

- In addition to spending time with your baby, a great early role for dad can be taking over household responsibilities and letting mom bond with her newborn baby.

- Although dads can't breastfeed, they can still help with feedings by bringing baby to mom and changing baby after feedings.

- Develop a good balance between work and family life.

- Don't forget to ask your partner what she thinks your role should be.

13

GETTING BABY HOME

Choose and install car safety seat ahead of time for stress-free ride home

Preparation is the key to making the transition between hospital and home easy and stress-free. No doubt a layette and baby's first bed are set up and waiting. At the same time, baby's first car seat should already be purchased, installed, and inspected so all parents have to do is open up the car door, carefully load in baby, adjust the safety harnesses, and be on their way.

Regardless of how much a car seat costs or its comfort features, even the highest-quality model may not protect your baby in a crash if used improperly. While fabric and color choices are considerations, be sure to read carefully about safety ratings, any recalls or advisories, and recommendations before purchasing a car seat. If possible, avoid used car

Before Using Baby's Car Seat

- If using an infant carrier–car seat combo (in which the carrier snaps into a car base), practice loading and unloading it. Know how it operates.

- Inspect carrier handle and make sure there are no cracks and that it performs as designed.

- Know how to properly adjust all safety harnesses and tethers.

- Many community groups offer free car seat safety inspections. See if a safety check is available in your area.

Placing Baby in Car

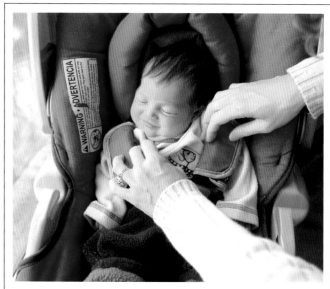

- Infant car seats must always be rear facing until a baby is at least 1 year old and 20 pounds.

- Rear-facing car seats help protect babies from spinal cord injuries and whiplash motions in a crash.

- The safest place for children to ride is the backseat. Never place baby in the front seat of a vehicle with an air bag.

- Make sure to protect baby's head from accidental bumps or scrapes when loading and unloading.

seats and invest in a new one, which should be manufactured using the latest safety standards. Parents can choose between infant car seats that will safely accommodate a baby up to 30 pounds, or convertible models that adjust and change to accommodate a baby's growth. Some carriers also snap into a car base or stroller for added convenience. Be sure the car seat you select fits correctly in your vehicle. Not all car seats fit all vehicles due to backseat designs and available space.

Plan ahead for baby's comfort on long car rides by dressing her in layers and in soft "breathable" fabrics. Avoid too-big clothing that can bunch up and scratchy embellishments.

Car Seat Comfort

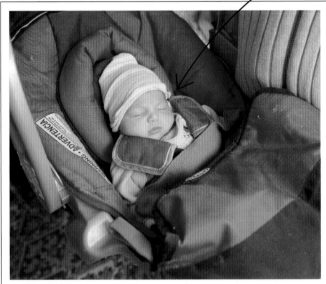

- Newborns lack neck muscle strength, often resulting in their heads wobbling to the side or falling forward. Make sure baby's head and neck are properly supported.

- Position harness straps at or below baby's shoulders. Padded strap covers can provide additional comfort.

- Keep a light blanket and hat in the car for baby, but be careful of overheating.

- Since sunshine streaming through car windows can agitate baby, consider a car seat sun shield or similar shade product.

LATCH Safety System

- Look for LATCH (Lower Anchors and Tethers for Children), an attachment system that eliminates using the seat belt.

- Vehicles with LATCH have anchors in the backseat. Car seats with LATCH have attachments that fasten to these anchors.

- Most vehicles and all car safety seats made after September 1, 2002, feature LATCH.

- Unless both your vehicle and car seat have this system, seat belts must be used.

15

HOLDING BABY

These tried-and-true positions help ensure proper head and neck support, safety, and comfort

Holding a newborn can be intimidating—especially if you have never held a baby before. Newborns flop, flail, and squirm, in part due to their lack of muscle tone. They also startle and jerk easily, and you may worry about dropping your infant or whether he's comfortable. When your baby is crying, you may feel insecure about whether you are holding baby correctly. Relax. Holding a baby is easy once you get the hang of it and become more comfortable. Then, you won't even remember what all the fuss was about.

Newborns may exhibit strong preferences for how they are held, so if baby starts to fuss while being held one way, try another. Don't be afraid to experiment and see what works

Cradle Hold

- Hold your baby faceup with head positioned in the crook of your preferred arm for support and elbow bent slightly.

- Secure the small of baby's back with the lower part of your arm. Use your free arm to provide additional support where needed.

- This hold allows baby to curl up in a familiar fetal position.

- The easy cradle hold can be used while seated or standing, and is a good hold for feeding baby as well.

Shoulder Hold

- This is a favorite cuddle hold and feels very natural.

- Place baby up on one shoulder (use a burp rag under baby's head) and wrap the arm on that side around baby's bottom. Use your other arm to support baby's neck and back.

- If seated, lean back slightly and baby should contentedly sleep in this position.

- This hold allows you and your baby to hear each other's heartbeat and breathing.

best for both of you. Also, if your baby begins to cry when you are holding her while sitting down, try standing up. Many babies prefer to be held while you are standing up and moving around. Since constant motion can calm infants, find ways to easily and safely create movement with your body. While seated or standing, try holding your baby while softly swaying from side to side or slightly rocking forward and backward with your arms. Consider walking with a slight bounce in your step.

. . . . YELLOW ● LIGHT . . . .

Babies may not weigh much, but many new parents develop back pain from holding their babies. Keep ergonomics in mind when picking up your baby by bending your knees and not your back. When standing up while holding baby, keep legs slightly bent. Use pillows to support your arms while holding baby while seated and use care when carrying a diaper bag or carrying baby in an infant carrier.

Belly Hold

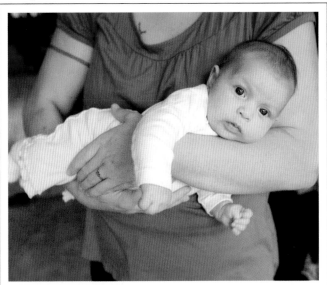

- Place baby facedown over one of your forearms, with head either cradled in the crook of your elbow or in your hand. Baby's legs can drape to either side of your arm.

- Try this hold first while seated with baby across your lap.

- Babies may be calmed by gently rocking your arms back and forth.

- Gassy or hard-to-burp babies may get relief from this hold.

Hip Hold

- This is a favorite on-the-go hold for older babies who have developed head and neck control.

- The hip hold allows one hand to be free while the other securely holds baby.

- Position baby on your favored hip bone facing outward and wrap the arm on that same side around baby's waist area.

- This hold allows baby a chance to be upright and look around while you are on the move.

INTERACTING WITH BABY

Bonding through touch, eye contact, and speech is essential for baby's growth and development

Bonding is the natural attachment that normally develops between parents and their baby. This strong and sometimes overpowering emotion is what drives parents to protect their offspring, as well as to nurture, feed, and respond to a newborn's every need. Newborns bond with their parents by using their senses—especially sight, hearing, and smell.

Bonding is essential for babies to thrive and develop.

Typical day-to-day parental interaction is the easiest way to form a strong attachment to your baby. Share tender moments by holding and touching your baby, through eye contact, and by talking or singing. Baby kisses, caressing, rocking, snuggling, and gazing at baby during feedings, help

How Babies Bond

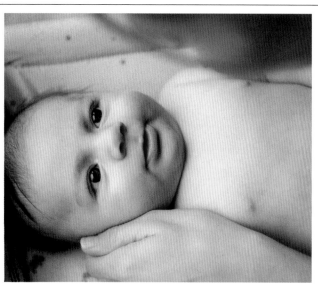

- Close-up eye contact helps foster closeness, and babies will follow their parents with their eyes.

- Most infants are ready to interact with their parents immediately after birth and are comforted by being held or touched.

- Premature babies or those placed in intensive care with medical needs may grow and function better through extended bonding times with parents.

- Babies quickly learn where their food source is and how to communicate when hungry.

The Magic Touch

- Get to know one another by gently caressing baby's skin in a calm and soothing manner.

- Gently applying baby lotion to arms, legs, face, stomach, and back is comforting and reassuring.

- Parents can stroke baby's head and face while snuggling. Recline slightly in a chair and place baby on your chest where you can see one another and touch baby's cheeks, nose, head, hair, neck, and even ears.

- Gentle infant massage promotes bonding.

affirm that ever-important connection. Parents may not know they are bonding, but they will certainly realize it when baby rocks their world!

Bonding may come easiest for moms who breastfeed or have primary bottle-feeding responsibilities. Dads, however, should play an equal role in interacting with baby and developing a loving bond. Fathers may have a different schedule, but should make it a priority to be an integral part of an infant's early life. Parents and baby benefit most when loving infant interactions are a shared family experience.

Use Your Voice

- Talk out loud whenever baby is awake, even if the two of you are alone. Converse with baby about everything that is on your mind. He may not understand, but he is certainly listening!

- Many newborns react better to higher-pitched voices, so for dads and anyone with a booming voice, try talking higher and softer.

- There's nothing wrong with using baby talk as a way to engage a newborn.

- Babies may try to vocalize—their first attempts at communication.

Ways to Play

- "Itsy-Bitsy Spider" and "Ten Little Piggies" games are ideal because they involve touching, eye contact, and singsong words. Your newborn won't yet giggle, but may respond.

- Gently uncurl baby's fingers and place your hands together, palm to palm.

- Hum whenever you change or feed your newborn as a way to connect.

- Place baby on your chest and breathe in tandem.

VISITORS AND FAMILY

Showing off baby while establishing a new routine and getting rest requires balance

Friends and family will want to see your new arrival as soon as possible. Part of the fun of being a new parent is introducing your wee one to others. It can be stressful at times as well, especially if the doorbell or telephone rings just when you've put baby down for a nap or are about to catch up on some much-needed rest.

If possible, establish your new family routine before having lots of visitors over to your home. By delaying visits, you can learn when your baby is most likely to be alert and content. Remember that being woken up and held by numerous strangers can be unsettling to baby and can delay the establishment of the solid wake-eat-sleep routine that you'll soon be craving.

Introducing Family to Baby

- Siblings will want to hold the newest family member as soon as possible, and parents should make sure it is a positive and rewarding experience.

- Establish safety rules about how young siblings should never pick up or hold baby without your approval and presence.

- Give siblings tasks like covering baby with a blanket so they feel like helpers. Children want to feel important.

- Give your children extra love and attention. Jealousy of baby is normal.

When Visitors Arrive

- Keep in mind that sudden noises and loud voices may frighten a newborn, so keep greetings calm and low-key.

- Have visitors touch baby, speak, and maintain eye contact (although baby may be asleep) as a first introduction.

- Turn off cell phones and avoid having older kids play with loud toys, or else you may end up with a shrieking baby.

- Keep hand sanitizer nearby. Guests will get the hint.

Set a schedule for baby's show-off times, and try to keep to it. Don't worry about having a clean house or snacks; visitors really don't expect it and the focus will be on baby. Don't hesitate to ask parents with young children if they are healthy (no colds or other illnesses, please!) and ask guests to wash their hands carefully before touching your newborn. Baby's immune system is not yet strong, and the last thing new parents need is a sick newborn.

YELLOW ●LIGHT

It may not be love at first sniff when it comes to your pet meeting baby. Introduce them with care. Let your pet explore baby's room before baby is born. Provide blankets or clothes with baby's smell for your pet to sniff before the actual introduction takes place. Shower your pet with plenty of love. Never leave your pet alone with baby, even if introductions went well.

Handing Off Baby

- Handing off baby may result in a jerking or startling reflex, as some are uncomfortable with the sudden movement.

- A swaddled baby may be most comfortable being handed off to others.

- It's best for visitors to hold baby while seated.

- Offer a pillow for people to place on their laps for additional comfort.

What Visitors Want

- Many visitors want a close-up inspection. Let them look over baby (fingers and toes are favorites) while safely seated.

- Provide quality time for grandparents and other family members to snuggle and caress baby.

- If guests offer to help in some way, let them! Parenting is hard work.

- Many family members and visitors want to feed baby. If the time is right, place baby in their arms while seated and give them the bottle and a rag.

BABY SLEEP SAFETY

Place baby on his back in a bed free from toys, pillows, and blankets

A newborn may spend most of his or her first month sleeping. Your baby may sleep about 16 hours a day, typically 3 to 4 hours at a time. As babies mature, the amount of time they remain awake will increase. This sleep regimen may influence where babies sleep when they are first born.

Safety should always be kept in mind when putting baby down to sleep. Do not place anything in a newborn's bed that could interfere with breathing. No-no items include cuddly toys or stuffed animals, pillows, blankets, and even crib bumpers (which are often sold in bedding sets but shouldn't be used with newborns). Make sure that baby's bed is free from any sharp edges or corners, ties or cords, or items that can

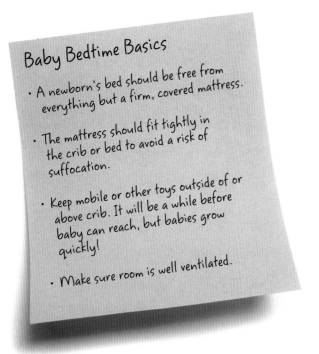

Baby Bedtime Basics

- A newborn's bed should be free from everything but a firm, covered mattress.

- The mattress should fit tightly in the crib or bed to avoid a risk of suffocation.

- Keep mobile or other toys outside of or above crib. It will be a while before baby can reach, but babies grow quickly!

- Make sure room is well ventilated.

Safety Checkup

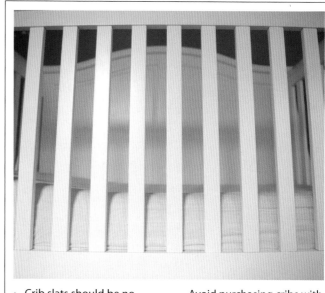

- Crib slats should be no more than 2⅜ inches apart. Inspect slats for loose, missing or cracked pieces.

- Double-check that baby's bed is installed correctly, and look for any exposed or improperly fitting hardware.

- Avoid purchasing cribs with cut-out designs to eliminate risk of baby getting trapped.

- Steer away from cribs with corner posts or knobs higher than 1/16 of an inch to avoid risk of baby's clothing getting caught on them.

become detached. Check that the bed complies with current safety guidelines. Be sure that baby sleeps on a firm and level sleeping surface to avoid the chance of accidentally rolling and getting trapped against a surface.

Babies should always be placed on their backs to sleep, not on their stomachs. Make sure there is plenty of ventilation in baby's room (a recent study suggested using a fan in baby's room). Placing babies on their backs decreases the chance of suffocation or re-breathing their own carbon dioxide.

Safe Sleep Time

- Dress baby in temperature-appropriate clothes or swaddle a newborn instead of using a blanket. Blankets can be used with supervision or when baby is at least 6 months of age.

- Install a night-light for your middle-of-the-night wakeup calls in baby's sleep area.

- While baby can be placed in your bed for comfort or to nurse, most doctors recommend that infants sleep in their own bed.

- Putting baby's first bed in the parents' room provides convenience for late-night feedings and greater peace of mind.

SIDS Awareness

- Sudden infant death syndrome (SIDS) tragically claims the lives of about 2,500 infants each year in the United States, and the reason remains a mystery.

- Infants age two to four months are at greatest risk of SIDS.

- SIDS strikes without warning and in seemingly healthy newborns.

- Most occurrences are associated with sleep. Placing babies on their backs to sleep has reduced deaths.

BABY'S BED

Ample choices provide plenty of designs, colors, and options for baby's first bed

Baby's bed is perhaps the most exciting purchase new parents make, because setting up space for a newborn makes the end result of pregnancy more realistic. Many families create a complete nursery with crib and furniture from the get-go, and a crib can safely hold baby until he is old enough for a toddler bed. Convertible crib-to-bed models even take a

child all the way from newborn to teen.

A majority of parents may opt for keeping baby in their bedroom for the first few months of a newborn's life, however, and a crib may be impractical due to its size. There are many newborn bed options to choose from that are both safe and comfortable for baby and easy for parents to pick

Moses Baskets

- These are portable baskets typically made of wicker or straw, and are so named because baby Moses was placed in a bed of similar design.

- The basket typically includes a snug-fitting mattress, pad, and basket liner.

- These newborn-size baskets are great for keeping baby close at hand or when on the go. They can be used later for toys and supplies.

- Avoid baskets with plush fabric, loose-fitting bumpers, or pillows. Remember safety first.

Bassinets and Cradles

- Bassinets and cradles are essentially the same furniture.

- The key difference is that a cradle is designed to rock back and forth while a bassinet is stationary.

- Both are harder to move around than a Moses

basket, but more portable than a crib. If casters are featured, make sure they lock in place.

- Make sure the bassinet features a wide base to avoid tipping over, especially when young children grab onto sides to peer in.

up and move, depending on desired location of baby. While babies will quickly outgrow these first beds, they offer flexibility and convenience.

Regardless of baby bed preference, parents need to do their research on federal safety standards. While you may want to use a hand-me-down crib for nostalgic purposes or to save money, chances are that unless it was purchased after the late 1990s, the crib may not comply with the latest safety regulations. Keep in mind that use and storage may also have damaged the crib.

Cribs

- Bumper pads should be avoided. If using one, make sure it fits snugly and isn't too puffy. Remove the bumper when your baby is old enough to stand.

- Many cribs allow for different mattress heights that can be adjusted as baby grows.

- Cribs should feature a railing that can be easily raised and lowered. Make sure the dropdown locking mechanism works properly.

- Make sure the crib never wobbles or shakes—a sign of inferior craftsmanship or improper construction.

GREEN ● LIGHT

It's not hard to find eco-friendly baby bedding items. More stores are stocking organic cotton bedding and nursery fixtures, including fitted sheets, mattress pads, mobiles, diaper stackers, and burp rags. Consider green mattresses made from materials like organic wool or rubber, which meet federal safety standards. Baby beds made from solid hardwoods limit baby's exposure to chemicals like formaldehyde, which are more common in laminated, pressed, or particle board.

Co-sleeping

- While safety experts advise against co-sleeping arrangements with infants due to increased risk of suffocation or the baby being rolled on, some families still choose this option.

- Research risks carefully before choosing a family bed.

- If you want to sleep with your infant, consider a style of infant bed that is like a sidecar attached to parents' bed. This provides the advantages of sleeping together while keeping baby safe.

25

HEALTH

Baby will get checked out from head to toe frequently during the first year

You'll make several trips to your child's pediatrician for well-child exams throughout the first year when baby's growth and development are most rapid. While schedules may vary, most pediatricians would prefer to see your healthy newborn in the hospital, then again within a few days, and at two weeks. Subsequent well-child visits occur around two

months, four months, six months, nine months, and one year. Babies with any health concerns will be seen more often.

What happens at each checkup? You'll need to undress baby so the doctor can carefully examine your newborn's overall health. You'll also be asked about how baby is adjusting, eating, and sleeping; your newborn's overall temperament; and

Eyes, Ears, and Mouth

- The doctor will look for blocked tear ducts, eye discharge, and crossing of the eyes. Baby should be able to focus on objects 8 to 12 inches away within the first month.

- Baby's ears will be checked for fluid or infection and overall shape.

- Baby's sucking reflex and overall mouth structure will be examined.

- A look inside baby's mouth can detect oral thrush, a common and easily treated yeast infection.

Abdomen and Extremities

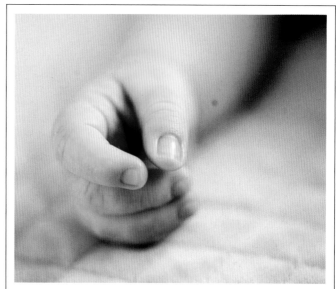

- The doctor will press baby's abdomen to detect tenderness, enlarged organs, or hernia.

- A hernia is the protrusion of an organ through the lining that normally contains it. Some newborns have umbilical hernias, where intestine or tissue near the navel extends through the abdominal wall. Most repair on their own.

- The doctor will move baby's legs to check hip ligaments and joints. Muscle tone will also be reviewed.

- Feet and hands will be checked for proper shape.

even the number of diaper changes each day. The doctor will examine a newborn's umbilical cord stump to make sure it is drying properly. Male newborns will have a quick check to make sure both testicles have descended properly, and if circumcision was performed, whether it is healing correctly.

These frequent doctor visits are a prime opportunity for parents to ask questions about their baby's health and vaccine safety, so make a list ahead of time to get concerns or questions addressed.

ZOOM

Choose your baby's doctor before birth, if possible. First determine which pediatricians are in your area and whether they accept your insurance. Research options and ask friends who they use. Visit the office you are considering and request a quick meeting with the pediatrician. Let the doctor's office you choose know your decision, your due date, and where you plan to deliver.

Heart and Lungs

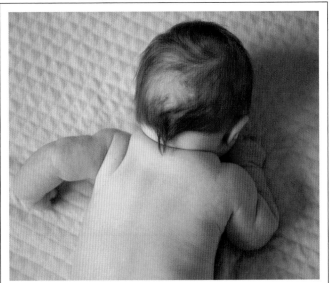

- The doctor will listen to baby's heart for irregular rhythms or sounds. Heart murmurs are fairly common in infants and are rarely a concern, as most babies outgrow them.

- Baby's lungs will also be checked for breathing difficulties.

- Premature or low-birth-weight babies are at greater risk of respiratory distress and apnea (meaning baby stops breathing temporarily).

- Keep newborns away from pollutants, irritants, and smoke.

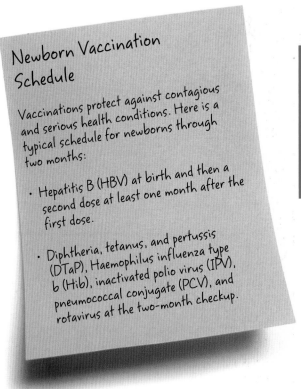

Newborn Vaccination Schedule

Vaccinations protect against contagious and serious health conditions. Here is a typical schedule for newborns through two months:

- Hepatitis B (HBV) at birth and then a second dose at least one month after the first dose.

- Diphtheria, tetanus, and pertussis (DTaP), Haemophilus influenza type b (Hib), inactivated polio virus (IPV), pneumococcal conjugate (PCV), and rotavirus at the two-month checkup.

GROWTH

Baby will experience several rapid growth spurts during first few months

Your teeny newborn will be "on the grow" at a record pace during the first few months. Most newborns lose weight after birth due to the loss of extra fluids from childbirth, combined with newfound activity levels (babies use a lot of energy after they are born) and adjusting to a new way to eat. Initial weight loss should be regained by about two weeks in

healthy newborns. From there, there's no stopping them!

Newborns typically gain about five ounces a week and will grow about 1 to 1½ inches during the first month. Babies on average will double their birth weight by five months. Most newborns will go through three growth spurts between birth and four months, including a first between seven and

Growth Charts

- Most pediatricians maintain a standardized growth chart on your baby to monitor development.

- Ask the doctor where your infant appears on the chart compared with other babies the same age. The charts are different for boys and girls. You should receive two percentiles each time—one for height and one for weight.

- Patterns will most likely stay consistent over time, but not always.

Baby's Head

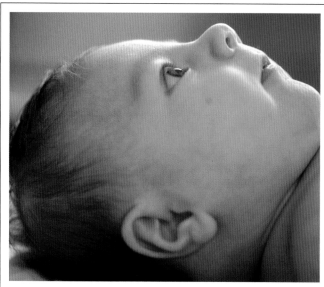

- Head circumference is measured using the distance around the largest part of the head.

- The measurement can provide clues about brain development.

- If baby's head is bigger or smaller than normal

or stops increasing or increases too quickly, it can signal a problem.

- A large head may be a sign of fluid building up inside the brain, while a smaller head could mean the brain is not developing on schedule.

ten days old, a second at around six weeks of age, and then a third at four months. Growth spurts may last a few days on average, and baby will lead the way in terms of feeding. Parents may notice the growth spurts when those adorable newborn outfits—too big a few weeks earlier—are suddenly too tight or short!

These milestone averages are just that. Infants born prematurely should not be compared to growth and development stages of a baby who was carried to full term.

Length and Weight

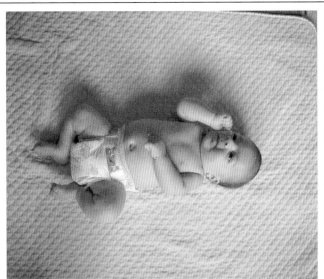

- Some pediatricians use measuring devices, but most determine baby's length using a tape measure or by laying an infant on paper and marking the crown of head and heels and measuring the distance.

- Genetics influence baby's height and weight.

- Your baby's doctor will likely lay baby down (naked or in a diaper only) on a scale with a stainless steel cradle for accurate weight.

- Chubby cheeks and fat rolls don't mean baby is overweight. Many newborns quickly lose their baby fat.

Milestones: Birth to Three Months

- Baby will turn head in search of nipple when cheek is touched and begin suckling when nipple touches lips.

- Newborn will close hand and grip your finger.

- Newborn will step when both feet are placed on a surface while body is supported. Baby will extend leg when the sole of foot is stimulated, and flex toes and forefoot.

- An infant should be able to lift and turn his head when on his back.

EMOTIONS
Parent expressions and mood can influence baby's happiness and comfort in environment

Your newborn is born with emotions, but they are limited and straightforward. In the first few months of life, baby is either happy or unhappy. Babies are typically happy when they are comfortable, have been fed, are well rested, receive attention and love, and are protected from loud noises and overstimulation. Change any of the variables above and the likely response will be that baby is unhappy and unafraid to let caregivers know.

As babies begin to tune in to their surroundings and focus on faces and objects near them, they also begin to respond to loved ones and expand their range of emotions. Baby will quickly transition from having a reflexive smile (instinctive) to

Emotions

- A baby's primary emotions focus around basic needs for survival: food, comfort, and sleep.

- Newborns won't show much emotion at first, but eventually they show pleasure by flapping their arms, kicking, squealing, and cooing. For the most part, a brand new baby expresses contentment by not crying!

- A newborn craves attention and love and will cry to get that emotional need fulfilled. He will stop crying when a caregiver picks him up, holds him, and interacts with him.

Temperament

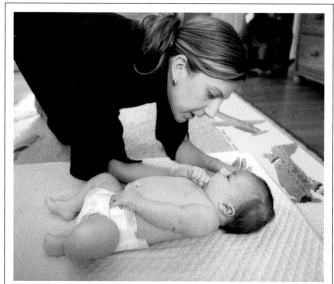

- How babies respond emotionally to a situation depends on their temperament, which is the way they experience the world.

- Temperament affects whether a baby is outgoing or shy, easygoing or easily frustrated, curious or intimidated.

- Temperament is inborn, but it is adaptable.

- Parents can help baby overcome emotional reactions to certain situations by learning how he best responds to new experiences.

a social smile (happiness at seeing someone he or she loves, for example). At the same time, babies may begin to mimic their parents' expressions and will respond based on how people around them react to stimulus. In other words, a parent's outburst or panic may quickly reduce an infant to tears.

A baby being in sync with loved ones expands past the expressions on your face or tone of your voice. An infant can sense emotions through body temperature, pulse, tension in your muscles, voice inflections, and even the way you hold them.

Alertness and Responsiveness

- Babies quickly advance from automatic startling and jerking reflexes to more controlled physical and emotional reactions when scared or excited.

- Doctors may test for baby's alertness by shining a light around his face, talking to him, and checking his grip.

- Newborns may turn their heads away from a situation they don't like.

- Babies who seem sluggish or nonresponsive should be seen by their pediatrician to rule out illness.

Colic

- All newborns cry. But beginning around two weeks of age, some newborns may develop a fussy period in the late afternoon and evening.

- Other newborns develop what is called "colic," a dreaded term that describes inconsolable bouts of extended crying for hours, for which nothing seems to provide relief.

- The good news is that most infants outgrow colic by around four months.

LANGUAGE

Deciphering the crying code will help parents to better understand their baby's needs

Your newborn is trying to talk with you. You just have to figure out what she's saying. Different types of crying, especially when coupled with gestures or flails, are ways that baby first communicates.

A baby's first language can be quite basic, and certain cues are easy to figure out. A crying baby who yawns and rubs his or her eyes may simply need to sleep. Many babies become overstimulated quite easily. Infants who suddenly close their eyes and attempt to turn away while beginning to cry may be overwhelmed. Babies can also express displeasure and fear. At the same time, they can show contentment, excitement, and joy.

Different Cries

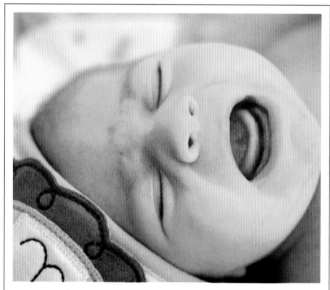

- Low-pitched and brief sobs may mean baby is hungry. Babies who aren't full after a feeding may cry at the end and also before the next one.

- Whiny or continuous wails may denote baby is uncomfortable or overtired.

- Intermittent fussiness or whining may signal boredom.

- A sudden or shrill cry may mean baby is in pain, while moaning or a soft, pitiful cry may indicate your baby is sick.

Body Gestures

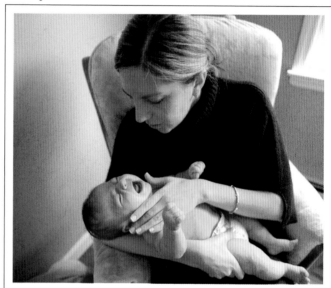

- Squirming or arching of the back may denote discomfort. This is a good time to check baby's diapers, clothing, or temperature. It can also mean baby is overly tired.

- Frog kicks and arm waves indicate excitement.

- Frantic rooting or finger or fist sucking is a surefire sign of hunger.

- A baby may root, not for hunger, but for comfort. You may try a pacifier, breast, or just holding and talking to baby.

Between one and two months of age, babies will use their bodies to show excitement and will begin to smile regularly at people they know, and even the family pet. Most likely, babies won't initially respond to visitors or strangers but will warm up to them in time.

Baby begins babbling at around two months. Repetitive single-syllable sounds like "ooh-ooh" and "aah-aah" are generally first. By three months baby may begin a pattern of communication, in which he speaks, waits for you to respond, and then talks back or responds with a smile or gesture.

Voice and Expressions

- Your baby may begin to mimic your facial expressions.

- Smiles, frowns, and even grimaces may become common around age two months.

- Baby may blow bubbles and begin to coo. Try cooing or making sounds to baby and delight in his efforts as he tries to imitate them.

- Baby may begin to reach out to you for attention, food, or comfort, or to grasp at something, at age two or three months.

Stopping the Tears

Here are tips for ending baby's tears:

- Dance with your baby (think "waltz" and not "jitterbug").

- Give baby a massage.

- Sing to your baby while maintaining eye contact.

- Change your environment. Go outside if weather permits or take a walk around the house while talking to baby.

- Go for a stroller ride or car ride. Many babies calm down with movement.

33

SAFETY

Choking, falling, and equipment breaking are hazards to watch for around baby

Your newborn is too young to crawl or get into much trouble just yet, but there is no better time than right now to conduct home safety checks. At this age, your newborn's personal safety tops the list. Safety hazards include parents tripping over objects left on the floor or bumping into furniture while holding baby. Hallways and baby's nursery should be kept clutter-

free to avoid late-night stumbles when baby awakens, as well as during routine feeding, clothing, and changing tasks.

Keep in mind that a baby's mouth can be likened to a vacuum cleaner (the "suck zone"), so parents must be vigilant in keeping small or unsafe items away from baby. Choking hazards are everywhere, especially in households with older

Safety in the Home

- Carefully inspect hand-me-down equipment, and call the manufacturer or the Consumer Product Safety Commission for a list of recalled products (1-800-638-2772).

- Install smoke detectors and fire extinguishers, and consider a carbon monoxide detector.

- Set the temperature of your hot water heater to 120 degrees Fahrenheit to prevent scalding.

- Keep small items out of baby's reach to avoid choking hazards. Keep household cleaners and medicines in a childproof container and out of reach.

Baby Personal Safety

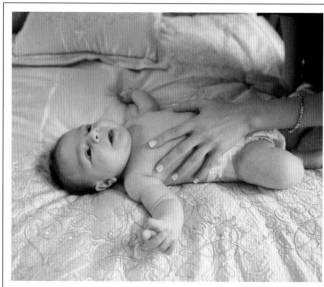

- Never leave baby unattended on a table or bed—even for a quick dash across the room to grab something. You never know when baby will roll over for the first time.

- Dress baby in a flame retardant sleeper when putting down for the evening.

- Make sure that all toys are disinfected before giving to baby and make sure they feature no small parts.

- Check your home for any hazards that could trip you while holding baby.

siblings (just think of all the toys with small, break-off parts).

Newborn equipment can also cause injuries. Placing baby in a carrier or similar device without properly applying safety locks can cause the item to flip over with baby inside. Carefully read and follow all safety warnings and don't let inexperienced helpers use carriers, swings, and bouncers without receiving proper training first.

Discourage visitors from walking around with a newborn, and encourage them to sit down with baby while ensuring proper head and neck support.

Out-and-About Safety

- Double-check handles of infant carriers, bracing of strollers, and straps on equipment to avoid spills.

- Don't attempt to carry items and baby at the same time to lessen risk of dropping your newborn.

- Keep baby away from pets while on a stroll or at someone else's house. Be cautious of homes with reptiles, a common source of salmonella.

- The safest place for baby when you are at someone's home is in your lap.

·············· GREEN ● LIGHT ··············

Along with childbirth classes, new parents should sign up for an infant CPR and first aid class. Infant CPR is modified for children under 12 months, whose delicate ribcages are susceptible to damage if chest compressions aren't performed correctly. Most hospitals and communities offer CPR training. However, if you cannot find a class, basic information is available online to help parents be better prepared in life-and-death situations.

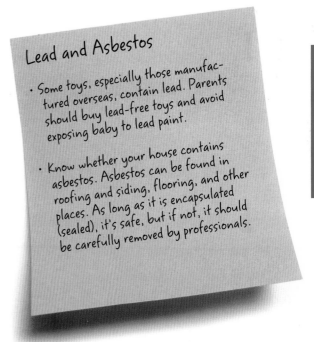

Lead and Asbestos

- Some toys, especially those manufactured overseas, contain lead. Parents should buy lead-free toys and avoid exposing baby to lead paint.

- Know whether your house contains asbestos. Asbestos can be found in roofing and siding, flooring, and other places. As long as it is encapsulated (sealed), it's safe, but if not, it should be carefully removed by professionals.

NEWBORN: MILESTONES

GEAR

Diaper bags, slings, carriers, bouncers, strollers and travel systems provide tempting choices for parents

It's hard not to go overboard with purchasing baby gear. A stroll through a baby store showcases an array of useful and colorful items designed to make life with a newborn easier. Keep in mind that your baby doesn't actually require these items. Most likely you already have the essentials, purchased before baby was born. But many of these designs do provide

practical options to let parents organize bottles and diapers while on the go, keep their hands free while holding baby, or allow baby to recline safely while being a part of the family during activities. That's worth a lot to busy parents or ones who want baby to have the absolute best.

Before buying any baby product, ask friends or family with

Diaper Bag

- Diaper bags range from inexpensive to couture, and designs include styles made specifically for men.

- Diaper bags come in an array of textures, fabrics, and strap designs (like over-the-shoulder or backpack). Consider your lifestyle and primary occasions when a

- diaper bag will be utilized.

- Most bags feature water-resistant liners, a portable changing pad, and an insulated area to hold bottles.

- Consider a stroller bag design, which attaches to the handles of a stroller to eliminate carrying.

Sling, Pouch, or Wrap

- Many parents opt for a sling, pouch, or wrap as a way of safely and securely carrying an infant while keeping hands free.

- Many designs feature a fabric "tail" that can used as a covering to make breast-feeding discreet, for sun shade, or as added warmth.

- Designs of these usually inexpensive carriers vary based on whether they are padded or unpadded, single or double shoulder style, and material used.

- Rings lock the fabric, and proper knotting techniques prevent unraveling.

babies for their recommendations on products and their advantages or disadvantages. Shop at stores where you can actually view the product outside the box to gauge comfort, craftsmanship, and durability. Some gear is intended only for newborns while other styles may transition to be used for older babies and even toddlers.

When looking at wheeled gear, such as a stroller, ask to take it for a test spin around the store, and try out how it folds and whether you'll be able to lift it on your own.

ZOOM

Full-term newborns are nearsighted, meaning they can see objects about 8 to 15 inches away quite clearly. Bright patterns and contrast are preferred, second to familiar faces. Consider placing a baby crib mobile and soft infant toys with vibrant colors and extreme patterns within viewing range. Pastels won't capture baby's attention as much at this age.

Stroller

- Stroller varieties include basic models, lightweight varieties, and jogging styles. Features may include storage, cup holders or trays, and toy bars.

- Travel systems feature an infant car seat that snaps into a stroller base for convenience.

- Alternatives include prams or carriages, although most cannot be taken apart or folded for transport.

- Strollers for multiples or for baby and older sibling allow parents to transport everyone at once, but can be challenging to navigate.

Diaper Bag Checklist

What should be in baby's bag?

- Baby wipes in an airtight container so they don't dry out and become useless

- Extra diapers

- Plastic bags for transporting wet clothes or smelly diapers

- Two changes of baby clothes, such as T-shirts or footed sleepers

- If bottle-feeding, extra bottles and formula

- A pacifier, if your baby uses one

SWADDLING

Age-old custom may calm fussy newborns by providing warmth and security

Swaddling, the custom of snugly wrapping newborns in lightweight cloths, blankets, or sheets to sleep or provide comfort, has been practiced in many parts of the world throughout history. Swaddling infants so that movement of their arms and legs is restricted is thought to provide warmth and security to a newborn who is accustomed to a confined space in the womb. It is also intended to keep babies from suddenly waking due to their startle reflex.

Swaddling babies when they are laid to sleep may also help reduce the risk of SIDS, but the primary reason in favor of the practice is that it may help infants who are otherwise uncomfortable or fussy being placed on their backs to be more

Swaddling, Step One

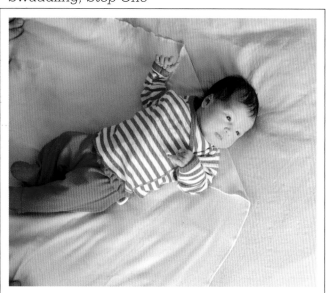

- Choose your swaddling cloth. Your selection should match the general climate by not being too hot or too cold. Receiving blankets work well.

- Specialty triangular-shaped blankets are also available at stores (or make your own).

- Place blanket on bed and fold top right corner down about 6 inches.

- After making sure baby is dry and fed, lay baby in the middle of the fold, face up with shoulders just below the edge and head above the edge.

Swaddling, Step Two

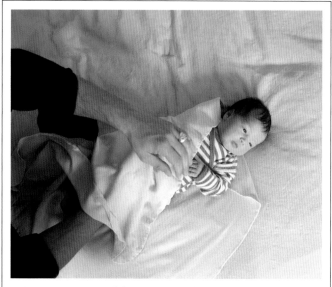

- Bring one corner of the swaddling blanket across baby's chest, making sure the covered arm is closely wrapped to his body.

- Pull the blanket over as far as you like, depending on how tightly or loosely you prefer to swaddle your infant.

- Lift your infant's opposite arm and securely tuck the blanket underneath his body.

- A variation is to keep baby's arms outside of the blanket while you swaddle, as some babies don't like their arms confined.

likely to go to sleep and stay asleep for a longer period. Some parents swaddle their babies to keep them from scratching themselves with their fingernails during sleep.

Swaddling is a personal choice, and some babies may like it while others do not. A variation to traditional swaddling is to leave hands free for babies who may prefer to have less restriction. Whether or not you choose swaddling, most babies outgrow swaddling around three to four months of age when additional movement is desired and baby may start rolling over.

Swaddling, Step Three

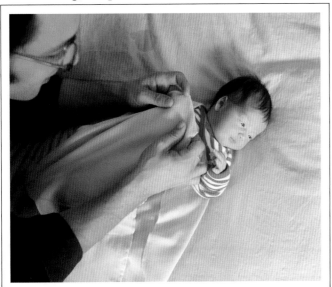

- Lift bottom corner of blanket over baby's feet and underneath chin. If blanket is too long, either fold back the edge or tuck it into the first swathe.

- Wrap the remaining corner of blanket across baby's chest and toward the opposite side, securing the

remaining arm near his body (unless it is an arms-free swaddle).

- Tuck the blanket under your baby's back as far as it will go.

- Be careful when picking up baby to keep the swaddling intact.

Swaddling Variations

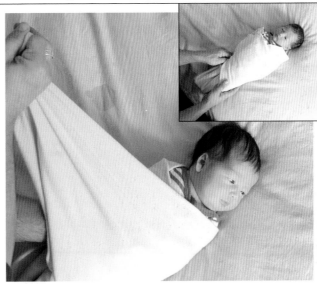

- The "burrito wrap," as it is affectionately called, is the most common swaddling method.

- There are also swaddling blankets with built-in feet and wearable swaddling styles featuring a stretchy blanket that becomes a sleep sack later.

- Preemie-size swaddling blankets are available for infants too small to be swaddled in normal-size receiving blankets.

- Loosely swaddling infants allows more movement and comfort for babies who don't like the snug feel.

DIAPER OFF

Preparation, proper cleaning, and practice make changing your newborn's diaper a breeze

Changing a newborn's diaper can unsettle even the most experienced parent. That's because newborns are so small and diapers—even those made for newborns—can sometimes seem so large. There's also the queasy factor, something you'll have to overcome, because lots of diapers will need to get changed before baby is potty trained.

Whether to use disposable diapers, cloth diapers, or a combination of both is a personal preference. Both types have benefits and drawbacks. Cost, convenience, and concerns about leakage top the list of why families may choose one variety over another. Environmentally conscious parents may want to avoid adding disposable diapers to our landfills. Families on

Diaper Station Checklist

- Make sure these items are on hand and in easy reach:

- Baby wipes or washcloths (you'll go through lots of these)

- A supply of clean diapers

- A diaper pail with an air-tight lid or a diaper disposal product that practically eliminates odors

- Hand sanitizer for you

- Diaper cream to apply in case of diaper rash

Changing Station

- Changing tables are sold independently or as part of a nursery set. Some playpens also feature changing pad inserts. Changing tables are waist-high and include a changing pad and storage space.

- Keep all essential supplies within arm's reach.

- Always maintain contact with baby to prevent accidental rolling or falling.

- A blanket on a floor can work just fine. Make sure the floor is carpeted or padded for infant comfort.

the go may like the ease of disposable diapers and not having to buy the liners and fasteners accessories that often go with cloth diapers. Some parents who utilize cloth diapers use a diaper service, while others wash diapers themselves.

If you plan to go the cloth route, research your options so you are familiar with the choices. Some diapers have Velcro fasteners while others still rely on pins. There are pre-folded and fitted varieties. Disposable diapers come in different shapes and sizes, and you and baby may quickly develop a preference for what style works best for you.

Removing Diaper

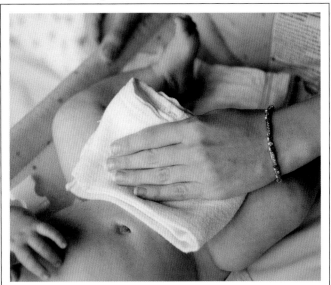

- Wash your hands thoroughly. Talk while you lay baby down for reassurance.

- Remove clothing from the waist down for accessibility and to avoid soiling clothes.

- Lift off diaper fasteners while keeping diaper area covered. To avoid acciden-

tal urine sprays by male newborns, place a washrag on top of penis. The release of a diaper or exposure can cause some babies to urinate.

- Grasp baby's legs together around the ankles with one hand, and lift up bottom.

Wiping Baby's Bottom

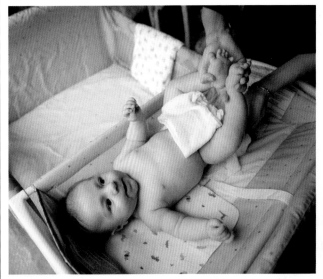

- Fold front of diaper over wet or soiled area and place underneath baby.

- While keeping legs lifted, use a warm washcloth or wipes to clean baby from front to back to avoid infection. Make sure you thoroughly clean skin folds and around genital areas.

- Inspect baby's umbilical cord stump area, and if using alcohol to clean it, do so now. Also check for any diaper rash and treat if needed.

- Remove baby's diaper.

41

DIAPER ON

Avoid diaper contact with healing umbilical cord area and make sure fit is snug

With the sometimes unpleasant task of taking off a soiled diaper accomplished, the easy part is putting a clean diaper back on!

While older babies may squirm and try to roll over, newborns are likely to be well behaved during diaper changes. Keep in mind that baby may not like to have clothing removed, or

may dislike the feel of a wet washcloth or wipe against his or her bottom.

A common mistake of inexperienced parents is putting on diapers too loosely, whether they are cloth or disposable. As a result, messy leaks may occur. Parents sometimes also put diapers on too snugly, causing baby discomfort, in which

Positioning New Diaper

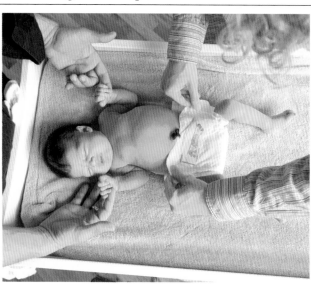

- Unfold new diaper and then slide it underneath baby while still holding up baby's legs.

- It is not uncommon for a newborn to wet or soil a diaper in the midst of changing. Episodes will decrease as baby gets older.

- Lower newborn's legs while holding the front of the diaper in place.

- Remove washcloth shield from over penis as you lower the front flap.

Fastening Diaper

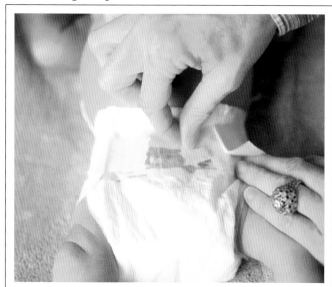

- Fold down front of diaper to avoid contact with the umbilical cord area. Remember, this area may still be sensitive for a short time after the stump falls off.

- Open tabs, adjust diaper position, and then secure diaper in place.

- If using cloth diapers with diaper pin fasteners, slide your opposite hand underneath the cloth to protect baby's skin from being accidentally poked.

- Other cloth diaper options include nonsharp diaper fasteners, Velcro, or adjustable snap closures.

case your newborn will be certain to let you know about it.

Diapers put on incorrectly can also chafe delicate skin. Look for telltale signs of chafing around a newborn's legs and stomach area. Until baby's umbilical cord stump is completely healed, you'll need to fold down the diaper to avoid any contact with the area. Some disposable diapers come with newborn "notches" so that the area remains diaper-free without extra effort on the part of the parent. If time allows, you can also notch regular disposable diapers yourself and save some expense.

Checking for Fit

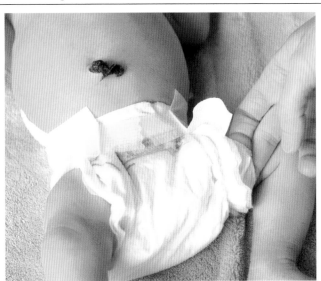

- Most disposable diapers have "fringes" near leg openings. Make sure one fringe is touching the skin and the other faces up, not tucked in, to protect against leaks.

- Diaper should not be too loose and not too tight so it is comfortable for baby.

- Your finger should be able to fit in between baby and the diaper.

- Check for any leg or waist irritations at the next diaper change. Experiment with different brands and styles.

····· YELLOW ● LIGHT ·····

If your baby's bottom is red, irritated, or has red spots, diaper rash is the likely culprit. Diaper rash is common, but can be uncomfortable for baby. It is usually caused by chemicals, moisture from urine and stools, and diaper rub. Damaged skin is also at an increased risk for bacterial and yeast infections. Consider applying a cream that is either a petroleum ointment or a white zinc oxide. Ask your child's pediatrician for recommendations for treating chronic rashes.

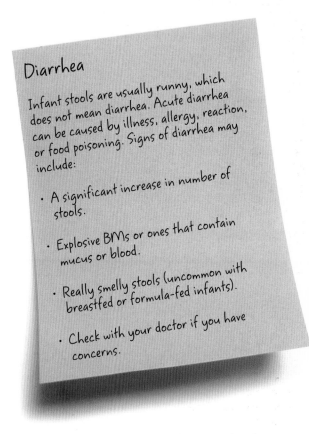

Diarrhea

Infant stools are usually runny, which does not mean diarrhea. Acute diarrhea can be caused by illness, allergy, reaction, or food poisoning. Signs of diarrhea may include:

- A significant increase in number of stools.

- Explosive BMs or ones that contain mucus or blood.

- Really smelly stools (uncommon with breastfed or formula-fed infants).

- Check with your doctor if you have concerns.

DRESSING
Lack of muscle tone and floppy head can make dressing newborns a challenge

Most parents can't wait to dress their newborn in the adorable outfits they've received as gifts. But often those first outfits look better on hangers than they do on your baby. A lack of muscle tone, floppy neck and head, and a tendency for newborns to prefer the fetal position make outfits cumbersome. In truth, all your newborn needs initially are plain T-shirts and onesies (once the umbilical cord area is healed) or just swaddling blankets. Regardless of whether baby is dressed in simple attire or more elaborate outfits, successfully dressing a baby who can't support himself creates a challenge.

Parents quickly learn that easy-on outfits that don't require removal for diaper changes are preferable. Most newborn

Dressing Tips

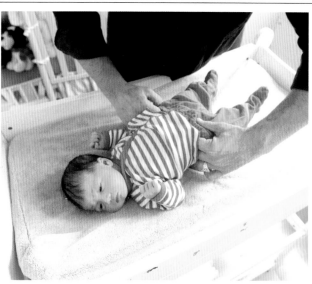

- Remove tags and wash new clothing to minimize exposure to chemicals or germs.

- Dress baby in layers. You may need to put on or take off layers to keep baby warm without becoming overheated.

- Look for booties or socks that are made to stay on your newborn's feet, which can become cold easily. Newborns do not need shoes; avoid hard soles.

- Be careful when zipping up jackets or closing snaps that can catch baby's skin.

Dressing Baby

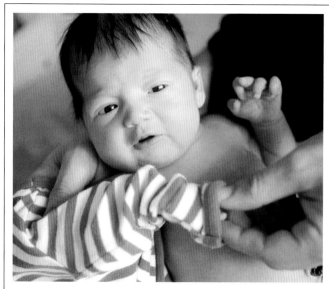

- Be gentle when dressing baby. Your newborn won't be cooperative with bending arms and legs into shirts and pants, so you will need to gently position limbs into clothing.

- Remember to support your newborn's neck while dressing or undressing. If possible, avoid clothing that must be pulled over a baby's head.

- Hold your newborn close to you on your lap facing outward, in a slightly reclining position, or use a changing table.

- Interact with your baby.

outfits are made from soft cotton material, although some may feature materials that look great but are irritating to the skin. Backing and embroidery can chafe. Manufacturer tags, snaps, and buttons can also cause discomfort, especially when babies are on their back, where they initially spend most of their time.

Most babies don't particularly like being dressed up and changed, so in-the-know parents try to keep clothing changes to a minimum. Spitting up and diaper leaks can require changing baby more frequently.

ZOOM

If you're taking baby outdoors, consider a hat or cap a dressing essential. During cooler weather, a hat helps regulate baby's temperature and keeps ears from getting cold. Babies should wear hats during warm weather as well to protect their delicate skin from sunburn, which can result from even minimal time spent outdoors.

Arms and Legs

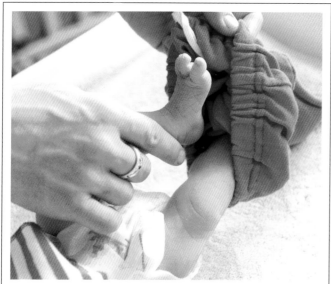

- It can be awkward to try to stick baby's arms or legs through clothing and pull them out on the other end, but practice makes perfect.

- Unbutton or unfasten baby's clean outfit before placing her on your lap, or else you'll be fumbling with it while holding onto baby.

- Stretch out arm and leg openings while sticking limbs through.

- If dressing baby in footed pajamas, put feet in first and pull up over body, putting arms in last.

Baby Bibs

- Frequent spit-ups make bibs a practical wardrobe accessory.

- Some baby clothing designers now offer bibs that match outfits so babies can be fashionable and practical at the same time!

- Bibs come in different sizes to fit the growing stages of babies.

- Styles include snap-on, Velcro, and tie, and often feature cute sayings and designs.

NEWBORN: CARE

SPECIAL CARE

Aspirating baby's nose, clipping nails, and taking a newborn's temperature are part of the job

Just what part of your baby doesn't require care and cleaning? Truth is, your newborn is totally dependent on you and that means every nook and crevice requires your attention and care. Babies may need their nose aspirated to clear out mucus (they can't yet blow their own nose), nails clipped, lotion applied, body washed, and ears and eye areas cleaned.

An uncircumcised penis in male infants also requires basic care, which is essentially washing with soap and water. The foreskin should never be pulled back in infancy or young childhood. While the majority of care for baby can be done with simple water or gentle baby soap, some care items require practice. After a few times, however, most new

Aspirating Baby's Nose

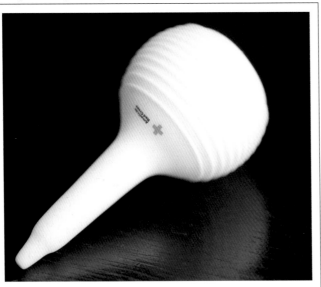

- A simple rubber aspirating bulb is all that you need. Parents often receive one at the hospital after delivery to take home.

- Tilt baby's head back slightly and squeeze the round base of the bulb with your thumb.

- Insert the tip into baby's nose. Release the bulb to suction mucus from the nose.

- If needed, put a few saline drops in each side of your newborn's nose before suctioning. Only suction when baby seems congested.

Clipping Nails

- Clip your newborn's nails while asleep, if possible, and following a bath. Newborns tend to clench their fists when awake.

- Only use baby nail clippers or baby scissors—they are the right size for tiny fingers.

- Clip a little bit at a time so you don't overdo it.

- Use an emery board if you are afraid of hurting baby, but be careful not to file the tender skin under the nail bed.

parents feel like pros when it comes to suctioning, clipping, and cleaning. That's why parenting newborns is such an exhausting, yet rewarding, job!

Even though baby is most likely months away from a first tooth, pediatric dentists urge parents to regularly wipe down infants' gums after feeding. You can purchase an inexpensive baby toothbrush or simply use a damp gauze pad or wash-cloth wrapped around a finger.

If you suspect your baby has a fever, you'll want to take your newborn's temperature with a rectal thermometer for the most accurate reading. While there are a variety of thermometer styles on the market, ones that require readings to be taken from the mouth, ear, or even forehead are typically not recommended for taking a newborn's temperature.

Taking Baby's Temperature

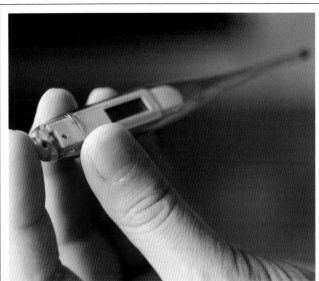

- Take a newborn's temperature rectally for the most accurate reading. Use a rectal thermometer with a security tip to prevent over-insertion.

- Place baby face down across your lap and separate buttocks with your thumb and forefinger.

- Gently insert the bulb with one hand while using other hand to hold and comfort your baby.

- After two minutes, remove the thermometer, wipe it off, and note the temperature. A reading at or above 100.4 degrees Fahrenheit indicates a fever.

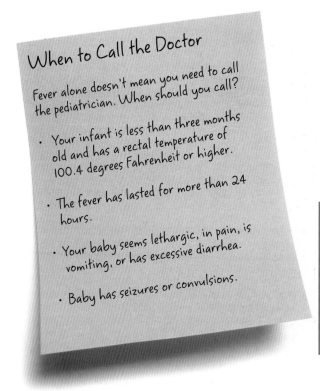

When to Call the Doctor

Fever alone doesn't mean you need to call the pediatrician. When should you call?

- Your infant is less than three months old and has a rectal temperature of 100.4 degrees Fahrenheit or higher.

- The fever has lasted for more than 24 hours.

- Your baby seems lethargic, in pain, is vomiting, or has excessive diarrhea.

- Baby has seizures or convulsions.

GEAR

Blankets, monitors, bouncers, and diaper disposal systems head up list of what parents want

There are numerous convenience and comfort products available to make your job as a parent easier. You may find yourself stressed from frequent checks on your sleeping newborn or may need hands-free solutions for completing household tasks. If you have multiples, these "nice to have" products may likely become essentials.

Items high on parent priority lists include baby monitors, safe infant seats for when baby is awake so you can keep your eyes on one another, and diaper disposal systems. Baby monitors provide parents with peace of mind while baby sleeps or is in another room. Monitors today range from very simple and inexpensive models that transmit basic baby

Blankets

- Receiving blankets are generally used to cover baby for comfort, warmth, shade, or breastfeeding privacy. Receiving blankets can also be used for swaddling.

- Specialty swaddling blankets often feature a triangular shape for easier wrapping and may even have built-in fasteners.

- Wraps may have built-in foot areas to allow baby kicking room.

- Bunting blankets keep baby nice and warm while in a stroller or car seat. Fabrics often feature soft fleece and styles may include zippers.

Monitors

- A monitor lets you know when your baby starts to cry or whine when in another room. They are also great for curious parents who are always wondering what baby is doing.

- There are two basic models: portable and plug-in.

- Audio-only monitors are inexpensive, while more elaborate and expensive models feature a video component so you can view your baby's actions.

- Dual parent monitors provide additional flexibility (his and hers or two locations).

sounds to ones that can provide a visual recording for review later or for use with caregivers for extra peace of mind. Infant seats, often called bouncers because they do just that, have reclining options that are ideal for newborns.

When you consider that babies soil around 10 diapers a day, the volume—and smell—can quickly add up. Some parents love the more elaborate designs, while others steer away from them due to cost and maintenance (the diapers still have to be removed, after all!).

Diaper Disposal System

- A plastic-lined pail with an air-tight lid meets the essential need, but consider an advanced diaper disposal system that practically eliminates diaper odors.

- Most designs feature bag inserts that hold from 25 to 50 diapers, depending on the model selected. Parents remove the bags when the system becomes full.

- Diaper services are available in many areas for parents using cloth diapers.

- Individual-size diaper disposal sacks are sold in large quantities and feature odor control.

Bouncer

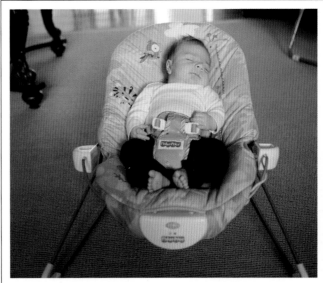

- Baby bouncers let baby recline while viewing the world. Maximum weight is typically around 25 to 30 pounds.

- Bouncers are lightweight and portable (some even fold up) so baby can follow you wherever you go.

- Most options feature a three-point harness and plush seating, and may have a canopy.

- Elaborate styles include battery-powered (or remote-controlled) vibrating or rocking options; music; or even a toy bar or mobile.

BREASTFEEDING

Convenience, cost, and baby's health are why many moms choose this option

Whether to breastfeed is a personal decision. About 85 percent of women around the world breastfeed, and when it comes to nutrition, research shows that the best first food for babies is breast milk. That's because it is perfectly suited to nourish infants. Antibodies found in breast milk help protect infants from common childhood ailments such as diarrhea, ear infections, allergies, and rashes. The American Academy of Pediatrics recommends that babies be breastfed for at least a year, and as long after a baby's first birthday as baby and mother desire. They also recommend that the baby breastfeed exclusively for the first six months, before which the baby doesn't need any water, juice, cereal, or baby food.

Should You Breastfeed?

- Are you comfortable with breastfeeding your baby?

- Are you willing to pump when away from your infant, or combine formula and breast milk feedings?

- Do you plan to return to the workforce soon after birth and find breastfeeding impractical for your lifestyle?

- Are you expecting multiples, so it may be challenging or too time-consuming?

Starting Breastfeeding

- Breastfeeding a newborn begins right after birth. A preemie or newborn with health concerns may not be able to breastfeed immediately, although mothers planning to do so should begin pumping.

- The more you nurse, the more quickly your mature milk will come in—usually in three to five days.

- Nursing for 10 to 15 minutes per breast, 8 to 12 times a day, is standard.

- Nurse whenever baby exhibits signs of hunger, such as rooting or increased alertness or activity.

In addition to the health benefits for mother and baby, breastfeeding is convenient and affordable. Nutrition is only as far away as the breastfeeding mother, and no preparation or temperature control is needed. While breastfeeding is natural, it is not always easy. Successful breastfeeding may require practice, and a rocky start without proper intervention may lead new mothers to switch to formula. Many hospitals feature lactation experts to help new moms, with proper techniques and positions so that breastfeeding is easy and satisfying.

Latching On

- Stroke baby's cheek or tickle the edge of her mouth with your finger or nipple to encourage your newborn to open up.

- Baby's mouth should cover a large part of the areola below the nipple, and your nipple should be far back into baby's mouth.

- If latch isn't correct, break the suction by inserting your small finger between baby's gums and your nipple, and try again.

- Remember that nursing should not be painful if done right.

Breastfeeding Gear Checklist

Stock up on these personal items if you plan to breastfeed:

- Nursing pads are usually worn inside your bra to absorb leaks.

- Nursing bras provide quick accessibility to breasts, especially when nursing in public.

- Button-down shirts or shirts and gowns with nursing panels offer ease in breastfeeding.

- Lanolin ointment soothes cracked nipples.

NURSING HOLDS
Best hold is the one that is comfortable and gets the job done

Since breastfeeding sessions may take as long as 20 minutes on each side, moms should carefully establish a comfortable spot for nursing. A variety of positions are intended to make breastfeeding easier for mom and baby, but the best choice is one that is successful for you both!

If a nursing mom prefers a seated position, she should choose a chair that glides, rocks, or reclines, or at least a chair with a comfortable cushion and one that doesn't leave her with a sore back or aching arms. Supporting baby at the right height by using a nursing pillow can prevent a stiff neck. Some nursing moms prefer a lying-down position. Whichever position you choose, make sure you're comfortable,

Cradle Hold

- Cradle your baby with your arm, tummy-to-tummy, and head resting in the bend of your elbow.

- Tuck baby's lower arm underneath your arm or under your breast so his mouth is close to your breast. The key is for baby to be pulled in very close and to be supported.

- A nursing pillow is particularly useful for this hold.

- This position is often preferred for babies with better head control and who don't need nursing assistance.

Cross-Cradle Hold

- This hold is recommended for newborns who may require help.

- It is similar to the cradle hold, but mom uses her hands to shape the breast and better guide baby's head to latch on.

- Mom's forearm is positioned up the length of baby's back, and she supports baby's head with her thumb and forefinger behind the ears.

- If you're feeding from right side, your right hand manages your breast, while left arm supports baby and left hand supports the head.

because you'll be there for a while.

Consider establishing a nursing station with reading material, a music player, and access to the television's remote control, telephone, and lamp. Having a beverage such as a glass of water at hand's reach is also recommended, as nursing moms may become thirsty more easily. Keep a supply of burp rags, blankets for baby and mom, nursing pillow, footstool, or any other desired comfort items nearby. Ask family members not to disrupt this area so you don't have to gather what you want beforehand each time.

Football Hold

- Position baby so legs and body are under your arm with your hand at the base of head and neck (as if holding a football).

- Place your fingers below your breast and have baby latch on while pulling in close.

- Keep legs tucked under your arm and baby's body flexed.

- This hold is good if you have had a cesarean and want to avoid placing baby against your abdominal incision.

Breastfeeding Multiples

- The more you breastfeed, the more milk you will make. Many moms successfully breastfeed twins or multiples.

- Try criss-crossing babies in the classic cradle hold with pillows for support, use the football hold, or even switch babies between breasts during each feeding.

- Some parents with higher-order multiples may pump to let others help out with feeding, or may alternate breastfeeding with formula.

- Keep a breastfeeding chart to keep straight who is getting what (as well as on which breast when nursing) and when.

BOTTLE-FEEDING

Bottle and nipple shapes, designs, and styles provide an array of feeding options

Whether you choose to breastfeed or bottle-feed your baby, you'll need to stock up on bottles, nipples, and accessories. There may be times when breastfed babies will drink expressed milk from a bottle, such as when mom is away or it is an inconvenient time to nurse. Parents who opt to bottle-feed their infant using formula will need a larger supply on

hand to keep baby fed every three to four hours. But what should you buy?

There is an almost overwhelming selection of baby bottles to consider. Bottles come in different shapes and styles, are angled or straight, may feature disposable liners, and typically come in four-, six- and eight-ounce sizes. Nipples vary

Should You Bottle-Feed?

- Consider bottle-feeding if you choose not to breastfeed or are unable to breastfeed, even after getting help from a lactation consultant.

- Baby formula is the best alternative to breast milk and provides healthy nutrients for your infant.

- Bottle-fed babies are at higher risk of gastrointestinal ailments, so bottles and nipples should be thoroughly washed in the dishwasher or sterilized.

Bottles

- Newborns may only take one or two ounces at each feeding, increasing up to six to eight ounces by their first birthday. That's why there are different size bottles.

- Standard bottles are straight, with some featuring wider necks.

- Disposable bottles use a liner inside the bottle holder so a nipple can be attached. After feeding is over, the liner is thrown away.

- Many bottles tout designs that reduce baby's ingestion of air that results in gas.

from slow to fast flow, are made of latex or silicon materials, and also come in a variety of shapes and designs.

Most parents in the know caution against the temptation to stock up on bottles before baby is born. Instead, consider buying a few assorted newborn bottles and nipples and seeing which particular design you and baby prefer. Once you know whether baby prefers latex over silicone and with which bottle design baby takes in less air, for example, then you can feel more confident in stocking up.

Nipples

- Latex nipples are golden brown and highly flexible.

- Silicone nipples are clear, heat-resistant, and typically last longer than latex nipples.

- Babies may develop a strong preference for a particular nipple.

- Nipple shapes may include naturally shaped with a wider base; orthodontic with an irregular shape and indention in the center; or traditional. Nipples may be vented (to prevent nipple collapse and reduce gas) or slotted, and have either a slow, medium, or fast flow rate.

Bottle-Feeding Tips

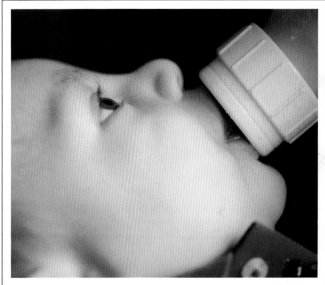

- There is no health reason to feed baby warmed milk. Feeding your baby milk served at room temperature is fine.

- Listen and observe your baby drinking. If your baby makes noisy or sucking sounds, too much air may be taken in. Be sure to hold bottle at a 45-degree angle.

- Don't let your baby fall asleep with a bottle. Tooth decay could result.

- To prevent choking, never prop a bottle in baby's mouth.

BABY FORMULA

Baby formula provides nutrition for baby, flexibility and shared care for parents

Breast milk may be best for baby, but baby formula also provides proteins, fats, vitamins, minerals, carbohydrates, and water needed to grow and thrive. There are many types of formula sold on the market, and parents should consider consulting with their baby's pediatrician for recommendations on which variety to use.

Standard formula is cow's milk–based, but the nutrients are different from that of cow's milk sold at stores. Regular cow's milk should not be given to a baby until one year of age. Most infants tolerate standard formulas, which are strictly regulated by the Food and Drug Administration, although nutritional fine points may vary slightly by brand.

Formula Basics

- Formula is available in powder, liquid concentrate, and ready-to-feed form.

- Powder varieties come in multiple-use cans. Single-serving packets provide convenience.

- Always check recommended use-by or expiration dates. Concentrated and ready-to-feed formula must be refrigerated after opening and is only good for 48 hours.

- Not all formula tastes the same and most babies develop a preference. Avoid switching brands unless recommended by a doctor.

Measuring Formula

- Concentrated formula requires a 1:1 dilution (one ounce of water per one ounce of formula).

- Powdered formulas are typically prepared by mixing one scoop of formula with two ounces of water. Single-serve sizes mix up into four ounces of formula.

- Make sure your water is safe for babies; if in doubt, mix formula with bottled water or boiled water.

- Don't make extra formula simply because you have a large bottle. Measure enough for baby's mid-point range to avoid excess waste.

Specialty formulas meet specific needs for baby, and may include lactose-free, soy, hypoallergenic, low-iron, gentle, added rice starch, follow-up (used to transition between regular formula and cow's milk) and preemie varieties. Specialty formulas cost more than regular formulas and may taste bitter to babies because of the changes required to make the formula more easily digestible. If a certain specialty formula is recommended for baby's health, note baby's reaction to it, and do not make any changes to baby's feeding or schedule without your pediatrician's advice.

Mixing Formula

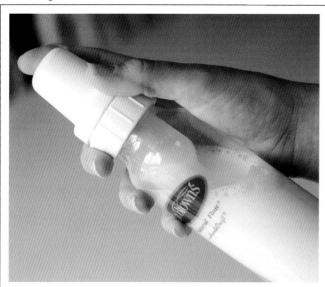

- Most parents simply cap the bottle and shake it to make sure contents are well mixed.

- If you mix formula with a nipple on the bottle, avoid touching the nipple with your hands as much as possible.

- Use a clean towel over your finger on nipple opening or use a formula stirrer (a small spoon with a long handle) to mix formula.

- Always discard any formula left in the bottle after baby finishes feeding.

Preparation Tips

Consider these tips when preparing baby's bottle:

- Make sure to cover the nipple opening when shaking bottle to blend formula and water, or you may be showered by the mix.

- Never warm a baby's milk in the microwave. It can heat unevenly, and hot spots can burn baby.

- Test temperature of warmed milk before feeding to baby.

- Always double-check nipple flow and the seal between bottle and nipple.

NEWBORN: FEEDING

57

BURPING

Burping clears the air and may keep gassiness to a minimum

Burping clears the air that many babies swallow during a feeding. Some babies take in a lot of air and need to burp often and loudly, while others take in very little air when they feed and may not burp at all. Too much swallowed air can lead to spitting up, gassiness, or discomfort in babies—which means unhappy parents as well—so burping a baby after every meal is generally recommended.

Babies may sometimes spit up when burping, and this is considered normal as long as they aren't spitting up their entire feeding. As long as baby is gaining weight appropriately, he or she is getting plenty to eat. On a practical note, it's always a good idea to keep those burp cloths handy to avoid

Shoulder Burp

- Sit upright and let baby's chin rest on your shoulder while supporting his head and back. (Lay a burp cloth on the shoulder you are using.)

- Use your free hand to pat your baby's back gently. Avoid giving hard or firm

- pats; they can cause discomfort or distress.

- Leaning back slightly, rocking, or gliding may help your baby to burp.

- Try burping when switching breasts or after two to three ounces of milk.

Lap Burp

- Hold your baby in a seated position on your lap.

- Position baby facing forward (looking out) or to the side.

- Support baby's head and chest with one hand by cradling your infant's chin in the palm of your hand

- (with a burp cloth handy) and resting the heel of your hand on your baby's chest. Make sure you don't hold baby around the throat area.

- Use your free hand to pat baby's back.

smelling of and wearing spit-up after a burping session.

There are a variety of positions that are effective when burping a baby. Repeated, gentle patting or massaging of your baby's back typically gets the desired action—a nice burp—with no pounding needed. If baby doesn't burp after repeated tries, don't force the issue. You can always try again later or after the next feeding.

While anti-gas baby products are available in stores, doctors do not consider them an effective way to treat gas in infants.

Belly Burp

- Lay your infant belly-down on your lap. While most people prefer to lay baby down across their laps, some parents prefer a lengthwise position, with baby's head near the parent's knees. Be sure to keep a burp cloth under baby's head area.

- Support baby's head and make sure it is higher than his chest.

- Gently pat your baby's back.

- Some parents use slight foot-tapping (raising and lowering legs) to lightly bounce baby to aid in burping.

ZOOM

If baby fusses during feedings or spits up when laid down flat but your doctor has ruled out any serious health concerns, there are products available to help make baby more comfortable. Incliners or wedges can lessen heartburn and indigestion by positioning baby at an angle during feedings or diaper changes. Most babies outgrow reflux within the first year.

Signs of Infant Reflux

Infant reflux occurs when food in the stomach comes back up into the esophagus. Symptoms may include:

- Projectile vomiting

- Constant or sudden crying (as if in pain)

- Arching of back or neck during or after feeding

- Wet burps or frequent hiccups

- Swallowing problems, gagging, choking

- Spitting up a lot after feeding

- Failure to gain weight

GEAR

Products offer solutions to make feeding convenient and comfortable, whether by breast or bottle

New parents will spend much of their days (and nights) feeding their infant. After all, "liquids in and liquids out" are the core of baby's needs during the few first months.

Parents settling in for another round of feeding may decide that baby feeding gear that offers comfort and convenience is well worth the expense. Bottles and nipples will need to be cleaned, possibly sterilized, stored, and maintained at the right temperature (when preparing for feeding). Although bottle-feeding basics such as nipples, collars, bottles, and pacifiers are dishwasher-safe (usually on the top rack), you'll still need a basket to avoid them getting tossed around the dishwasher and landing on a heating coil. A bottle brush for

Feeding Pillow

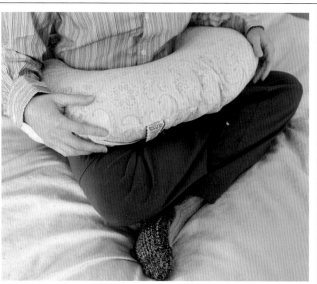

- Whether baby is breast-fed or bottle-fed, a pillow prevents you from stooping to baby's level while sitting down by positioning him at mid-waist, which keeps your back straight.

- A regular bed pillow can meet the need to support baby while feeding.

- Specialty pillow products are designed to have additional uses beyond feeding, and can be used for baby tummy time, reclining, and sitting support.

- Consider pillows that feature slipcovers.

Bottle Accessories

- Bottle storage systems allow you to keep bottles clean and ready. Many varieties feature spindles for bottle storage with a separate area for nipples and collars. Make sure your style of bottle fits.

- Bottle warmers allow parents to quickly and conveniently warm bottles to a consistent temperature.

- Powdered-formula dispensers allow parents to pre-measure formula so they don't have to travel with a large can.

- Travel gear like bottle lids and stirrers are available for parents' convenience.

cleaning out bottle crevices is a must for most families. Look for a smaller brush—often sold as part of a set—to clean out the ends of the bottle nipples as well.

Once everything is clean, you'll probably opt for some type of organizer system. And, once you are ready to begin bringing baby out and about, you may need an insulated bag (some diaper bags have this feature) to keep milk at the right temperature until it is feeding time.

Breast Pump

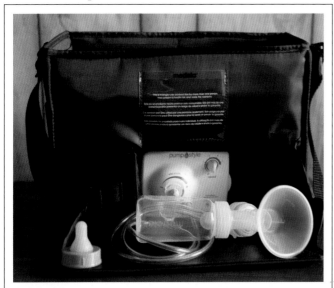

- Breast pumps provide flexibility and are essential for working moms.

- Manual pumps are inexpensive and small. They generally don't express much milk.

- Battery-operated or single-breast pumps express milk more quickly than manual pumps.

- Electric pumps are bulky but express milk efficiently.

- Dual-breast electric pumps that pump both breasts simultaneously are the most costly, but may be rented.

Pacifier

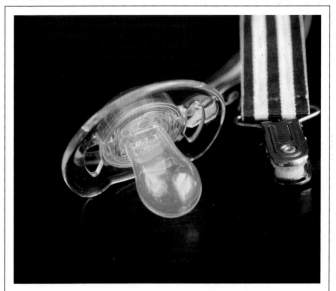

- Offering a pacifier every sleep period during the first year may provide additional protection against SIDS.

- Don't begin offering a pacifier until feeding patterns are firmly established (around one month of age). Some infants will refuse a pacifier.

- Pacifiers should never be offered as a substitute for feeding.

- Pacifiers come in many nipple shapes and types, and baby will most likely have a strong preference. Never tie a pacifier around baby's neck.

SPONGE BATHS

First baths provide baby-cleaning basics while keeping umbilical cord area dry

You'll want your newborn's first baths to be a positive and comfortable experience for you and baby alike. It will be a while before baby splashes in a big tub; your goal until then is to keep your newborn clean and fuss-free. While bathing a floppy infant can be a tad overwhelming at first, you'll quickly gain confidence, transitioning from initially awkward sponge baths to full-out bathtub fun in no time!

Baby should not be immersed in water until the umbilical cord stump has dried and fallen off. If your son was circumcised, that area needs to be healed as well. Since this typically takes two to three weeks, baby's basic cleaning can be accomplished until then with a simple sponge bath.

Sponge Bath Supply List

Keep these sponge-bath essentials handy:

- Baby body wash (some brands double as shampoo)

- Washcloths or sponges

- Towels (a soft hand towel and hooded towel are recommended)

- Two bowls of warm water

- Scalp brush

- Cotton balls, gauze, or thin cloth (used for cleaning delicate face areas)

- Clean diaper and outfit

- Baby lotion (optional)

Prep, Face, and Hands

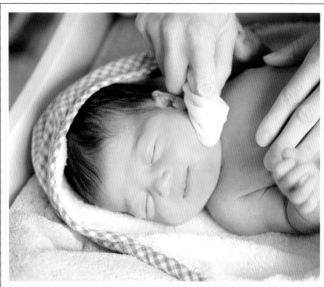

- Talk to your baby and offer reassurance about having a bath. Your newborn won't understand your words but will find comfort in your tone.

- After supplies are in place, lay baby down. While keeping baby fully dressed, wash baby's face.

- Use cotton balls, gauze, or thin cloth to clean inside baby's ears, around baby's mouth and nose areas, and baby's eye areas. Wipe eyelids from inside corner out.

- Wash baby's hands with wet washcloth.

Since only minimal water is used, sponge baths can be performed just about anywhere. Some parents use baby's changing table, keeping newborns at waist height to avoid bending over. Others may lay baby down on a pad or blanket on a bed or on floor. Whatever your choice, make sure you have all supplies prepared and within easy reach so baby can be bathed quickly and efficiently. Spot-cleanings, especially around mouth and face areas, are all that many newborns really need at first to avoid overly drying their skin.

YELLOW ● LIGHT

Even the simple act of removing clothing or the sensation of water can frighten some newborns. Since a flailing, wailing infant isn't the best way to begin a bath, try to pick a time when baby is most likely to be alert and content. You can keep baby's diaper on throughout the sponge bath, and only remove it briefly when you need to clean the genitals and bottom areas.

Hair and Head

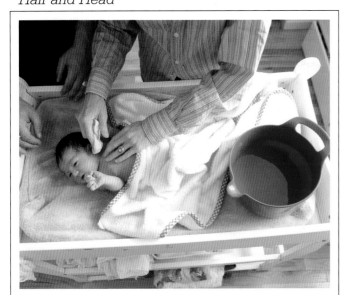

- Remove baby's top and cover baby with a towel while washing hair.

- Lift baby up slightly and while supporting baby's back, slightly recline head and lightly wet hair with warm water. Squeeze a small amount of shampoo or body wash onto wash-cloth, and lather, scrub with scalp brush, and rinse with the washcloth.

- Use one water bowl to rinse cloths or towels while keeping second bowl for clean water.

- Dry baby's head with a towel.

Body

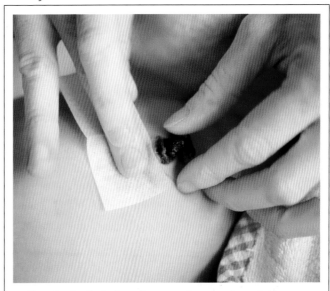

- Clean back of baby's neck and upper back and then lay baby flat.

- Remove baby's clothing, leaving diaper on. Quickly clean neck, stomach, arms, and umbilical stump area, while keeping stump dry.

- Remove diaper (place a washcloth on genitals to avoid being sprayed) and clean thighs, legs, feet, genitals, and bottom, remembering to wash front to back.

- Wrap baby in hooded towel for warmth, place clean diaper on, and apply lotion if desired.

FIRST BATH: GETTING READY

Transitioning newborn to infant bathtub and water immersion takes proper preparation

Once your newborn's umbilical cord area has dried, you're ready for a new phase in baby's hygiene: taking a real bath! There's nothing quite like a freshly bathed infant wrapped in a warm towel, smelling clean and baby fresh. A bonus is that most babies, although not all, quite enjoy the experience of a bath and thrive on the various sensations and all

the attention. Those who do fuss and dislike baths altogether may make bath time a greater challenge, but most who initially cry will grow to at least tolerate the experience in time.

Transitioning your infant to a first "real" bath in a specially sized infant bathtub requires planning. As with sponge baths, you should have supplies on hand before you bring in

Infant Bath Safety Checklist

- Do a safety check before placing baby in an infant tub.

- Know how your tub works. If it folds, make sure it can be secured in an open position.

- Check that feet or bottom grippers are in order to prevent risk of tub turning over.

- Give your tub a test run with water to look for leaks.

Getting Ready

- Gather supplies—including body wash, washcloths, towels, cotton balls, and a clean diaper and outfit— and store within arm's reach of the tub.

- Run warm water into tub and then pour out to avoid having parts of tub or foam padding cool to baby's skin.

- Fill tub with two to three inches of water and add body wash.

- Water temperature should be slightly cooler than your personal preference, as baby's skin is more sensitive.

baby for bath time. Infant tubs generally provide a comfortable position for baby while allowing a few inches of water to fill the bottom portion of the tub. Not all tubs are created the same, and you'll want to carefully consider styles and whether they fit safely and securely into a sink or bathtub or on the counter before making your selection. Since some water may end up on the floor during bathing, protect yourself from spills and slipping hazards by placing a rubber mat or bathmat where you will be standing.

GREEN ● LIGHT

In response to growing consumer demand, a number of organic baby care products are available on the market. Make sure you read labels carefully for nonirritating and tear-free formulas. While some products are scent-free, others are enhanced with earthy or floral scents. Many green products do not utilize animal testing, promote minimal impact on aquatic life, are hypoallergenic and chlorine-free, and use biodegradable packaging. The downside is that they typically cost more.

Preparing Baby

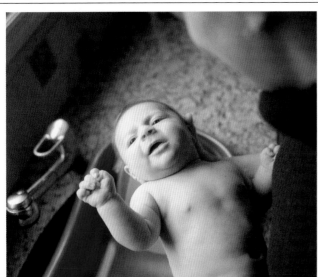

- Undress your infant and carry him to the bath wrapped in a warm towel for comfort.

- Gently lower your infant into the bath while supporting head and neck with your arm. Make sure the infant bath stays secure under baby's weight.

- Keep a washcloth over baby's genital area to avoid accidental spraying.

- Maintain eye contact and give plenty of smiles to help baby feel more at ease with taking a bath.

Bath Basics

- Be prepared that your baby may urinate, or, less frequently, even defecate when first laid into water. If that happens, you'll need to remove baby from the tub and start all over.

- Keep hold of your baby at all times while in the bathtub. Babies can flop and hurl their bodies without notice due to lack of muscle control.

- Having both parents or an older sibling help with bath time provides an extra set of helping hands.

- Baby's water will turn cold quickly, so keep baths brief.

FIRST BATH: IN THE WATER

Many babies love the splish-splash sensations and fun of taking a bath

Cleaning out all those creases and crevices that can hide waste and make your baby smell not so sweet is a primary reason for giving your infant a bath at this stage. After all, newborns aren't exactly rolling in the dirt. While daily spot-cleaning of baby's face and hands along with careful wiping during diaper changes can mostly do the trick, a bath keeps

newborns smelling clean and lessens the chances of irritation from wet diapers, spit-up, or drool.

Most likely, you'll want to position baby's bathtub close to a faucet for convenience in changing out water, if desired. If your baby isn't so sure about baths, you may prefer to stick with a few inches of water and a warm washcloth and use

Bath Tips for Parents

- Consider your comfort when choosing where to bathe your baby. Using your bathtub will require you to bend over, while selecting a counter or sink lets you remain standing.

- Position your infant's tub away from the bath faucet, or consider buying a faucet

- cover to avoid accidental contact with your baby.

- Avoid getting stressed over giving your baby a bath.

- Keep a firm grip and use a towel for lifting out of bathtub to make baby less slippery.

Interactions

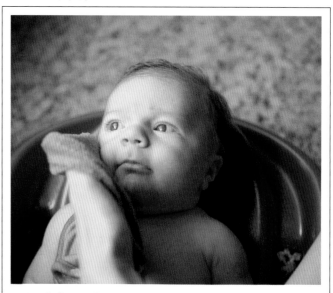

- Your baby needs reassurance that baths are okay. Maintain caressing-style contact with your baby at all times during a bath.

- Baths provide a great opportunity for quality bonding time.

- If your baby is comfortable in a bath, take time to stroke baby's skin with your hand or a soft sponge or mitt and caress baby's hands, toes, and chest areas.

- Sing or hum to your baby or play music in the background.

bowls of water for rinsing. For a baby who delights in bathing, you can heighten the bath experience by positioning the tub in the sink or bathtub and pouring warm (but not hot) water over baby's body. A recommended temperature is about 90 degrees Fahrenheit, and you can dip your elbow in the water as a good way to test that it's not too hot. Be sure to constantly drain old water to avoid over-filling the tub while keeping baby warm and comfy.

MAKE IT EASY

What can you do if your baby hates baths? Don't force baby into an infant bathtub. Rather, return to sponge bathing your infant for now. A warm washcloth, water, and body wash can still accomplish the basics. Slowly ease baby back into a bathing routine over time. Avoid potentially scary sounds of running water or bright lights, and let baby feel water in the bathtub with hands and feet.

Wash and Go

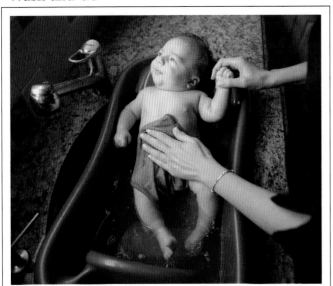

- Clean baby from top to bottom and from front to back.

- Dried mucus can sometimes collect in the corner of baby's mouth and nose. Use a small cotton ball to dab those areas first to moisten them before wiping with a washcloth.

- Don't forget to clean behind the ears, under the arms, and underneath the chin!

- Pat baby's skin dry softly rather than rubbing vigorously.

Bathing Frequency

- Daily baths for newborns are not recommended.

- Most infants only need to be bathed two or three times a week. Too-frequent baths invite dry skin or even rashes.

- If your baby develops dry skin, apply a moisturizer made specifically for infants a few minutes after a bath. Fragrances and other ingredients in adult lotions can irritate sensitive skin.

WASHING HAIR

Shampooing your newborn's hair and scalp doesn't need to be a hair-raising experience

Washing your newborn's hair can be the most frazzling part of a bath. Many infants enjoy bath time right up to the shampooing stage. Inexperienced parents may oversuds baby's hair, requiring excessive rinsing. A bald baby still needs the scalp washed, although using a washcloth with a small amount of baby shampoo or wash gets the job done.

Scalp brushes can feel good on a newborn's head and help treat cradle cap, a common skin condition. Cradle cap is a crusty and scaly rash that is found on scalps of healthy babies, and usually doesn't hurt or itch. Check with your infant's pediatrician before trying any specialty shampoos because they may contain harsher chemicals and could cause irritation.

Wetting Hair/Scalp

- Avoid pouring water on baby's head. Use a small fistful of warm water or wring a small amount from a washcloth.

- You can easily wet a bald baby's head by rubbing a damp washcloth onto the scalp.

- Make sure baby is in a reclining position to avoid any sudden lunges, and maintain a firm grasp in case of a reaction to the water.

- Keep in mind that less is more when bathing baby.

Shampooing

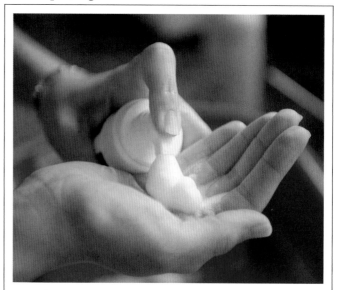

- Apply a tiny (dime-size) amount of shampoo to baby's scalp brush or washcloth and apply to head.

- Work into a small lather and then quickly rinse or remove with a dampened washcloth.

- Babies with little or no hair need only a trace amount of shampoo or body wash, which is then wiped off with a clean washcloth.

- Many babies like the sensation of a brush or cloth on their scalp. It's like a mini massage!

A shampoo shield prevents water or shampoo from running down baby's face during a bath. It resembles a visor and fits snugly around an infant's head. The material is usually foam, neoprene, or nylon and is offered in a variety of designs and colors to meet the preferences of parents (your baby doesn't yet have a favorite color, after all!). Infants usually outgrow the need for a shampoo shield as they become used to the bathing experience, and may begin to reach for it and remove it themselves when they are able.

ZOOM

Is there a difference between shampoo products? The answer is definitely yes! Baby shampoos gently clean, moisturize, and protect sensitive scalp and hair. They are designed to be free of soap and alcohol, and are hypoallergenic and dermatologist-tested. Many varieties are fragrance-free while others tout "clean scents" from natural oils or chemically derived fragrances.

Rinsing

- Double-check that the water you plan to use to rinse baby's scalp is at the right temperature and has neither cooled off nor is too hot.

- Infants at this age are too young to enjoy bath games like silly hair shapes; save that for when they are older.

- Infants may respond to seeing themselves in the mirror while you bathe them.

- Try using a baster or squirt bottle to maintain better control of water flow when rinsing.

Treating Cradle Cap

- Rub a small amount of baby oil or olive oil on baby's scalp. Wait a few moments for oil to soften scales, remove them with a brush or cloth, and then wash the oil off.

- Apply cortisone cream to scalp to reduce redness or irritation.

- Cradle cap doesn't usually require treatment as long as it doesn't bother baby. But its appearance often bothers parents.

BATH GEAR

Products promote convenience and comfort but are typically extras and not essential supplies

There's no shortage of bath gear for parents to buy. Determining whether certain items are necessary may depend on your pocketbook and baby's temperament during a bath, although most baby bath items are fairly inexpensive.

"Nice to have" gear items may include knee pads if you plan to bend over the tub, a bath organizer so you can keep all needed items together, towels designed just for baby that may include a hooded towel with matching washcloths, and rubber-backed bath mats to avoid slippery floors. Baby toys can be tempting, although at this age and stage, the one who will most likely play with items like a squish ball or squirter is you!

Infant Bathtubs

- These basic tubs are typically made from a single-piece plastic design, and aren't usually foldable.

- Some designs feature built-in accessory trays and built-in temperature strips.

- Supportive backrest with slip-resistant pad is usually standard.

- Infants will outgrow this first tub, but at under $20, it's a relatively small expense. The next step for baby can be bathing in the big tub, eliminating the need to buy a second tub.

All-in-One Bathtub

- Tubs typically offer head support pads that can be easily removed as baby grows.

- All-in-one tub designs are bigger. Since they are made for various stages of baby's growth, they may seem large for newborns.

- Seats may either have adjustable reclining positions or a removable sling to meet baby's various developmental stages and preferences.

- Some all-in-one bathtubs use quick-drying fabric and fold for easier travel and storage.

The most important decision, however, is what type of tub you want to use to bathe your newborn. Some styles stick to the basics with simple foam pads and an all-in-one design and are very inexpensive. Others offer variable reclining positions so that you can raise or lower baby depending on preference, growth, and muscle control. Still others feature elaborate features such as built-in storage areas and removable supports to transition from reclining to sitting styles to match baby's development. Some even fold up for easy storage or for travel convenience.

Baby Bath Organizer

- Over-the-door bath organizers provide pockets and pouches all within arm's reach of parents while being too high for siblings or babies to reach.

- Some organizers use removable adhesive or suction cups to attach to most bathtub surfaces.

- Plastic or rubber bath buckets or caddies keep bath supplies together in a waterproof organizer. Many designs feature a center handle for ease in transporting essentials.

- Drawstring bags provide a simple solution.

Baby Towels

- Hooded towels are sized for infants and provide a simple hood flap or curved design. They are more than cute; they keep baby warm and avoid them losing body heat from their head and neck areas.

- Towel sets often come with matching washcloths and accessories in varied designs.

- Look for towels that are soft to the touch; some towels are scratchy or have trim that could irritate baby's sensitive skin.

- Organic towels are readily available.

COGNITIVE DEVELOPMENT

Phenomenal brain growth quickly transforms your newborn's needs beyond just food and sleep

While at first glance your infant seems so utterly helpless and dependent on others, a closer look at all the things your newborn can already do is nothing short of amazing. Babies are born with many natural reflexes and survival instincts, and their intelligence along with motor and social development will grow and flourish with each passing day.

It's true that newborns spend most of their time sleeping, eating, crying, and eliminating waste, but that quickly changes. By the end of the first month, your baby is more alert and responsive, is more coordinated, and is becoming more social. It's almost inconceivable that a tiny baby who relies on parents for everything will eat solid food, begin to

Seeing and Hearing

- Newborns can focus on objects 8 to 12 inches away, so bring your face and any objects in for a close look!

- Newborns will prefer a human face above all else, although they may find high-contrast patterns and items of interest as well.

- Newborns will recognize and may turn toward or away from certain sounds and voices.

- Newborns are born with mature hearing. Check with your doctor if baby doesn't seem to respond to sound.

Motor Skills

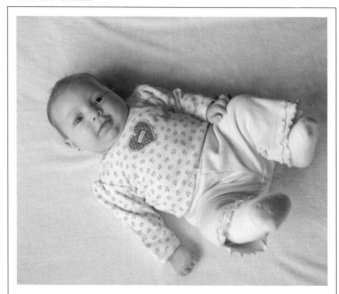

- While newborns make jerky and flailing thrusts and movements, they will quickly develop greater control and coordination.

- Newborns will be able to turn their heads. Most infants can turn their own body to respond to you by the third month.

- Infants will learn to bring their hands to their mouths, and open and close fists, by the third month.

- Infants will begin to stretch out and kick their legs.

talk, transition to drinking from a cup, and crawl or perhaps walk in the course of one year.

Newborns are also born with a developed sense of taste and smell, and may turn away from something they find unpleasant while turning toward something they want, such as the smell of their mother's milk. Infants can communicate their needs and excitement for their environment, and aren't afraid of telling everyone within when they are hungry, tired, or just want to be held. Greater changes are in store in the upcoming months.

YELLOW LIGHT

Parents may want to check with their pediatrician if their baby displays certain development flags. This doesn't mean anything is wrong, but warrants getting checked out. Flags may include a lack of reaction to loud sounds or never turning toward voices; does not blink, close eyes, or turn head in bright lights; does not focus on or follow an object; isn't gaining weight or has a poor sucking habit; or seems excessively stiff or floppy, especially after the first month.

Touch and Smell

- Newborns will prefer soft fabrics and avoid scratchy or coarse ones, and may grasp onto blankets.

- Caressing touches calm most babies, while grabbing them in rougher holds can cause newborns distress.

- Babies have a developed sense of smell, and will especially root and turn toward the smell of their mother's milk.

- Sweet smells in general are preferred over acrid smells.

Understanding Your Newborn

- A newborn's alertness will increase rapidly.

- Babies are born with all five senses.

- Newborns are naturally curious. They may stop what they are doing, including eating, to respond to a sound or something that captures their interest.

- Watch how infants widen their eyes, try to look for sound, track movement, or study your face.

SOCIAL DEVELOPMENT

Newborns' first emotions typically revolve around adjustments of fitting into their new world

Babies crave attention, and except for when hunger is the motive, snuggles and hugs from loved ones are usually the best ways to comfort a wailing infant. Infants will quickly develop temperaments—or behavioral styles—that determine at least initially how they may respond to the world around them. Infants may show strong differences in how they react to various sights and sounds, how they first communicate their basic needs, and how accepting they are of changes and different people. Parents quickly learn which tactics to use to (hopefully) achieve a desired behavior with their baby.

During an infant's first three months of life, baby is adjusting to pretty much everything. Your baby starts to learn to stay relaxed

Focus

- Your newborn will quickly begin to stay alert and focus for greater lengths of time.

- Infants find human faces the most interesting, and may seem to study your eyes and facial expressions intently.

- Focusing on your face is a way that baby first figures out how to relate to people.

- Spend quality time just gazing into each others' eyes and let baby explore your face while you talk, sing, or make facial expressions.

Love

- Most babies will experience a sense of "love at first sight" with their parents and will begin to show their emotions within the first few months of life.

- Look for early love responses from baby such as reaching for you or patting your face or body.

- Babies may begin to smile at you when seeing you or responding to your voice at around two months.

- Reciprocate those tender emotions through frequent holding and caressing.

and calm in the midst of what can be a world filled with potential sensory overload. As newborns begin to develop a sense of their environment, they may gradually begin to respond with increasing curiosity, focus, love and adoration, and mimicry. More tentative babies may exhibit anxiety, become overwhelmed, or be withdrawn and shy. Knowing what to do and what to avoid, sheltering babies from situations in which they become frightened and upset, and introducing them to situations at a comfortable level are strategies that parents learn to employ as part of getting to know their baby.

Responses

- Newborns may begin to look toward their parents as a clue to how to react to things around two to three months.

- Babies may begin to mimic and respond to their parents' facial expressions, especially exaggerated, overly silly ones, by three months.

- As infants become more aware of their surroundings, they may react more strongly to being overwhelmed, anxious, or overstimulated.

- Quivering lips and chins are ways babies express being scared or unsettled.

ZOOM

Babies are born with six states of awareness. Four levels occur while baby is awake and two are when baby is asleep. Awake states are drowsy, quiet alert, active alert, and crying. The sleep states are quiet, or what is called deep sleep, and active, or light sleep. Newborns spend more of their time sleeping in the light sleep stage, which is why they are disturbed or awakened easily.

Predicting Baby's Temperament

Is your infant's behavior an indicator of his temperament later? Maybe . . . or maybe not. An inconsolable, high-maintenance infant may grow to be a well-balanced youngster. Certain traits can be indicators, but not always. Still curious? Look for:

- How easily your baby is soothed.

- Length of focus or distractibility.

- Whether your infant seems easygoing or craves routine.

A GOOD ENVIRONMENT FOR BABY

A consistent schedule, attentive caregivers help newborns adjust to life outside the womb

Establishing a consistent schedule helps to provide an optimal environment for baby. Setting times when baby eats, bathes, interacts with family members, and even ventures out of the house in a stroller or other adventure helps infants begin to learn that that they will be taken care of in a predictable fashion. If you are parenting multiples, establishing

a schedule will become even more important so that babies are awake, asleep, and fed on a similar timeframe. Otherwise, you'll find yourself rotating the same activities throughout the day and night without an opportunity to accomplish anything for yourself or other family members.

While babies will initially eat and sleep at totally random

Air Quality

- Consider running a fan or using a ceiling fan in baby's nursery to help air circulation, which is thought to lessen the risk of SIDS.

- If baby seems congested, consider using a cool-mist humidifier to aid with breathing and coughs.

- Keep pets out of baby's room at all times to avoid pet dander or pet accidents.

- Keep baby's room free of odor from soiled diapers and use a disinfectant regularly.

Home

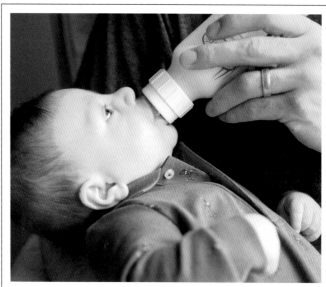

- Separate baby's environment by purpose. Baby's sleep area should be low-key and tranquil, with nightlights so that you can do middle-of-the-night feedings or diaper changes without stimulating baby.

- Have brighter lighting and high-contrast toys and objects for when baby is awake and alert.

- Bath area should be well-lit and warm. Try playing music.

- Feeding area should be quiet and calming to lessen distractions.

times, and may even have their days and nights mixed up, parents should be able to begin using sleeping and feeding as the cornerstones of baby's schedule beginning at around one or two months of age. Waking up baby when the rest of the family wakes up and then incorporating feedings into mealtimes are ways to blend baby's routine with your own. Encouraging alertness and activity in your baby during peak family busy times further helps to make your newborn involved with everyday activities. Your infant will soon transform from a passive observer to an active participant.

MAKE IT EASY

Since newborns spend most of their time sleeping, establishing a nursery environment that is calming and comfortable is key. Keep baby's nursery simple and serene to aid undisturbed and deep sleep. Consider using lamps instead of overhead lights, and change the bulbs to provide a soft glow. Curtains or child-safe blinds on the windows allow you greater control of lighting.

Sorting Days and Nights

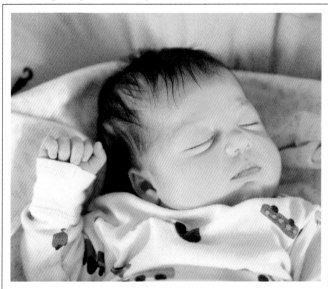

- Many newborns have their days and nights mixed up at birth. Getting used to a new sleep routine may take time, but baby will eventually adjust.

- Energetically interact with your newborn during the daytime while remaining quiet at night.

- Establish different day and night environments. Allow sunlight to stream in baby's room in the mornings, and keep room dark at nighttime.

- Don't let your baby sleep too long between daytime feedings.

Away from Home

- Healthy newborns will enjoy outings as long as they are kept comfortable and protected from the sun, if outdoors.

- Most babies enjoy exposure to new sights, sounds, and experiences.

- Seemingly harmless sounds, lights, or even wind gusts can create anxiety for a newborn, so provide frequent reassurance that you are nearby.

- Strangers may want to look at, touch, and even hold your newborn, so determine in advance how much you want to share your baby.

CONTACT THAT BABY NEEDS

Don't worry about spoiling your newborn; now's the time to meet baby's every need

There's absolutely no truth to the adage that you can shower your newborn with too much love and attention. Spoiling can indeed occur later, but for this age and stage, your newborn thrives from constant holding, attention, and love. Parents should forgo any guilt and comfort their newborn when she cries, and rock her back to sleep when she awakens in the

middle of the night. Responding to your newborn's needs in a timely fashion helps to build a loving relationship and foster trust and dependence.

At the same time, parents learn quickly that a baby's cries don't always signal distress, and that some babies seem to just cry for crying's sake. While crying is the key way baby

Settling In

- Give baby a home tour as you walk around holding your infant, pausing to let him take in the various lights, sounds, and sensations.

- Introduce your baby to household sounds while holding him for reassurance.

- Encourage your baby to track you as you move from area to area, and provide constant reassurance that you are nearby.

- Encourage your baby's tactile curiosity by holding his small hand to reach for and feel certain objects.

Family Contact

- Broaden baby's world to other loved ones beyond mom and dad.

- Let siblings assist with baby care basics such as dressing, bathing, and diaper changes in an age-appropriate fashion.

- Let baby get to know your family pet through constant and safely monitored exposure to one another. Many babies delight in a pet's soft fur or swishing of a tail.

- Provide constant caresses and reassurances with each new experience.

communicates, parents can help their infants to learn better coping skills and how to soothe themselves. Newborns need consistent care and to have constant contact, but that doesn't mean that weary parents need to provide round-the-clock care. In addition to providing them with milk when they are hungry, other ways to comfort and settle down a crying baby may be by speaking to him, playing music to calm or soothe him, changing his diaper, rubbing his face or head, or reassuring him just by being there.

Keeping in Contact

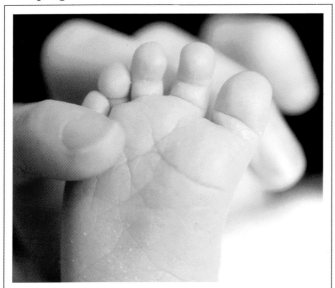

- Place a monitor in reverse so that baby can hear the family talk and laugh when in another room.

- Hold baby's hand or encourage baby to grab your finger. Stroke the back of his hand or feet with your other hand.

- Place baby in a sling or carrier while performing household duties such as vacuuming. Many newborns find the noise and repetitive back-and-forth motions calming.

- Use a soft baby brush to gently brush and massage your infant's hair or head.

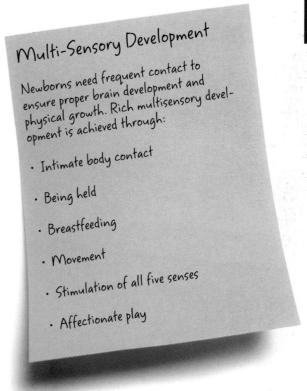

Multi-Sensory Development

Newborns need frequent contact to ensure proper brain development and physical growth. Rich multisensory development is achieved through:

- Intimate body contact

- Being held

- Breastfeeding

- Movement

- Stimulation of all five senses

- Affectionate play

PLAY

Playtime with baby is a surefire way to bring on the smiles, kicks, and flaps

Newborns won't be able to throw a ball or even truly laugh at this stage, but by the end of their first three months of life they will begin to interact and engage in simple play. Play is critical for your baby's cognitive, emotional, physical, and social growth. Besides providing ideal bonding experiences, play lets infants use their senses and learn about themselves and their world. Newborns are born explorers and are curious about their surroundings. That innate desire to check things out and to touch, feel, see, taste, and hear something of interest is the foundation of basic play. Why do you think babies want to take everything in, almost as if saying, "What's that?"

Early play for newborns may focus on the study of faces

Face and Expressions

- Newborns will mostly focus on faces at this stage, and will find your expressions and voice of greatest interest.

- Play simple face games with baby. Show baby your eyes, nose, mouth, ears, and hair and then point to hers.

- Exaggerate your expressions to the point of being really silly and clown-like. Show baby "happy," "sad," and "mad" faces, and anything else you can create.

- Put on and remove accessories like glasses or hats for baby.

Movement

- Newborns enjoy watching movement. Bob your head up and down and in each direction and encourage baby to watch.

- Juggle a small ball and encourage your baby to watch the ball's movement. Show excitement every time you catch it and encourage your baby to react.

- Play simple finger games with your baby. Your fingers can become a silly spider, crawling on baby and then soaring into the air.

- Watch a slow-moving ceiling fan together.

and contrasts, watching actions and reactions, and use of the senses. Brightly colored mobiles promote an early visual interest and encourage focus. At between two and three months, infants begin to grip and grab objects, and a basic rattle may become a favorite first toy. Infants like to squeeze, hold, and shake things, and then usually whatever they grasp goes straight to their mouths for a taste test. This form of early cause-and-effect experimentation is how newborns learn and explore their environment.

· · · · · · · YELLOW ● LIGHT · · · · · · · ·

Your infant won't yet have good muscle control, and may accidentally strike himself with toys while grasping them, only to get frustrated and then accidentally do it again. Keep your baby from hurting himself by making sure that initial "grab" toys are soft and have no sharp edges. Some baby rattles are made of hard plastic, and should not be given to infants until they demonstrate mastery of hand control.

Silly Sounds

- Whisper to baby and make soft, silly "sshhhh" and "ssppp" sounds. Watch her reaction.

- Introduce baby to wind chimes, a ticking clock, or other soft sounds that won't scare her.

- Turn on some music (not too loud!) and dance around for baby's entertainment. Your newborn will enjoy watching you move while listening to accompanying sounds.

- Carry baby while performing some safe and secure dips and sways to the beat.

Playtime Tips

- Many infant toys feature high-contrast color schemes, but you can also create fun at home.

- Make simple flashcards using white paper and a red or black marker to create shapes or patterns for show and tell.

- Use the cards to play paper peek-a-boo. Hold one in front of your face, and then pull it away suddenly while saying, "Peek-a-boo! Guess who?"

FOR DADS

Dads provide an extra set of helping hands and heart for bonding and care

The role of dads today and the ways they interact with their babies are typically very different from those of generations past. More dads desire to be active and equal participants in bringing up baby, opting against traditional roles and expectations. A growing number of men today become stay-at-home dads with baby while mom returns to work. The more

that parents share in duties, the more comfortable your newborn will be with different types of handling and involvement. Dads often bring a sense of play and adventure to their interactions. With many activities, an extra set of hands provides additional safety and confidence all around. And it's impossible for a baby to be loved and nurtured too much!

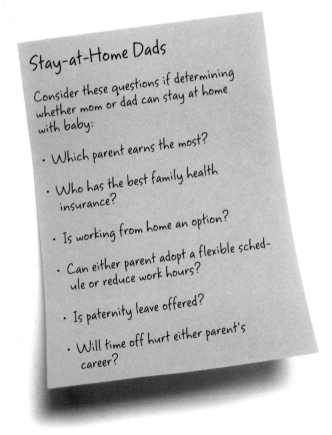

Stay-at-Home Dads

Consider these questions if determining whether mom or dad can stay at home with baby:

- Which parent earns the most?

- Who has the best family health insurance?

- Is working from home an option?

- Can either parent adopt a flexible schedule or reduce work hours?

- Is paternity leave offered?

- Will time off hurt either parent's career?

Dads and Bonding

- Newborns may respond better to higher voices. Dad should be careful to keep his voice volume quieter and even raise his pitch initially with baby.

- Dads should not be fearful of hurting baby. Dad can snuggle and caress baby just like mom.

- Chest or facial hair may irritate baby's soft skin, so keep that in mind when holding your newborn.

- Carrying baby, helping with feeding, changing diapers, and giving baths are great ways to bond.

In spite of all the changes in parenting, a new dad still may sometimes feel left out of caring for and nurturing his newborn. Breastfeeding moms share intimate time with baby that can't be totally replicated, and men who work long hours may feel they are missing out on important milestones. New parents need to work together to find positive and beneficial ways to build and maintain a strong connection between dad and baby. Consider simple approaches such as rotating diaper changes, scheduling baby baths when both parents can participate, and learning basic care together.

MAKE IT EASY

Dad classes are offered in many communities, and provide the basic training dads need to transition from the role of husband or partner to father. Classes are usually taught in "guy-speak" by dads for dads. Besides basic care, topics often address establishing or maintaining a work/life balance, relationship dynamics, and where to go for additional male support.

Dads and Newborn Care

- Most dads are very willing to learn basic newborn care, including diaper changes and middle-of-the-night feedings.

- Dads may be reluctant to step in and help because they are afraid of doing things wrong.

- It's okay for moms and dads to do things differently as long as baby's basic care is provided. There is no single "right way" to do things.

- Parents can learn together and agree on certain ways to do things.

Dads and Routines

- Dads can establish their very special place in an infant's life by creating special routines or traditions—something they can build on and continue throughout baby's childhood.

- Take turns soothing a fussy baby, and try out new calming sounds, holds, or regimens that are uniquely yours.

- Incorporate your new baby into your routines, such as taking baby in a jogging stroller on your morning run.

HEALTH

Stronger muscle control, better sleeping habits, and early crawling movements mark baby's progress

If your baby is healthy and growing on schedule, it's been a while since your last visit to the pediatrician. A lot has changed since then, and your infant is no longer as helpless and small. Most pediatricians schedule a well-child visit for babies at around four months of age to make sure your infant is growing on schedule and that normal milestones are being reached. Your

doctor will want to review your baby's asleep and alert periods, feeding routines, cognitive development, emotions, and overall adjustment. Above all, your doctor will determine that your infant is healthy, growing, happy, and making progress.

Your baby will receive several immunizations, including DTaP, IPV, and hepatitis B (which may be combined in the

Four-Month Health Checkup

Here's what to expect at your baby's four-month checkup:

- Baby's weight, length, and head will be measured for proper growth.

- Baby's body will be examined.

- Baby's heart and lungs will be checked.

- Your infant's eyesight, hearing, reflexes and basic skills may be checked.

- Several immunizations will be given.

- Parent concerns and questions will be addressed.

Vision

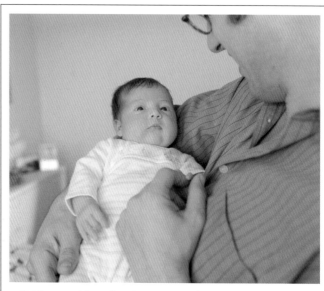

- Babies are able to focus easily and will follow you with their eyes as you move around a room.

- Babies will be able to recognize people when they walk in the door.

- Babies will be able to track fast movements, such as watching a moving car or a cat racing across the yard.

- Babies will be able to judge distance by the end of this stage and will see three-dimensionally.

single combination vaccine Pediarix) along with Hib. You may also ask your child's doctor about Prevnar, a vaccine that helps to prevent infections by the pneumococcal bacteria, which is a common cause of ear infections among other things; and RotaTeq, a vaccine that provides protection against different types of rotavirus, which may cause vomiting and diarrhea, and even dehydration, in children.

Your baby's motor skills have really started to blossom. Between three and six months, babies have become more alert and in control. They are developing skills for crawling, have gained control over their still-oversize head, are learning how to play, and are sleeping on a more consistent schedule. If your baby had colic as a newborn, most parents are happy to report that the symptoms usually lessen and go away during this stage. Your baby also seems to be genuinely happy more often than he is not, making him more fun to be around. While baby is not yet mobile, a growing independence and mastery of basic skills make this an exciting stage for parents and baby alike.

Coordination

- As baby gains better muscle tone and control, early innate reflexes are lost.

- Hand-eye coordination is improving to the point where baby may be able to reach for an object, grasp it, and bring it to the mouth successfully.

- Baby can bring hands together and may begin to play with the fingers and toes.

- Babies may sit with support, although they may require lots of propping and can easily tip over.

Signs of Concern

- Ask a doctor if your baby doesn't smile or try to engage people, doesn't show pleasure, or avoids eye contact.

- Check with a doctor if you don't see neck and head control or an improvement in baby's overall muscle tone.

- Have your baby's eyes checked if they seem crossed, if baby doesn't follow objects or people, or the eyes themselves don't seem "quite right."

- Diminished alertness could be a flag that something is wrong.

GROWTH

Most babies double their birth weight at five months and begin to roll and go

There's rarely a day that goes by when baby doesn't exhibit a new milestone or skill that seemed totally unattainable only days before. You'll need to keep your camera charged and ready, as baby's personality and desire to delight and show off for loved ones will keep you busy capturing those adorable expressions and toothless smiles. Your baby is now exploring

with all her senses, so expect to have glasses grabbed, hair pulled, and even your eye poked as baby begins learning about her world.

Most babies have doubled their birth weight at around five months. During this stage, babies gain approximately 1½ pounds and grow about an inch every month. Boys tend

Sleep and Growth

- Infants sleep so much due to rapid brain and body growth during this stage.

- Proper development requires that babies sleep a lot. Growth hormones are secreted by the pituitary gland at a faster rate while babies sleep.

- It is normal for infants to interrupt sleep for food and attention before returning back to sleep.

- Total sleep time will continue to diminish as length of alertness continues to increase, and basic routines are now possible.

Growth Spurts

- Milestones are often achieved about the same time growth spurts occur.

- Infants may act fussy and want to eat more than usual during a growth spurt. They may also want to eat more when they are working on developmental skills such

- as rolling over or head control.

- Growth spurts are typical during this stage, at four and six months of age.

- A spurt may last two or three days, but sometimes as long as a week.

to be longer and heavier than girls, although there are lots of factors that may determine a baby's size. The main criterion that doctors and parents will expect to see is progress. Regardless of where your child falls on the chart, it's a sure bet that those adorable newborn outfits that baby may have only worn a few times are already too little.

As babies continue their rapid growth, their fat stores increase, giving infants a chubby appearance. Not to worry . . . the rolls that are typical for babies at this age usually disappear as baby becomes mobile.

ZOOM

Are you concerned that your chubby baby is overweight or that your infant isn't getting enough nutrition? If you are worried that your baby is too fat or thin, check with your baby's doctor. In the meantime, don't make any changes to his diet or feeding schedule. There are many factors that affect a baby's size.

Coordination

- Babies may begin to amuse themselves with new noises, sounds, and playing with their fingers and toes.

- Sitting up (usually help is still needed) opens up a whole new perspective of what baby sees and begins to desire and reach for.

- Babies will learn to pass objects from hand to hand at around six months.

- Infants are becoming increasingly alert, and interest in just about everything helps with overall coordination.

Strength

- Infants have a strong grip that can surprise unsuspecting parents. Just try to get them to turn a coveted item loose!

- Babies learn that their hands are tools and will reach and begin to use hands in a raking fashion to bring desired objects closer.

- Babies will begin to support weight on legs when being held in a standing position.

- Infants aren't yet ready to stand on their own, but may test out their legs by doing "steps" and even bouncing up and down in standing position (with support!).

EMOTIONS

Squeals, smiles, laughter, and concern showcase baby's growing emotional development and awareness

Your baby has come a long way emotionally in the first few months of life. For many parents, the three- to six-month age provides the opportunity to relax a little and enjoy their baby's new social beginnings and more in-tune emotions. Your newborn has mostly settled in to her life and is beginning to truly understand her place in the world and how she fits into

it. Parents too have a better grasp of baby's communication style. Your baby may not cry as much or may be more easily comforted when the tears do come, and is more predictable about basic needs. Parents live for the frequent smiles, belly laughs, and wholehearted squeals that will develop during this stage.

Expressions

- Baby is learning that inter-actions are important.

- Babies may become quite animated and demonstrate their emotions by waving their arms and kicking their feet while squealing.

- Infants can imitate basic communication. You talk,

they may respond in turn either with babble, giggles, or physical movement; and so on.

- Your baby may mimic or study your facial expres-sions. Try making a big O with your mouth and widen your eyes and see the response.

Moods

- Your baby will increasingly show different moods to convey likes and dislikes.

- Your baby may demon-strate frustration. An ankle rattle that irritates baby, for example, may result in kick-ing and crying.

- Your baby may begin to cry more for attention. Infants at this age are beginning to want to be around people and activities.

- Babies can get irritable or become withdrawn if they do not receive quality inter-action with others.

While your baby is more content and comfortable, it is still easy for him to become overstimulated and overwhelmed. Your baby's emotions can overload, causing excitement and grinning sessions to transform without warning into outbursts of crying. That's the cue for parents to help baby calm down.

Infants may flash anyone a smile because of the positive response they receive in return. Infants often giggle and smile for strangers, family pets, and even for situations they find funny—in part because of support and encouragement from loved ones.

Your baby is beginning to learn expressions, and may respond according to how he "reads" your face. Babies may look worried or concerned if their loved one looks the same. They may also show delight when you are happy or get upset and begin to cry when you are angry. So, be careful how you look and act around your baby, or you may find your expressions can get you in trouble!

Understanding

- Baby knows that your or certain loved ones meet her needs but doesn't yet understand she's a separate person.

- Infants may grasp the concept that they can cause things to happen.

- Baby doesn't yet understand the more complex concept of you being present but not visible. Either you are here or you're not.

- A frightened baby can be comforted by the sound of your voice without necessarily seeing you.

Emotional Highs and Lows

At this age your baby may:

- Smile a lot to anyone (babies aren't typically shy around strangers until they are older)

- Laugh and squeal out loud

- Enjoy social interactions

- Respond positively or negatively to activities or surroundings by demonstrating excitement over things that are desired or crying or making faces when something is not desired

LANGUAGE

Crying is still primary method for babies to communicate their basic needs and emotions

By now, parents are better judges at distinguishing one cry from another. Crying becomes almost a language unto itself, with certain cries meaning, "I'm hungry," while others may mean, "I'm bored and need attention." Babies whose needs are met in a timely basis at this age will actually cry less and for a shorter duration. Babies who are left to cry things out

may cry more and are harder to comfort, and may feel anxious or scared. For now, parents need to focus on meeting their baby's needs and shower their infant with attention, cuddles, and comfort.

Your baby is experiencing new emotions. Whereas cries before focused on hunger, attention, and sleep, cries at this

Giggles and Coos

- Your baby may giggle at himself in the mirror. At this age, he won't actually realize he's staring at himself, but it won't matter, because he'll find it funny regardless.

- Early play may include swatting at a toy and laughing at the attempt.

- Babies may develop a deep belly laugh at this stage, and will find many situations and objects absolutely hysterical.

- Babies may begin to utter oohs and coos as early sounds.

Frustration and Irritability

- Babies may attempt to grasp objects, and become frustrated when they are not successful.

- Infants may cry to express frustration or anxiety, and show their unhappiness through body gestures and mad faces.

- Infants may become irritable over certain sounds or being held in a way that they don't like, and aren't afraid to express it.

- Infants at this age may become moody and don't necessarily want to do things at the same time you do.

stage may also signify fear, pain, loneliness, boredom, and frustration. Babies may become overstimulated and begin an all-out wail that takes time to be shushed, in part because babies don't know how to effectively turn off their emotions and soothe themselves.

Continue to encourage language by talking out loud throughout the day with your baby. Working together as a team, parents and their infants will navigate needs and wants in the coming months. At the same time, baby begins to learn early sounds and pre-words as a warm-up to language.

Reading to your baby is a great way to interact while promoting early understanding and familiarity with language. Baby books are fun to read and are visually stimulating, but don't limit yourself to those. Parents can read articles from the newspaper, nutritional information found on cereal boxes, and even recipes out loud to baby. The main goal is for baby to hear your voice and language patterns.

Tiredness

- Baby is becoming increasingly used to an awake/sleep routine and may suddenly become overly tired and cry to be laid down.

- Babies who are ready for a nap may begin to rub their eyes and act inconsolably cranky.

- Babies may push away the bottle or breast while crying and grasping a blanket or trying to turn to a favored sleep position.

- Infants may begin to reach for their pacifier or whine as a cue that they need sleep.

Babbling

- Babies start to babble at age four to six months.

- Babbling consists of infants learning and repeating many more sounds than expressed the first three months.

- Babies are literally practicing the rhythm, intonation, and sounds of language before they begin to speak actual words.

- Parents can initiate and encourage babbling by repeating sounds back and forth.

SAFETY

Baby's emerging mobility and curiosity mean parents need to childproof home and keep closer watch

While your baby isn't exactly mobile and won't be able to get into too much trouble yet, abilities and curiosity are quickly emerging. That means something that may be out of harm's way today may be a safety risk tomorrow, so parents should begin anticipating what baby may soon be able to do and make sure areas are secured and rooms are childproofed accordingly.

Your baby is (or soon will be) rolling around, grasping at objects, pulling on things, and putting just about everything in her mouth. Crawling or early mobility in some form or another will likely happen during this stage as infants become better aware of their growing abilities and want to explore. That means babies need to be protected from

Watch for Rolls

- Many infants are injured each year from rolling off furniture. Never leave baby on your bed unattended.

- Propping pillows around baby may no longer do the trick to prevent falls. Keep your baby within easy arm's reach when on furniture.

- Babies can now grasp railings on changing tables and dressing areas and roll or flip over with a surprising amount of strength.

- Remain with your baby when on the floor or during tummy time to prevent rolls into furniture or sharp corners.

Childproofing Basics

- Childproof electrical outlets with inexpensive and easy-to-use inserts or covers. Outlets near the floor are among the first things that babies may want to explore.

- Install or check your home's smoke detectors and consider purchasing a carbon monoxide detector.

- Protect sharp corners on furniture and around fireplaces by placing plastic, rubber, or padded cloth inserts on corners.

- Lower your water temperature setting to 120 degrees Fahrenheit to avoid accidental burns.

electrical outlets, extension cords, sharp objects, and anything else that catches their eye.

Baby's caregivers should never leave them alone or unsecured—even for a second—because the opportunity to roll, twist, or reach for things may be tempting. Colorful mobiles that were safely positioned just above baby's eyes only a short time ago need to be raised out of arm's grasp. Diaper changing areas and bathing centers that hold a variety of lotions, shampoos, products, and wipes need to be positioned out of reach as well.

There is often a gap in baby's mobility and abilities between four and six months of age, but since all infants attain milestones differently, parents should not procrastinate and begin performing safety checks as soon as possible.

Top occurrences for infant injuries include cuts and abrasions, burns, choking, and other soft-tissue injuries. Head injuries often occur due to an infant beginning to get mobile, and rolling around or falling over when sitting up, so parents need to make sure baby's surroundings are well padded and protected from sharp edges and objects.

Check Doors and Cabinets

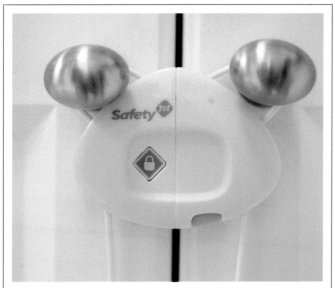

- Consider placing childproof guards on cabinets and drawers to which baby will have access, such as in the kitchen.

- Keep a single cabinet with "baby-safe" items that baby can open and close and get things out of safely.

- Place childproof handle covers on important doors, such as those that go outside or down to a basement.

- An option is to install flip latches at adult height to keep babies from opening and closing doors.

Secure Potential Hazards

- Drapes are tempting for baby to pull, and may need to be raised or the room be made off-limits. Older mini-blind styles have dangling cords and will need to be secured. Consider replacing them with a cord-free design.

- Make adjustments to where certain objects may be plugged into outlets. Electrical cords are a potential strangulation or pulling hazard.

- Secure heavy furniture, especially televisions, that could fall on baby.

- Move lamps and other lightweight items that can easily topple.

GEAR

Array of baby products for this age focuses on entertainment, exploration, and education

You can just look at your infant's face and see how he is starting to process information and figure things out. Babies are all about learning what things are, what they do, how they feel, what they may taste like, and how they sound, look, or move. That's why products for babies at this age focus on exploration. In addition, babies are becoming more vocal in their desire for attention, and won't hesitate to cry as if to say, "Pick me up! I want some attention!"

An array of products also helps busy parents with safe ways to provide baby with short-term entertainment while they try to accomplish a few things around the home that aren't baby-related every now and then. In addition, once baby

Activity Mats

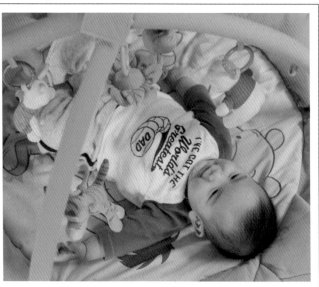

Indoor Swings

- Activity mats provide entertainment for infants to explore while lying on their backs.

- Mats are usually padded and feature soft fabrics along with textured areas and response pads for babies to touch.

- Activities often include dangling objects that can be safely grabbed, and some deluxe models include music, lights, and a variety of sound options.

- Most mats can be folded up and transported from room to room and may include a case for easy travel.

- Portable swings can safely entertain or soothe babies weighing up to 25 pounds (be sure to double-check weight recommendations).

- The slow, repetitive back and forth can help babies relax, while a higher speed and music can provide entertainment.

- Variations may include wind-up swings, battery-operated models, simple open-top designs, and ones that feature music, lights, and sounds.

- Five-point safety harnesses offer the safest protection.

gains head and muscle control, carriers in the form of front packs or backpacks let parents keep their hands free while holding and interacting with baby at the same time. Most babies really like adventures in which they are on the go with mom or dad while feeling snug and secure at the same time.

Convenience and cleanliness are also popular themes for baby products. Look for items such as mirrors, shopping-cart inserts, and toy bars that can go on the stroller or car seat.

YELLOW LIGHT

Germs can linger for days, so products such as shopping-cart covers that limit baby's exposure to surfaces that are used by the public can help prevent a baby from becoming sick. Research shows that cold viruses can lurk on shared toys, doorknobs, faucets, and other commonly touched items. Since babies constantly put their fingers into their mouths, limiting what baby can touch or share may indeed be a safety "do!"

Convenience Gear

- Soft mirrors that fit on the passenger seat where baby's rear-facing car seat is positioned let car drivers safely keep an eye on their infants.

- Shopping cart inserts allow parents to keep baby's hands away from handles and other often-touched areas.

- Soft activity books, clip-on toys, or entertainment trays provide convenience for baby.

- Pacifier keepers safely latch to baby's clothes to keep them handy when on the go. Similar products keep bottles from being thrown.

Baby Packs

- Infant front carriers provide positions for carrying infants in front, either face in or face out, and adjust to parent's back. Look for adjustable backrests and head support.

- Front carriers for babies who have mastered head control provide them with a safe and comfortable way to get a look at the world while parents keep their hands free.

- Backpack carriers often feature sunshades and even netting to protect babies from outdoor elements.

- Look for storage pockets.

BATHING

Baths become much more fun and may be entertaining as well as relaxing for baby

Bath time can be an absolute blast for most babies, although a few remain reluctant bathers who still dislike the whole water experience. Babies who enjoy bath time may begin to kick their legs, coo with excitement, and show their overall eagerness as you pull out the portable bathtub and ask, "Are you ready to take a bath?"

Since infants are now more mobile and may kick and splash, baths are most safe if you put baby's bathtub inside your own tub. However, that can be hard on your knees, so parents may want to invest in knee pads or bath cushions. While babies most likely still don't "get" funny hair shampoo shapes at this stage, many will like grabbing at suds and splashing

Setting the Mood

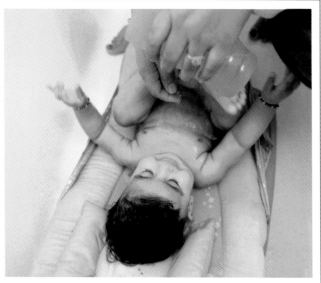

- Unless your infant still fusses, baths now are more leisurely and fun.

- Add baby body wash to water and fill baby's tub a little fuller.

- As you undress baby, talk up the bath experience.

- Encourage your baby to anticipate baths by talking about it, and let baby listen to the sound of the running water and watch as you prepare the tub and gather supplies.

Safety

- Your baby may be more active in the tub now and may twist her body around and kick, so be prepared.

- Make sure the adult bath faucet is childproofed with a covering or towel to prevent baby from accidental contact. Remember that the metal can become hot.

- Use a temperature monitor if you are unsure what temperature is best for baby.

- Be extra careful in lowering and lifting baby from the tub before and after bathing.

their hands in the water. Many babies are also interested in very basic bath toys, which can be as simple as a sponge to hold, a terry washcloth, or plastic squirter.

Babies still aren't getting dirty at this stage, as most babies are still mostly stationary. If your baby is still on the same feeding schedule, nothing new will be occurring with what's going in or out, but you may notice an increased amount of drooling as your baby may be preparing for a first tooth. Only one to three baths every week are recommended, although you may want to increase spot wipes around the mouth and

hand areas for sanitary reasons and to avoid any irritation from increased saliva. (Remember, everything seems to go from hand to mouth at this stage!)

Parents should be sure baby doesn't get too cold during longer baths, and have warm (not hot) water nearby to continuously pour over baby to provide warmth as well as for rinsing. You can further add to the bathing experience by providing a gentle massage, especially on scalp, legs, and toes.

Fun

- Encourage your baby to explore and splash in the tub.

- Bubbly body wash can be interesting to look at and feel, and babies may be fascinated with how foam looks on their belly or other body parts.

- If you want to energize your infant, play some upbeat music while giving a bath and sing along to it. Or, just sing or make up your own tunes.

- Soft spongelike toys or rubber duckies are classic favorites.

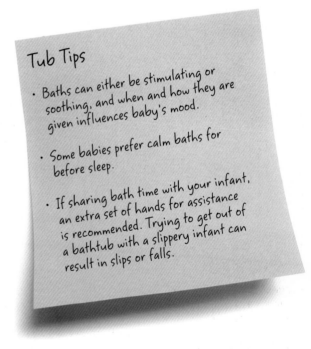

Tub Tips

- Baths can either be stimulating or soothing, and when and how they are given influences baby's mood.

- Some babies prefer calm baths for before sleep.

- If sharing bath time with your infant, an extra set of hands for assistance is recommended. Trying to get out of a bathtub with a slippery infant can result in slips or falls.

DRESSING

Styles may be cute but not comfortable or convenient, making dressing baby a challenge

Dressing your infant may be easier in some ways now that baby is gaining better body control. However, many babies start to voice their displeasure at having their arms and legs pulled through clothing, and may especially dislike pullover shirts. Parents become masters at distraction as they dress wriggly and whiny infants. Fashions may be absolutely adorable, but

cute doesn't necessarily translate to comfortable or convenient, and babies won't hesitate in letting you know!

Look for outfits with snap crotches that are made from comfortable fabrics. Beware of certain styles that require an almost complete undressing of your infant with every diaper change. Certain overall styles and jumpers may require

Fit

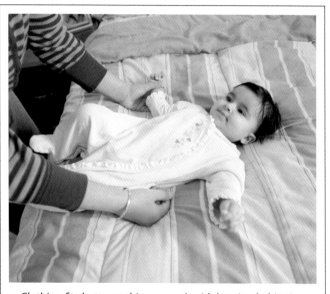

- Clothing fits better at this stage, since babies have better body control and now fully extend their arms and legs so outfits don't appear to have excess fabric.

- Buy big, but not too big, and not too much of any one size.

- Avoid dressing babies in clothes that are too long around the crotch. Excessive material keeps safety harnesses from fitting properly.

- Not all clothing styles work on all babies. Experiment with brands.

Layers

- Footed pajama styles can provide the easiest dressing, but thin fabrics may not keep feet warm in cooler temperatures and footed types may limit wear time.

- Long-legged and long-sleeved onesies without feet can be layered with socks or booties.

- Soft hooded jackets with hand coverings work well in cold weather. Mittens or gloves aren't practical at this stage.

- Remember that infants can overheat easily in car seats and strollers, even in cooler weather.

clothing to be removed from the leg area entirely for diaper changes, and others only snap down part of the way, requiring extra effort. Avoid clothing with snaps, buttons or zippers on the back, or bulky apparel that prevents baby from comfortably lying down or reclining.

Dressing your baby in layers helps moderate temperatures, and baby is now old enough to wear a jacket comfortably without being slumped over. While you won't be swaddling your baby at this stage, blankets still provide warmth, protection, and comfort.

Accessories

- Accessories are available for infant boys and girls, and are often too cute to pass up.

- Most babies aren't bothered at this stage by headband bows, simple barrettes, or caps or hats, and some outfits come with matching accessories.

- Infants don't really need any shoes, although the soft-sole types can be used for fashion and to keep socks on.

- Make sure head accessories aren't too snug and don't poke into the scalp or pull hair.

3-6 MO.: CARE

YELLOW LIGHT

To avoid chafes or rashes from scratchy fabrics, dyes, or trims found on many outfits, parents should wash their infant's outfits before putting them on baby. Tags located on the back of necklines can also be irritants to sensitive skin. If it seems like your baby is bothered by them, look for tag-free varieties or carefully cut off the tags after reading the labels for fabric construction and washing instructions.

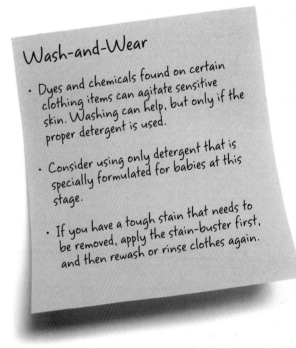

Wash-and-Wear

- Dyes and chemicals found on certain clothing items can agitate sensitive skin. Washing can help, but only if the proper detergent is used.

- Consider using only detergent that is specially formulated for babies at this stage.

- If you have a tough stain that needs to be removed, apply the stain-buster first, and then rewash or rinse clothes again.

DIAPERING

Changing baby's diaper in public means keeping an eye on safety and sanitation

As parents settle into their routine with baby, trips and outings seem not only feasible but simple as well. One common concern that may give pause to parents on outings, however, is changing baby's diaper in public.

Most restaurants and public places—but certainly not all—have portable changing stations located within restrooms.

Styles vary, and some may be located within certain privacy stalls or in the larger, wheelchair-accessible stalls. Others are in common areas and are sometimes in the traffic flow of people entering and exiting restrooms. More women's bathrooms than men's have changing stations, creating a dilemma for dad if he is the one with the tot in tow.

Average Wet Diapers

- Exclusively breastfed or bottle-fed babies may now have an established pattern as to the daily frequency of wet diapers and bowel movements.

- As baby's digestive system matures, the frequency of wet diapers may decrease while the amount of wetness increases.

- Expect about four to six wet diapers a day and around one bowel movement daily (although it can sometimes be more or less).

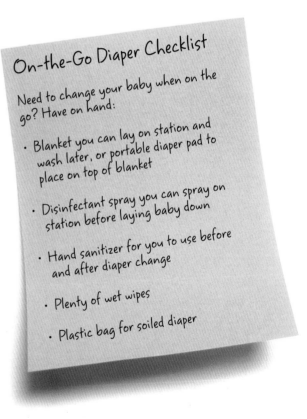

On-the-Go Diaper Checklist

Need to change your baby when on the go? Have on hand:

- Blanket you can lay on station and wash later, or portable diaper pad to place on top of blanket

- Disinfectant spray you can spray on station before laying baby down

- Hand sanitizer for you to use before and after diaper change

- Plenty of wet wipes

- Plastic bag for soiled diaper

Even if the facility has a portable changing station, some may appear to be unsafe or in an unsanitary condition. Before using one with baby, be sure to inspect the straps and make sure they are properly attached. Next, see if the station seems relatively clean. Changing an infant on a portable station will be more palatable if you come properly prepared. Parents should have the appropriate gear to minimize contact with the changing station and by beginning and ending with carefully washing their own hands, since they'll be handling the station. Since germs can last on a surface for days, you'll want to be extra careful to avoid picking up any bad bugs.

If your baby needs to be changed and a station isn't available or isn't suitable, you may elect to discreetly change baby's diaper using supplies from your diaper bag on a bench, on a public grassy area, or even in the backseat of your own automobile. Be sure to remain considerate of other people and place the soiled diaper in an airtight diaper disposal bag before depositing it in a public trashcan.

Quick Diaper Changes

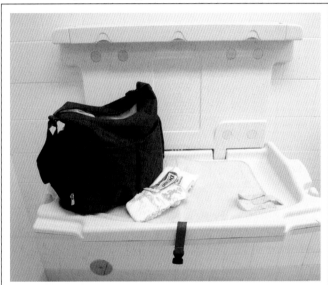

- Your car or baby's stroller may be a better place for a diaper change than many public establishments.

- Do the bare minimum necessary for baby's comfort; you can do a more thorough cleaning later.

- Never change a baby's diaper in a restaurant booth or similar environment. Food and diaper changes never mix, and you'd expect the same courtesy of others.

- Always keep extra baby outfits in your diaper bag, just in case.

Travel Tips

- Dress baby in simple clothing styles when away from home to minimize time spent on a public diaper station.

- Use distraction to prevent baby from grabbing the sides of a changing station.

- Make frequent diaper checks on car trips to avoid your infant developing a rash from being in a wet diaper for too long.

- Wrap a second diaper on baby if traveling on an airplane, where lack of space may make changing a diaper impractical.

101

SLEEPING

More firmly established awake/sleep cycles and decreased night feedings mean more rest for parents

It's probably too early to realistically expect to enjoy a full eight hours of uninterrupted sleep just yet, but the good news is that your baby may now be sleeping for longer stretches through the night. Your baby should have an awake/sleep pattern mostly established at this time, although parents may still face occasional howls in the night if baby is awakened, because she may not be able to successfully return to sleep. The need for most night feedings has also decreased, as most babies at this age receive enough nutrition during the day to sustain them for a longer stretch (typically five or six hours) at night than when they were newborns.

Infants will now sleep for a total of 12 to 16 hours a day,

Sleep Positions

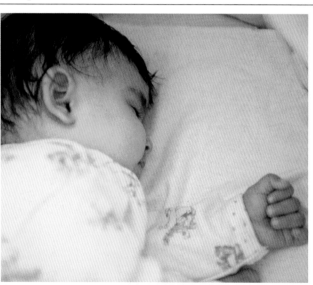

- Baby should be put on his back to sleep, but might roll onto his side or stomach.

- If your infant can roll over from back to tummy only, consider a sleep pad that prevents rolling (and middle of the night howls when baby can't roll back).

- Infants are less susceptible to SIDS risks after their fourth or fifth month—about the time they begin to choose preferred sleeping positions.

- Alternate the direction your baby's head faces when laying baby down to decrease the risk of a flattened head.

Sleep Strategies

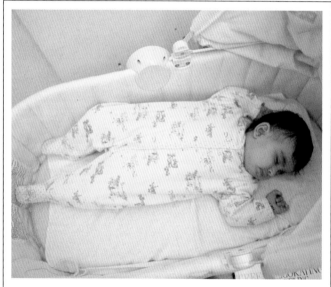

- Every child is different, and a sleep strategy that works well with one baby may be ineffective with another.

- A sleep strategy that works for a while may suddenly not work any longer, and parents will need to try something new.

- Establish a consistent routine and stick to it at all costs if your baby is having difficulty sleeping at night.

- Reinforce good sleep habits at as early an age as possible.

including naps. When they are awake, they are more alert and interactive, and their bursts of newfound energy often mean they will enjoy a deep sleep to rest up for what's next.

If your baby is routinely waking up every night, it may be time to take steps to change sleeping habits. Babies typically sleep better after active play. Following interaction and developmental time, establish a quiet sleep environment, and then make sure baby is relaxed, comfortable, and tired. Make sure that you establish and then maintain a consistent bedtime routine.

Exhausted parents whose baby is not sleeping for a longer period at night may consider basic sleep training. Approaches vary greatly, and parents should research options about whether they want to let their baby cry it out and learn to soothe and comfort himself, respond immediately to cries and comfort their infant without picking him up out of bed, or opt for timely attention that may include holding and rocking with the belief that secure babies will be less likely to cry out with time.

Sleep Routines

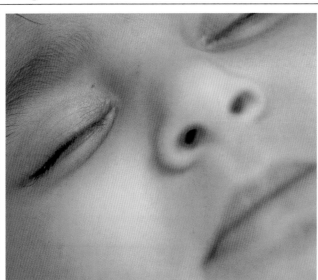

- Help set baby's clock by waking her up at the same time in the morning. If you let baby sleep in, then you're only encouraging her to stay up later in the evening.

- Encourage baby to learn to fall asleep independently by laying her down when drowsy but not asleep.

- Set naptimes based on your family schedule and baby's sleep cycle as much as possible.

- Create a special bedtime routine that baby can learn to anticipate.

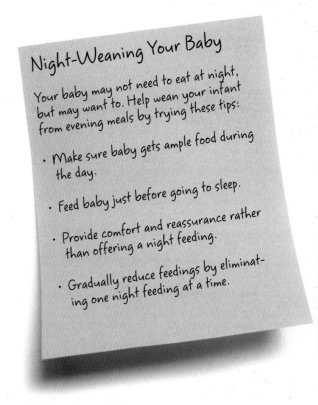

Night-Weaning Your Baby

Your baby may not need to eat at night, but may want to. Help wean your infant from evening meals by trying these tips:

- Make sure baby gets ample food during the day.

- Feed baby just before going to sleep.

- Provide comfort and reassurance rather than offering a night feeding.

- Gradually reduce feedings by eliminating one night feeding at a time.

ON THE MOVE

Exciting adventures and experiences beckon as baby begins to discover newfound mobility

Wherever did your newborn go? The transformation in just three to four months is nothing short of miraculous, as your baby is beginning to show personality combined with an earnest interest in movement and motion. Your infant isn't yet a whirlwind of activity (that will come later), but in this stage, your baby may likely begin to hold up his head without wobbling, use arms to push up his body while on his stomach, roll over, and maybe even sit up. Some babies even begin to crawl in a clumsy and uncoordinated fashion. Your baby's confidence in his abilities is growing along with his curiosity and determination, and mobility becomes a desired skill by the end of this stage.

Gaining Control

- Infants laid on their tummies may initially be reluctant to raise their heads because it's hard work.

- Parents should schedule daily supervised tummy time sessions with baby and provide encouragement with positive support and toys.

- Baby may initially whimper and cry when placed on her stomach but should quickly adapt to the new position.

- Neck, arm, abdominal, and leg muscles will begin to strengthen in preparation for crawling and eventual walking.

Heads Up

- Curiosity and alertness will encourage most infants to lift their heads and use their arms to push up while looking around when placed on their tummies.

- Infants can lift and hold their heads up at a 90-degree angle.

- By the end of this stage, baby will keep head level when pulled to a sitting position.

- Babies may roll over from their backs to stomachs, and with practice will learn to flip back.

Parents can also help to encourage motor skill development and movement through simple play. Interactions such as moving baby's legs in a bicycling motion, boxing, hand-jive clapping, and dancing are a lot of fun for both parent and baby and are activities you can do after diaper changes or during alert periods. Other motor control activities can include teaching baby how to "swim" the backstroke or breaststroke, do the "turtle dance," take your infant on an imaginary airplane flight, or any other silly movement or motion you can think of!

Encouragement

- Infants will be more apt to try new things if they receive positive reinforcement from loved ones.

- Some babies may be able to lift themselves from lying down to sitting up.

- Once babies develop better motor control, they'll quickly be on the move.

- Infants may begin early crawling motions, which may resemble wiggles or "commando" crawling in which they use their arms to lurch forward while on their bellies, dragging their legs behind.

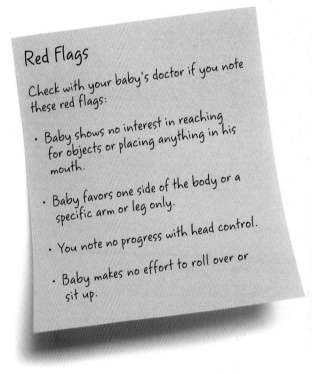

Red Flags

Check with your baby's doctor if you note these red flags:

- Baby shows no interest in reaching for objects or placing anything in his mouth.

- Baby favors one side of the body or a specific arm or leg only.

- You note no progress with head control.

- Baby makes no effort to roll over or sit up.

INFANT AILMENTS

Extra dose of TLC needed for treating common colds, ear infections, and stomachaches in babies

A fever is a telltale sign that your baby is sick. But your infant can also be ill without running a high temperature, and common ailments can transform your usually happy and babbling tyke into one who is either inconsolable or listless in a matter of hours. Most likely your pediatrician has already provided you with general information about what to watch for

concerning your infant's overall health. But sometimes your infant may not seem his usual self or doesn't seem hungry and you may be unsure of what to do next. Since dehydration can occur quickly in small infants, parents need to keep a careful watch on their baby's symptoms, and if in doubt, err on the side of caution and schedule a sick-child appointment

Vomiting

- It can sometimes be difficult to know the difference between excessive spitting up and vomiting in an infant.

- Warning signs of sickness include spitting up more frequently than usual, refusal to eat, diarrhea, arching of the back, or

incessant crying while attempting to eat.

- See a doctor if your infant has forceful or projectile vomiting.

- Vomiting is often due to a stomach virus or blockage.

Eye and Ear Issues

- Excessive tearing and possible discharge in one or both eyes can indicate blocked tear ducts.

- Massaging the inside corner of the eyelid and using warm compresses may help unblock the duct. Antibiotic drops or ointment may be prescribed.

- Ear infections are noted by increased irritability, fever, pulling or scratching on ears, or crying when attempting to eat.

- Middle ear infections are common. Infant immune systems are immature and Eustachian tubes may not effectively drain fluid.

with the pediatrician for an examination. More urgent cases may require a trip to the emergency room. Thankfully, many conditions are not serious and baby will feel better soon.

If your infant shows any signs of breathing difficulties, head toward the doctor as soon as possible. Breathing that appears to be labored or is unusually rapid or heaving is worrisome and requires prompt medical care. If your infant has a serious fall or injury, especially to the head, make the call right away.

······· YELLOW ●LIGHT ·······

Infants can suffer from car or motion sickness, although it can be more difficult to diagnose because babies can't say what is bothering them. Motion sickness has to do with a conflict between the eye and ear resulting in a sensory overload. Infants can have motion sickness from traveling in the car and even from being carried around in an infant carrier (some parents may unwittingly swing the carrier while carrying baby).

Respiratory Illness

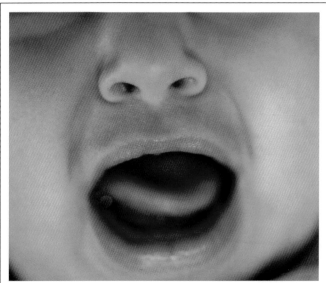

- Croup affects the upper airway and is noted by a hacking cough that sounds like a bark.

- Bronchitis is most common in the winter and may start with a low-grade fever, deepening cough, and then faster breathing and restlessness.

- A runny nose or nasal stuffiness, throat irritation, sneezing, cough, and possible fever may signify a common cold.

- Serious ailments in infants can include rotavirus, influenza, pneumonia, respiratory syncytial virus (RSV) and whooping cough.

Antibiotics: Do or Don't?

- Antibiotics can effectively treat a variety of illnesses. But growing concern about antibiotic overuse and the development of drug-resistant bacterial strains is prompting doctors to scrutinize symptoms before prescribing them.

- Antibiotics treat bacterial illnesses like strep throat.

- They are ineffective against viruses that cause colds and stomach flu.

- More powerful antibiotics may be reserved for harder-to-treat cases.

SCHEDULES

Establishing a feeding routine helps bring family life back to a sense of normalcy

As baby grows, feedings will become more predictable and length of time between when baby eats will increase. That's especially good news for parents of multiples, who may find that most of their day (and night) until now has been filled with a feed–diaper change–sleep routine repeated again and again. Most on-demand feedings have been replaced with a semblance of a feeding schedule, usually every three to four hours at this stage, meaning that a routine may start to take shape. That's not to say that your baby is always consistent, but it's now becoming possible to plan activities and to include baby's meals along with your own.

Premature babies may still eat more often than a full-term

Milk

- Even when solids are introduced into baby's diet, meals will still typically start with breastfeeding or bottle-feeding.

- Breast milk or formula will remain the primary source of nutrition for baby's first year.

- Nutritional value may vary depending on food, but none is as complete as breast milk or baby formula.

- Check with your doctor before switching to a different type of baby formula, especially if you are using a specialty formula for a special condition.

Hunger

- While most infants at this stage drink five to six ounces in a sitting, others may want more.

- Parents may begin using bottles in seven- or eight-ounce sizes instead of the three- or four-ounce bottles they used to feed their newborn.

- Bottle-fed babies may grow impatient and fussy over slow-flow nipples used when they were newborns, so parents may want to switch to a medium or fast flow.

- There's no mistaking now when baby is hungry; you'll know her cues that it's time to eat!

baby at this stage, because they have more catching up to do. While their schedule may be slightly delayed, they soon will begin a predictable routine as well.

What does a feeding schedule look like at this stage? Schedules vary based on your personal routine, but babies may eat upon awakening, mid-morning, around noon, mid-afternoon, at early evening, and again in the later evening. That leaves about two feedings in the night hours, although some parents may wake baby just before they head for bed, leaving one feeding in the wee hours.

Interest

- Incorporate your baby into mealtimes as much as possible.

- Your infant will enjoy the sensations of smelling food, seeing what it looks like, and watching and hearing people eat—even if all she eats at this time is milk.

- Feed your baby right before mealtime so she is not hungry while you eat.

- Once baby transitions to solids, she will already be accustomed to mealtime routines.

········· RED ● LIGHT ··········

As tempting as it may be sometimes, you should never prop your baby's bottle. A propped bottle can easily lead to choking and an infant may not be able to push the bottle away to avoid a serious or even life-threatening hazard. Bottle-feeding your infant is also intended to be a pleasant and interactive experience, and a propped bottle denies parent and baby enjoyable shared contact.

When to Replace Nipples

- Periodically inspect nipples for wear and tear, and always replaces ones that seem damaged.

- Silicone nipples may need to be replaced every three months; latex ones may require replacement sooner.

- When replacing nipples, consider whether to change the flow rate (slow, medium, fast, or variable) to coincide with baby's growth.

3–6 MO.: FEEDING

109

READINESS
Solid foods are typically added to baby's milk diet between four and six months

Typically between four and six months of age, your child's doctor will give you the green light to introduce solid foods to your infant's diet. The decision usually follows a satisfactory checkup to assess overall health and development. For many parents, the news signifies a significant milestone in their baby's first year. From now on, feedings and diaper changes will never be the same!

While breast milk or formula will remain the staple of baby's diet during the first year, solids provide additional nutrients and a more filling meal to satisfy growing hunger. But just because your baby can start solids doesn't mean that the early stages will be free of lots of trial and error and rejections.

Reflexes

- If your baby's tongue-thrust reflex is gone or mostly disappeared it may be a sign of readiness.

- This reflex prevents infants from choking on foreign objects but also causes them to push food out of their mouths.

- Baby may initially push food out with her tongue for you to scrape off with a spoon as she adjusts to the concept of swallowing.

- Babies may purposefully push food out with their tongues or spit when they dislike a taste or texture.

Sitting Up and Head Control

- Babies should be able to sit up without any or very little support before they are introduced to solids.

- A high chair isn't necessary at this stage; babies can also be fed in infant seats or while supported in your lap.

- Babies need to be able to control their heads.

- Babies should be able to turn their heads or push the spoon away with their hands when unwanted food is offered.

Your infant may be physically ready for food but simply uninterested in trying it at this time. Forcing your baby to eat before he is ready will only lead to frustration on both sides.

Your baby's senses of smell, vision, and taste are fully developed, so an infant who swipes at your food, seems overly interested in watching you eat, demonstrates an increased urgency while feeding, or acts hungry after a meal is signaling that he's ready for "real" food. There are other solid-readiness clues to consider as well.

Most pediatricians recommend a maximum formula intake of 32 ounces a day. For most babies, that equates to about five six-ounce bottles. If your baby drinks this much or more and still seems hungry, beginning solids may be the answer. However, don't start giving your baby cereal until his overall developmental readiness is confirmed at a complete well-child visit.

Gear

- Purchase feeding spoons designed for young babies that feature a small head covered with rubber.

- Bibs are a must, as most food initially will end up everywhere except inside baby's tummy.

- Since cereal is initially mixed with milk or formula, you'll need a bowl handy. Only prepare a small amount initially in case baby isn't interested. You can always mix more.

- Wet wipes or dampened towels are a must-have to clean up messes.

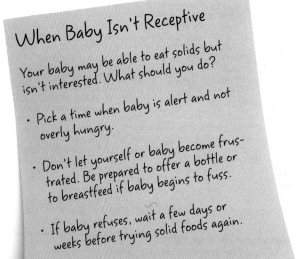

When Baby Isn't Receptive

Your baby may be able to eat solids but isn't interested. What should you do?

- Pick a time when baby is alert and not overly hungry.

- Don't let yourself or baby become frustrated. Be prepared to offer a bottle or to breastfeed if baby begins to fuss.

- If baby refuses, wait a few days or weeks before trying solid foods again.

CEREAL

Single-grain, iron-fortified cereal is usually recommended as baby's first taste of solid food

You've picked a time to introduce solids when your baby is most likely to be interested and alert and have started the meal with a bottle or breastfeeding. It's time to introduce solids! Most likely, baby's first taste will be rice cereal, and the mixture will be nothing more than a little bit of cereal mixed with a lot of either formula or breast milk. The appearance

should be runny, not like oatmeal. Your baby has a lot to get used to with these first attempts.

Initially mix only a tablespoon or two of the milk-cereal mixture while testing baby's reaction. With a small amount on an infant spoon, place the mixture near your baby's lips. Baby may want to smell before tasting. Don't be surprised

Preparing Cereal

- Mix one or two tablespoons of cereal with one ounce of formula or breast milk initially.

- You can either make cereal from scratch or choose a store-bought variety from a box or jar (check the ingredient list carefully so you

- don't feed baby something with more ingredients than you had intended).

- Cereal can be served at room temperature.

- Organic commercial baby foods are also available.

Consistency

- The initial cereal mixture should literally drip off a spoon.

- Experiment with the texture if baby seems to be rejecting eating from a spoon.

- Repeatedly try the same flavor before giving up. It may take time, so try again

- at a future meal and don't lose hope!

- Once baby learns how to swallow cereal and is receptive to eating from a spoon, gradually thicken the mixture to be more like the consistency of oatmeal.

if your baby doesn't want to open up her mouth at all and rejects the notion of being spoon-fed entirely. Talk with your baby about how yummy the food will be and how excited you are about eating solids, and try again in a minute. Parents naturally open their mouths as they bring food to their infant's mouth, and your baby may mimic the open mouth in response. Once food is in, don't worry if it almost immediately gets pushed or spit back out.

Set Up and Storage

- Use a clean spoon to place a small amount of mixture on baby's plate and then a baby spoon to feed your infant.

- You can refrigerate any remaining food mixture for up to two days.

- Praise your baby for trying a new food, even if you're not sure whether any of it was truly swallowed.

- Begin offering cereal once or twice a day.

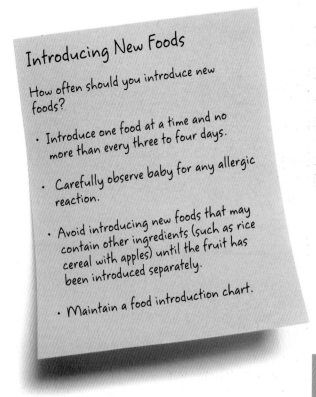

Introducing New Foods

How often should you introduce new foods?

- Introduce one food at a time and no more than every three to four days.

- Carefully observe baby for any allergic reaction.

- Avoid introducing new foods that may contain other ingredients (such as rice cereal with apples) until the fruit has been introduced separately.

- Maintain a food introduction chart.

FEEDING BABY

Babies have their own tastes and preferences when it comes to eating food

Most babies begin eagerly anticipating mealtimes and the new tastes and smells they experience. Not surprisingly, they'll quickly let you know that they favor one food over another, or even home-prepared over commercial-prepared (or vice versa). While baby may initially eat squash and peas, for example, he may show his displeasure at being served

those instead of sweeter peaches, over which he bounces and flaps. Once the first stage of feeding cereal has passed, and various foods have been safely introduced, you may find that baby rejects the previously acceptable rice cereal but will eagerly open his mouth for mixed cereal with bananas.

When choosing the next food to introduce (and your

Trial and Error

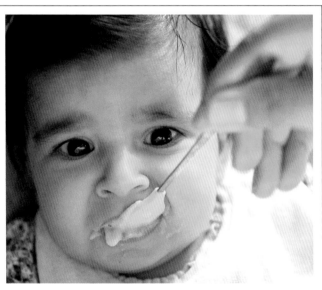

- Even if baby rejects a certain food initially, don't give up. Keep trying and if after a few days it's still a no-go, rotate it to the bottom of the list and try again later.

- Babies don't have to try all basic foods on a list, but make sure skipped foods

- are not blended into a multi-ingredient recipe later.

- Watch baby's cues for when to stop.

- Don't encourage baby to eat more or "finish up."

Flexibility

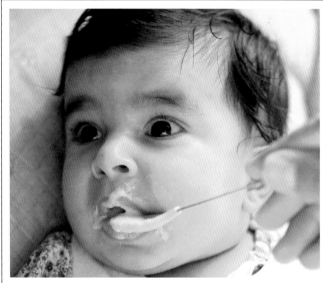

- Sometimes babies simply aren't in the mood to eat solid food. It's okay to skip a meal session!

- Don't worry about food being repetitive. Babies don't yet understand variety in their diets.

- Experiment with different times to introduce solids until you find when baby seems most receptive. Midmorning and evening often work best, but any time is okay!

- Baby should still take 24 to 32 ounces of breast milk or baby formula each day.

doctor may have a preferred order for you to follow), don't let your personal taste preferences dictate what baby may like. Parents are often quite surprised over which types make it on the "love it" list and which ones don't. Many babies like the taste of beets, for example, while many adults don't. But don't stock up too much on those ingredients; baby's taste may quickly change as the process of feeding continues.

When should you feed baby solid food and how often? Initially, you'll want to start with once or twice a day based on when you think baby will be most receptive. You can either start with breast milk or baby formula; end with milk after giving baby solid food; or both depending on your schedule and baby's preference. Keep in mind that the amount of solid foods baby will eat at six months of age may amount to only a few tablespoons.

The ultimate goal is to feed your baby solids when your family eats its meals (think breakfast, lunch, and dinner), but that comes at a later stage.

Feeding Fun

- Early feeding attempts should be fun and stress-free.

- A spoon is like a foreign object to your baby, and it's only natural that she may first reject the concept of opening mouth and swallowing food.

- Babies may react to new tastes with photo-worthy facial expressions.

- Parents of multiples should establish a shared mealtime routine, but maintain separate food logs of each baby as individual preferences or reactions may vary.

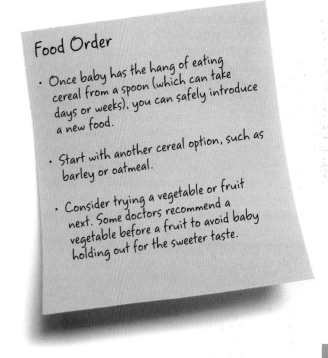

Food Order

- Once baby has the hang of eating cereal from a spoon (which can take days or weeks), you can safely introduce a new food.

- Start with another cereal option, such as barley or oatmeal.

- Consider trying a vegetable or fruit next. Some doctors recommend a vegetable before a fruit to avoid baby holding out for the sweeter taste.

115

ALLERGIES OR INTOLERANCE

Food reactions aren't common, but parents should know what to do if baby shows symptoms

Introducing foods one at a time and then waiting and looking for a reaction may add additional time to your already busy schedule, but it's your baby's health you're talking about. Allergic reactions to foods that are typically safe and allergy-free for babies are rare, but they do exist. And parents won't know which allergies might exist in their child until they see

a reaction for the first time.

Before starting a baby on solids, parents should know what to do in the event of an allergic reaction. A severe reaction that results in breathing difficulties requires emergency medical treatment, while most reactions that are minor (such as a rash) can simply be noted in baby's food log. Parents should

Signs of Allergic Reaction

- A skin rash, often in the form of blotchiness

- An increase in intestinal gas

- Bloating

- Diarrhea or vomiting

- Fussiness after eating

- Hives

- Breathing difficulty

- If your baby shows a reaction, don't offer that food again until you've talked with your doctor.

Risks

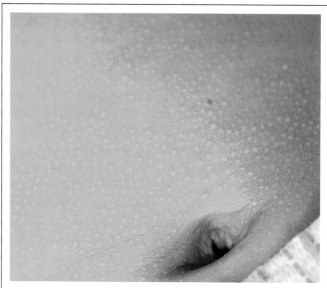

- Your baby has a greater risk of having food allergies if close family members also have food allergies.

- Know the foods to which family members are allergic, and closely monitor baby when introducing those items.

- Allergy-related conditions, like eczema or asthma, in close family members can be indicators for an increased risk of food allergies.

- Avoid citrus fruits because of their high acidic content, which can create painful rashes even if baby is not allergic.

116

also note whether baby has other ailments at the time, such as a common cold, that could also contribute to any minor symptoms. Try the food again later when baby is well. While some reactions are almost immediate, other symptoms of food allergies are harder to diagnose because they initially seem to be chronic problems like poor growth, lethargy, or diarrhea.

Food items that should be avoided until baby is at least two years old include nuts of any type and many kinds of seafood due to risks of high levels of mercury. (Consult with your child's doctor before adding any fish to your child's diet.)

Most/Least Allergenic Foods

- All foods are not created equal when it comes to potential food allergies.

- Least allergenic foods include apples, apricots, bananas, barley, carrots, oats, peaches, pears, plums, rice, and squash.

- Foods to avoid introducing until baby is older include berries, chocolate, citrus fruits like oranges or grapefruit, egg whites, honey, nuts and peanut butter, syrup, tomatoes, wheat, and yeast.

- Check with your doctor before adding fish.

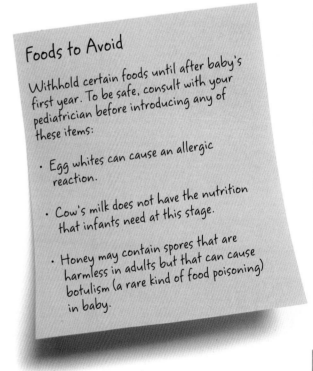

Foods to Avoid

Withhold certain foods until after baby's first year. To be safe, consult with your pediatrician before introducing any of these items:

- Egg whites can cause an allergic reaction.

- Cow's milk does not have the nutrition that infants need at this stage.

- Honey may contain spores that are harmless in adults but that can cause botulism (a rare kind of food poisoning) in baby.

FOOD OPTIONS

There are pros and cons to making baby's food versus purchasing commercial varieties

Choosing whether to make baby's food from scratch or purchase store-bought varieties may not be as clear-cut as you may think. While pureeing baby's first foods is fairly simple and straightforward, preparation does take time and the process involves washing, chopping, cooking, and then blending ingredients. And then there is cleanup afterward. But

making food yourself means you know exactly what is going into your baby's mouth, and you don't have to worry about added sugars, preservatives, or other ingredients.

On the other hand, added ingredients are actually a plus for some commercially prepared foods. Some brands fortify foods with 100 percent of the daily requirement of iron and

Rice Cereal Recipe

- 2 cups of brown rice, cooked according to package directions, and 8 ounces of baby formula or breast milk.

- Place cooked rice in a blender or food processor with formula or milk and puree until completely smooth.

- Add additional formula or milk if needed for preferred consistency.

- Extra cereal mixture can be frozen for up to two months.

Preserving Nutrition

- If you plan to prepare your own baby food, preserve nutrients by using cooking methods that retain the most vitamins and minerals.

- Opt for baking or steaming fruits and vegetables instead of boiling, which washes away nutrients.

- Freeze portions that you don't plan to use right away.

- Avoid preparing spinach, turnips, beets, and collards. They can contain high levels of nitrates, which can cause anemia. Serve commercially prepared varieties to be safe.

B vitamins, have added calcium, and have added prebiotics to help with digestion. Prebiotics exist naturally in certain foods like bananas and help good bacteria to grow and flourish in baby's digestive system.

Cost versus convenience is another factor to carefully consider. Undoubtedly, making baby's food yourself is the most economical way to prepare first meals since convenience packaging drives up the cost of baby foods. For busy parents, however, store-bought brands provide significant time savings and are worth spending a little more money. Many parents opt to prepare food when they can, but don't feel guilty when they buy commercially prepared varieties, allowing them the flexibility of choice based on their family schedule and routine.

A growing number of parents prefer to feed their babies organic baby food, and organic stores coupled with commercial organic food products make those preferences easily attainable as well. Organic labels cost more than other commercial products but tout that every recipe is made in accordance with organic production and growing practices.

Make-Ahead Food

- Make extra baby food and then freeze until needed.

- Pour pureed food into ice cube trays, cover with plastic wrap, and freeze overnight.

- Remove frozen food cubes from tray and place in freezer-safe containers or bags labeled with the food item and date made.

- Defrost cubes as needed and add breast milk or baby formula as desired.

Health Hints

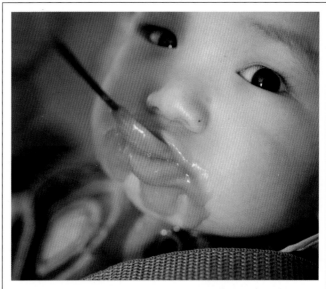

- Follow proper food preparation safety rules to protect your baby from food-borne illnesses such as salmonella or E. coli.

- Wash your hands frequently before, during, and after food preparation for baby.

- Do not feed your baby directly from a jar. Bacteria from baby's mouth can contaminate remaining food. Spoon out what you need onto a separate plate.

- Dispose of opened jars of baby food and fresh pureed food within two days.

PLAYTIME

Include baby in family fun while introducing physical interactions and expanding stimulations

About everything baby does involves some type of play or interaction at this stage, and that is what makes her so much fun! By six months, your infant may be enthusiastically waving her arms, kicking her feet in delight or just because she can, and rolling over . . . and maybe even sitting up and starting to crawl. Life is one big adventure, and while your infant most likely isn't yet very mobile, you and baby both know what lies ahead in the near future. For parents of multiples, your play opportunities will be doubled, tripled, or more, so get ready for plenty of giggles!

Your baby is now seeing the world more clearly in terms of vision, focus, and desire. Grabbing and gripping, responding

Seeing Fun

- Show baby a coveted toy or object, and then place it slightly out of reach and encourage her to look for it. Watch her reaction when she finds it!

- Let baby admire herself in the mirror.

- Your baby may now focus on finer details, so show her things like patterns on her room's wallpaper, colors on clothes, and details on favorite toys.

- Perform a light show with a flashlight for baby to watch.

Hearing Fun

- Give your infant noisemakers you can tolerate, such as soft rattles to clench and shake. Simple music toys provide sound stimulation as well.

- Start a ritual of loud and exaggerated "smack and blow" kisses as you say hello and goodbye to baby.

- Encourage basic sound associations such as that of a barking dog, a meowing cat, a car revving up, the telephone ringing, or the crunching of leaves.

- Vary music selections to energize or soothe baby's mood.

to sounds, mimicking what you do, and early communications are all in a day's work. Playtime is here, and your baby most likely wants to be the star attraction. Visual play can involve variations of jack-in-the-box, peek-a-boo, or even just simple opening and closing of fingers or eyes, where now you see something and now you don't. Add sound effects, such as a bumblebee buzz landing on her belly or a "pop" with your mouth when you hide your face and then reappear, and baby will be that much more enchanted.

Touch Fun

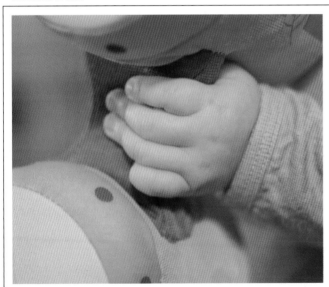

- Look for items around your house that baby can touch and feel. Why do you think the baby book *Pat the Bunny* remains so popular?

- Let your baby touch the grass, soft and rough fabrics, and hard and soft surfaces. Remember that infants will want to grasp and then place objects in their mouths.

- Introduce basic concepts of "hot" and "cold."

- Let your baby explore your face, skin, and dad's facial hair or stubble.

Buddy Pals

- Baby can increasingly become your buddy by accompanying you on simple outings.

- This is a great stage for carrying babies around in either a front pack or a backpack for a new perspective before they become too heavy.

- Keep baby safely nearby and keep conversations going while you fold laundry or cook dinner.

- Pal around together on walks.

EXPLORING AND LEARNING

Promote infant's curiosity and increasing focus through encouragement, reinforcement, and repetition

The best part of exploration and learning at this age is that you don't really need to buy anything to entertain your baby, although of course many parents do. You're the clown, the scientist, the explorer, and the teacher all in one, and baby will get all the entertainment and playtime he needs by simply engaging in baby play with you! Keep in mind that

repetition of the same action will delight baby again and again, until suddenly it doesn't. Overstimulation is a reality, so parents need to carefully follow baby's lead when enough is enough.

The more you can get down to baby's level and relate to him on his terms, the better. Lie on your stomach while your

Act and React

- Change what you do and watch baby's reaction. Babies will learn to anticipate as part of their learning.

- Spin a yo-yo, stretch a rubber band, or engage your baby in any activity that becomes predictable.

- Hide an object in a plastic cup and then turn it over. Where did it go? See if baby can learn to pick up the cup and get the object.

- Stack things up and let them fall, and do it again . . . and again.

Interactive Play

- Beyond watching you or a loved one, a ball can be a baby's best interactive toy at this stage.

- Bounce or dribble a ball while baby watches, and count or make sound effects.

- Roll a ball to baby. Have your partner behind baby to help roll it back. Most babies find the rolling game fun.

- Let baby hold a ball and watch how she explores it with her fingers, mouth, and eyes.

baby has tummy time and have a friendly staring contest. Be a friendly drill sergeant and encourage mini-pushups of keeping his head and chest off the floor with his arms. Show baby your personal snake slither, complete with sound effects, or play a game of rootin'-tootin' scooting fun along the floor, with your tyke at your side or on your lap. A great way to get baby active on the floor is to scatter toys or child-safe objects of interest around to encourage him to move from one object to another independently.

Move It!

- Pull baby up from a lying position to sitting while gripping his hands (once baby can support his head).

- Encourage baby to begin to pull up on things (with you there as support and for safety).

- Show baby how to touch or smack the ground or furniture with her hands while sitting (with your support to avoid topples).

- Help baby to clap hands and even stomp feet while standing (with you supporting him).

Exercising With Baby

- Your baby doesn't need formal exercise. But you might, and including baby can benefit you both!

- Always use a cushion or pad for baby in an open area.

- Think "slow and gentle" when bicycling baby's legs or moving baby's arms out and in or across the chest.

- Let baby watch you while you stretch and perform basic exercises.

SOCIAL DEVELOPMENT

Baby is ready for prime-time smiles and is into showing off and charming attentive visitors

Eye contact and smiles coupled with earnest attempts at charming someone or even an interesting object (sometimes babies may still not know the difference) are all part of baby's social development at this stage. Your little cherub will typically make an all-out effort to entertain and please you—as long as the mood strikes—and temperament is more likely to

be happy than not. Most likely, your baby enjoys the company of just about everyone, and likes to observe the activities of those around. These social engagements are what drive your baby's self-esteem and opinion of her environment.

Your baby's social development also allows you to begin to better understand which things baby enjoys and which ones

Prince or Princess Charming

Social Butterfly

- Your infant will make and maintain eye contact with you.

- Babies can literally read the expressions on people's faces, so if she sees you worrying or fretting, baby will likely do the same.

- He recognizes and understands that there are special people who care for him and meet his needs.

- Your baby is learning that relationships are rewarding and that his world is safe, predictable, and loving.

- Baby gets pleasure in smiling at people and having them smile back.

- Baby may initiate conversations with people, and respond back enthusiastically with babbles, sounds, and physical movement such as kicks or waves.

- It's too early for your baby to wave hi or bye-bye, but he may reward you with flaps and coos.

- Your tyke can become overexcited and may start to cry, and will need to be calmed down.

she doesn't. Body language, facial expressions, and enthusiasm (or lack thereof) let you know whether baby likes to take a bath or what she thinks about getting dressed or going for a walk. A full-fledged cry or belly laugh is clear-cut communication, but increasingly your baby is expressing opinions in other ways about everything!

If your baby doesn't maintain eye contact or seems unresponsive to people most of the time, it could be a sign of a developmental delay. Check with your baby's pediatrician if you have concerns.

ZOOM

Your baby still believes that her life is the world and that she controls making everything happen. The notion that events occur and people she doesn't know exist apart from her doesn't really come until a later stage. This lack of understanding is why babies may not have yet developed concern over "stranger danger" and are often less resistant to leaving mom or dad's sight.

Family Fun

- Let baby participate in as many family activities as possible, and don't shelter him from normal household noise.

- Your baby may show pleasure and begin to squeal when siblings interact with him.

- Family pets typically amuse baby (although they should still not be left alone together).

- While baby may sleep much of the time, stroller adventures, walks around the block, and watching older children at play provide new experiences and fun.

Symbiosis

- Symbiosis is a term describing the relationship between an infant and parent, and often, but not always, refers to the mother.

- An infant is dependent on the parent both physically and emotionally.

- Each person receives reinforcement, beneficial or detrimental, from the other.

- Parent and baby feel a strong sense of empathy with the other's emotions, such as frustration, joy, and impatience.

125

ROUTINE

Setting schedules can help to re-establish couple time and help balance family dynamics

Baby, baby, baby. It may seem that your baby is all you have thought about for the past several months. By now, you're more comfortable with the whole baby business and most likely you, your partner, and the rest of your family are craving a return to a sense of normalcy and the beginnings of a routine.

The basics of a routine are pretty simple. Sleep. Eat. Basic care. Repeat. But actually establishing when the fundamentals of baby care occur, especially on a busy schedule, may not be as easy. Start with one essential at a time, and build around it. Combine that with baby's cues about what he needs and when, and a basic structure begins to take shape.

Logging Z's

- Keep a log of what time and for how long baby sleeps.

- Record baby's temperament and ease in going to sleep. Does he fuss or cry? Settle in quickly? Seem ready?

- Note when baby typically wakes up in the middle of the night and how long before sleep is re-established. Write down efforts used to put baby back down.

- Use this information to create a basic schedule with sleep as the cornerstone.

Setting Schedule

- Fill in other activities on your schedule, including feeding times, playtime, and ongoing events.

- If a caregiver cares for baby, ask her to write down a schedule that you can use for weekends or days when your infant is not in care.

- Make sure your baby is "ready" for bed by making sure he is comfortable and fed, and that care needs have been met.

- Adjust schedule until it seems right.

Since most of baby's time at this point is spent sleeping, start by establishing nap times and bedtime. For sleep to be successful, you'll want to establish a plan and to make sure your infant is "ready" for successful sleep, meaning baby should be fed, dry, comfortable, and healthy. That means establishing feeding times around sleep times, and in between come periods for play and basic care. Remember that extended time in the car may serve as "naptime" for baby and may affect the schedule.

Having multiples can challenge even the most basic plans, as your babies' preferred schedules or cycles may be different.

With enough consistency and time, parents of twins, triplets, or more can establish a sequence of order, including who gets what and when, to maintain a functioning household as much as possible! Older siblings and their various activities can be integrated into a family's busy routine, and parents can adapt the schedule so that they can feed or incorporate a naptime when bringing baby along to a sibling's dance class or soccer practice.

Schedule Success

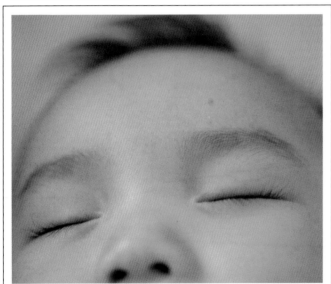

- A baby's routine will change as he does, so regularly review and adjust schedule.

- Baby's alert times are the preferred times for a well-child visit. Try to avoid scheduling that requires you to awaken your infant from his established naptime.

- Set other family activities around your plan as much as possible during baby's first year.

- Use baby's schedule to insert couple time and allow an occasional break from parenting.

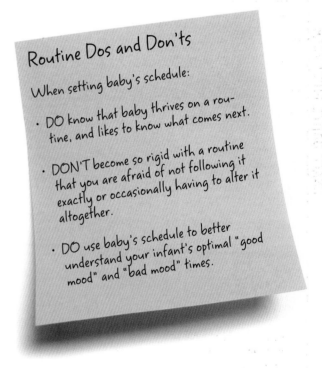

Routine Dos and Don'ts

When setting baby's schedule:

- DO know that baby thrives on a routine, and likes to know what comes next.

- DON'T become so rigid with a routine that you are afraid of not following it exactly or occasionally having to alter it altogether.

- DO use baby's schedule to better understand your infant's optimal "good mood" and "bad mood" times.

127

OTHER CAREGIVERS

Leaving baby with a child-care provider or babysitter provides new freedoms, worries for parents

Almost every baby will receive care by a caregiver other than a parent or close relative at some time. Parents who both work outside the home must find a child-care provider for their infant while they are away, and occasional babysitters are often needed so parents can attend an adult activity or just get away from parenting responsibilities for a while.

At the same time, no one said leaving your infant in the care of another is easy. Do your homework and carefully research various child-care options before deciding whether to take your infant for care at a daycare or family home setting, or whether you prefer having a nanny, au pair, or babysitter care for baby in your own home. Cost, flexibility, comfort level,

Choosing a Care Provider

- Ask friends and family for references for who they use for child care.

- Part-time, full-time, and occasional care needs may influence who you use as a child-care provider.

- Assess your family needs and budget first to know what you can afford. There's no sense interviewing applicants if their fees are outside your range.

- Check licensing, certification, and training of staff members and centers carefully. Many states feature online listings of licensed providers.

Options

- Daycare centers group kids by ages and feature longer hours. Staff turnover and an "institutional" feel at some centers may be concerns.

- Family care providers typically keep four to eight children of varying ages in their homes. Kids are treated like family members, but not all home providers are properly trained and licensed.

- Hiring a provider (such as a nanny) in your home typically costs the most.

- "Mother's helpers" help with baby while you remain at home.

caregiver qualifications, safety, and hours that care is needed may influence the choices working parents must make.

Using an occasional babysitter requires much of the same consideration. Weigh various factors such as reference checks, safety training, and your confidence in a person's care abilities and that your instructions will be followed before leaving baby with someone else.

Parents often find that taking a break from baby provides a chance to re-energize and be happier with their responsibilities when they are reunited.

ZOOM

Most child-care providers welcome infants for part-time or full-time care beginning at six weeks—about the time maternity leave for working moms ends. Some working parents can extend time home with baby by using vacation and sick days or combining maternity and paternity leave. Make sure the provider is set up to handle the special needs of a young infant.

Safe and Secure

- Always conduct reference checks of any caregiver, including a babysitter, before making a hiring decision.

- Watch how a potential caregiver interacts with your baby.

- Ask about child-care phi-losophies and make sure they match up with yours.

- Check out facilities or homes carefully for safety, cleanliness, comfort, and suitability for your age child. Not all settings are conducive for infant child care and their specialized needs at this stage.

Babysitter Checklist

Questions to ask:

- Have you received specialized training for child care (first aid/CPR, attended a babysitter class, or taken related school courses)?

- Do you regularly work or volunteer with kids?

- Are your immunizations current?

- Do you drive (in case of an emergency)?

- Do you have any health restrictions that could affect your ability to babysit?

129

FOR DADS
A new dad's role may change and grow as his baby gets older

New dads sometimes take a hands-off approach during baby's first few months, thinking they will spend more time with baby once he can walk, talk, and be more playful. This can be a big mistake. Dad will miss out on some of the most memorable moments of being a parent, such as baby's first smile, first words, and maybe even first steps. And they risk losing out on some prime opportunities to bond with baby. So get involved from the beginning and as baby gets older, continue to take a supportive role at home. Take turns with nighttime feedings or consider taking over extra household duties as mom continues to spend extra time with her baby, and go to as many pediatrician visits as possible.

Don't Be a Clueless Dad

- Understand safety rules, including proper use of a rear-facing infant car seat and not leaving baby where she can fall.

- Never shake a baby.

- Learn your baby's feeding schedule, including what she can and can't eat, and don't give inappropriate foods.

- Don't leave your baby in a wet or soiled diaper.

Dad's New Role

- New dads can usually still find time for hobbies and interests, as long as they prioritize their time.

- Make your family your top priority.

- In addition to helping take care of baby's day-to-day needs, a new dad should help his partner plan for baby's financial future.

- Life insurance, a will, and a college fund are all things that can help make your baby's future more secure.

YELLOW LIGHT

Postpartum depression (PPD) is a common problem among new mothers. Unfortunately, it is sometimes overlooked as being part of the normal baby blues that many moms have. Dads are in the perfect position to be on the watch for PPD, which typically lasts longer than the baby blues (a few days or weeks) and includes more severe symptoms. These can include feelings of sadness, hopelessness, having trouble focusing, or feeling overwhelmed. Moms with PPD may also cry a lot and have trouble sleeping. They withdraw from friends and family members, or even think about harming their babies. Be extra helpful with your baby and get your partner help from a doctor if you think she might have PPD.

Understanding Your Growing Baby

- Don't trust most old wives' tales, such as that it will hurt your baby to let her stand with support.

- Your baby will double her birth weight when she is about five months old.

- Rolling over, sitting with support, holding a rattle, and turning to sounds are some of the milestones your baby may reach by the time she is six months old.

- Many babies are sleeping through the night by five to six months.

Do it Dad's way

- Learn what techniques work best for you and your baby. They won't always be the same ones that work for mom.

- Dad can have his own songs, books, games, and special times with baby.

- Strap-on baby carriers can be a great way for dad to carry baby around.

- The easy way isn't always the best way to do something in the long run. Don't be afraid to take your time.

131

HEALTH

Well-child visit and another round of immunizations help keep baby's health on track

Another well-child visit starts this age and stage for baby, and your pediatrician will measure, weigh, and carefully examine your tot to make sure her health is good. By now, you're used to the frequent checkups, and may even look forward to them as an opportunity to learn where your baby is on weight and height charts, to get parenting questions and

concerns answered, and to receive reassurance that your baby is thriving.

Your doctor will most likely check baby's vision and hearing, lungs, and heart; examine the soft spots (fontanels) on his head; and look inside his mouth and check for any incoming teeth. The doctor will also press gently on baby's abdomen

Vision and Eye Contact

- Eyes will be examined. Many doctors shine a light and see if baby will follow it with his eyes.

- A regular avoidance of eye contact, especially if baby doesn't look parents in the eye, could signify autism or other developmental issues.

- If concerns are noted, most pediatricians will refer parents to a pediatric eye specialist for further testing.

- Babies often like looking at themselves in the mirror and closely examining objects.

Hearing and Response

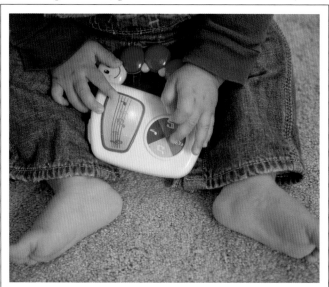

- Newborns receive hearing screenings in the hospital and more informally at every well-child visit.

- Early detection of hearing loss helps to ensure infants receive assistance to develop language and cognitive skills.

- An audiologist can check the hearing of newborns and infants with an auditory brainstem response (ABR) or otacoustic emissions (OAE), a more specialized test.

- Doctors will also ask about baby's response to sound in general.

for tenderness or problem areas and will check your infant's hips for developmental hip dysplasia to see if they are loose in the hip socket and whether thighs spread apart easily. Genitalia may also be briefly checked.

Most likely, the pediatrician will ask you about your baby's schedule, temperament, eating, social skills, and motor development. Your doctor may perform simple tests to determine physical milestones and whether baby maintains eye contact and reacts to toys or stimulation.

If baby is healthy, additional immunizations will be given.

Head and Neck

- Head and neck control will be checked.

- Doctor may pull baby from a lying to a sitting position to note muscle control.

- Excessive floppiness or stiffness or lack of muscle tone is a red flag for a developmental delay.

- Baby's head will be examined for proper shape. A misshapen or flat head, called positional plagiocephaly, may require further review by a specialist and perhaps treatment with a head band or helmet for a designated time period to help correct head shape.

Six-Month Immunizations

This is baby's third round of vaccinations. New combination vaccines mean that baby only receives two or three shots while still receiving the recommended vaccines. Here's what to expect:

- Hepatitis B (HepB)

- Diptheria, tetanus, pertussis (DTaP)

- Haemophilus influenza type B (Hib)

- Inactivated poliovirus (IPV)

- Pneumoccal (Prevnar)

- Rotavirus (RotaTeq)

- Flu vaccine if in season

GROWTH

Baby's on the move as growth, motor skills, and coordination start to come together

Rapid growth and motor control development occur between the ages of six and nine months, and by the end of this stage, your baby may be fairly mobile. A few babies may even be getting close to walking. Your baby is quickly figuring out how his body works together to achieve a desired movement (such as getting over to a toy or object).

Early movements may look quite strange, as babies don't all learn to sit up, crawl, or even pull up in quite the same way. Many babies never crawl, but scoot on their bottoms or even roll to get where they want to go. Some prefer to go straight from sitting up to first steps when they are ready.

Learning to Crawl

- Early crawling starts with the transition from a lying to a sitting position and then trying to move from there.

- Some babies crawl on all fours in traditional fashion, although they may go sideways or even backwards at first.

- Some babies commando crawl (like slithering snakes) while others scoot on their bottoms and use their arms to move themselves forward.

- As long as they are trying to move, babies are attaining a typical milestone.

Increasing Strength

- Hard-surface flooring can provide a safety challenge for a baby just learning to crawl. Use carpeted areas or mats to minimize spills.

- Baby may like to be on all fours and rock back and forth without actually moving.

- Many babies like to push themselves up to a standing position while you are safely holding onto them.

- Marching steps (with parent support) helps babies to build those needed leg muscles.

Most babies will be able to lean over while sitting independently and reach out for an object, usually without toppling once they have practiced and mastered the skill, and then pass it from hand to hand. While baby's primary focus until now has been learning to use and control larger muscles, hand-eye coordination is becoming a greater priority as baby's focus and desire for objects achieves a "want it, go get it, got it" drive. Carefully supervise your baby as she attempts movement, as successful body control isn't always consistent.

ZOOM

Fine motor skills use small muscles for grasping and basic hand-eye coordination, while gross motor skills involve the development of large muscles that baby needs to sit, roll, crawl, and eventually walk. It might be helpful to keep a log of skills your baby has accomplished to update your doctor, as baby may not be inclined to show off these abilities during a well-child visit.

Pull to Standing

- By nine months, babies may begin to transition from crawling or sitting to a standing position.

- Baby will use your legs or furniture to pull up. Keep items with wheels or objects that can tip over safely out of baby's reach.

- Once babies reach this milestone, most will likely just hold on until they topple down again. Some may start to stand without support.

- This new vantage point increases baby's interest in exploration and perhaps walking.

Exercises

- Help baby to build strength and have fun at the same time.

- Lay baby faceup on a mat and gently pull up to sitting position with her arms and make a silly expression or sound when she's upright. Lower and repeat.

- Hold baby around his waist, upright and facing you, while you're seated and encourage him to do leg bounces.

135

EMOTIONS

Baby is gaining awareness of desires and feelings and wants to interact with family

You'll notice some big emotional changes in your baby between six and nine months, with most of them being due to your infant's growing awareness of himself as a separate person, a better recognition of his own feelings, and the increasing desire to be an integral part of the family.

A big step in emotional development is baby's awareness

that she is an individual and not the extension of someone else. While the details may still be fuzzy at this stage, your infant is beginning to realize she is separate from loved ones, which can result in anxiety or concern when she can't see or hear you nearby. Babies are also starting to better understand their different feelings and what they can do to get

Feelings

- More complex feelings are starting to emerge at this stage.

- Baby is starting to process and identify different feelings, such as being hungry versus craving some attention.

- Babies sometimes may not

understand their awakening emotions, and react by becoming overstimulated or crying without apparent cause.

- Babies may begin to communicate with their parents better about what they are feeling and what they want or need.

Identity

- Baby begins to realize he is a separate person and not an extension of you and the world.

- Baby is starting to develop a basic understanding of the differences between outside influences versus what she feels on the inside.

- Baby may begin to "get" that the person in the mirror is her, although this may still come later.

- Your infant may begin to fuss or become anxious when he doesn't know where you are.

the desired response. Whereas your baby may only have felt the most basic of needs, emotions are beginning to become more complex at this stage.

A surprise for many parents is how baby's will is starting to emerge. Your tyke may become more assertive, even forceful, with demands. Patience is not a skill baby has at this stage. Incessant desires and the feeling of frustration can set the stage for initial clashes between parents and baby, especially when baby begins to understand the word *No!*

ZOOM

While some infants may begin to grasp the meaning behind the word *No* between the ages of six and nine months, most may not stop what they are doing in response to the word until they are older. That means you'll have to rein in your patience and explain to your baby why you don't want him to do what he's doing. A stern tone in your voice can transmit the message.

Willfulness

- You'll begin to see baby's willfulness emerge at this stage.

- When baby wants something, he will try to get it and most likely will become frustrated and impatient—emotions that weren't previously expressed.

- You and your infant may experience conflicts for the first time as baby begins to be more insistent on desires and demands.

- Babies can start to understand simple commands from parents, such as "No!" or "sleep time," and react to them accordingly.

Stranger Anxiety

- As babies learn to recognize loved ones, they will also understand that there are people they don't know.

- Babies may act shy or become anxious around strangers, and look for familiar faces.

- Normal reactions may include crying, hiding the head, or turning away.

- After a period of adjustment, most babies become comfortable with new people and surroundings.

SAFETY

Parents need to take precautions against babies eating things they shouldn't, choking, and accidents

Parents will need to be extra zealous about baby's safety from here on out. Curiosity combined with increased mobility, along with baby putting just about anything in his mouth, means there are lots of opportunities for injuries. Many babies at this age are absolutely fearless. Caution doesn't exist in most infants' ways of thinking, so parents have to protect their baby against accidents, injuries, and ailments as much as possible.

Since your infant's lips and tongue are the most sensitive parts of his body, he will put everything he can in his mouth to learn about shape, taste, and texture. Unfortunately, that means pet food, small toys, and even dirt and grass can end

Preventing Choking

- The Heimlich maneuver isn't recommended for infants under the age of one. If you cannot remove an object from the mouth or airway of an infant who is choking, immediately call 911.

- Toys that fit through a 1¼-inch circle (about the diameter of an empty toilet paper roll) or are smaller than 2¼ inches long are unsafe for young children.

Choking

- Choking is a prime worry at this stage, as it is a common cause of accidental death in children under the age of one. Avoid all foods that could lodge in a child's throat (e.g., grapes, popcorn, raisins, hot dogs), and stick with recommended baby food.

- Keep baby's environment free from any small objects that could be swallowed.

- Check floors and tables for coins, batteries, rings, nails, deflated balloons, plastic, and other small items.

- Always supervise your baby's exploration.

up in baby's mouth until he learns that some things just aren't meant to be eaten!

Grabbing and knocking over heavy objects, pulling over things on tables, and tasting house plants are among the activities that busy babies may attempt during this stage. Your baby simply doesn't know right from wrong yet, and so everything is a learning process or an experiment. You'll need to be on your guard for possible safety concerns at all times and wherever you take your baby, as other homes and places may not be as child-friendly as you'd prefer.

Home Décor Hazards

- A tablecloth or runner—and any potentially hazardous decorative objects on it—can easily be pulled down by a curious infant.

- Certain varieties of houseplants are poisonous if ingested. Keep them out of baby's grasp.

- Pet food and litter box areas can be tempting playgrounds for babies on the go.

- Keep floors vacuumed, swept, or mopped and be on the lookout for trash or small objects.

Heavy Objects

- Crushed limbs, or worse, can occur when a curious tyke topples over a heavy object. Parents should be vigilant against unsteady items within baby's grasp.

- Within seconds, baby can smash breakables and touch broken pieces, or even put them in her mouth.

- Guard against babies climbing on furniture or using furniture against walls or windows as a ladder for greater heights.

- Watch baby's limbs when closing a car door.

CHILDPROOFING

Reaching, pulling up, and growing mobility mean it is time for childproofing baby's environment

Most families consider their home a safe haven, but for babies, curiosity and accessibility to potential dangers result in unexpected and avoidable trips to the emergency room each year. Some adventures can end in tragedy. Parents must keep baby's safety in mind by childproofing everything they can, because they may not always be prepared for their infant's next quest. Mechanical suffocation and suffocation by ingested objects cause the most home fatalities to children. Drowning, accidents such as burns or falls, and home fires are also leading contributors to tragic deaths of youngsters. There's no such thing as being too careful when it comes to childproofing your home.

Hallways and Stairs

- Use child gates to prevent access to the top and bottom of stairways, especially if baby's room is upstairs.

- Dark hallways can lead to many avoidable accidents, especially if there are toys or other items in the pathway. Add childproof safety lights in dark areas.

- Accent rugs can bunch up or get caught in busy feet, so should be removed or safely secured.

- Consider installing carpeting or a secured padded rug on landings around stairs or steps.

Edges and Ledges

- Fireplace hearth edges are often sharp. Install bumpers on front and corners, and place a screened barrier around the fireplace opening.

- Run your hands over countertop ledges and edges of furniture to identify and cover any sharp surfaces.

- Glass tables are a particular safety concern, and should be covered, or baby's access should be restricted.

- Be careful of any outdoor areas, which may have sharp landscape edging and jutting brick or stone accents.

Now is the time to carefully inventory your home for safety concerns. Beyond securing cabinets and drawers, parents should now consider installing locks on toilets, securing any chemicals or poisons up high and locked away, keeping matches and lighters safely out of reach, and making sure your child can't access oven doors, stovetops, fire places, space heaters, or box fans. Rugs that can slip, stairs, and doors that shut on their own can all hurt newly mobile babies. Windows can harm small fingers, and open sills can shut, trapping and even suffocating babies.

Doors and Windows

- Make sure all windows and doorknobs have proper safety latches and covers.

- Babies may experiment with opening and closing doors, and often hurt themselves as a result.

- Consider placing plastic guards along the hinge side of easily accessible interior doors to avoid babies accidentally pinching or smashing their own fingers or toes.

- Remove plastic ends commonly found on doorstops or replace them with a one-piece design to prevent choking.

Additional Childproofing Tips

- Make sure plastic bags and plastic trash liners are kept out of baby's reach.

- Never leaving cooking food unattended.

- Store tools and garden and lawn equipment in a locked area.

- Never let kids near a grill.

- Know what types of trees and bushes are on your property in case your baby ingests leaves or berries.

GEAR

Array of products are geared for babies on the go and babies on the grow

A significant number of baby products are targeted at infants between the ages of six and nine months, and with good reason. Your infant wants to play, explore, and be on the move, and her newfound abilities make it easier for her to be where the action is. Stationary seats that let baby use her feet to jump or spin while pressing buttons that make music or provide stimulation at all angles are popular toys for babies. These easily movable jumpers or exercisers allow baby to sit safely upright, and height can be adjusted to provide a custom fit for your baby. Make sure you buy one with safety harnesses. Many babies like playing in these while you are cooking dinner or doing other household chores nearby.

Upright Baby Gear

- Babies like to be upright at this stage to see the world from a new viewpoint.

- A jumper lets baby bounce up and down and twirl around without going anywhere, and typically features a 360-degree entertainment station. Baby's feet touch the floor surface.

- Exersaucer activity centers are a variation of the jumper, but baby's feet are on a platform.

- Some jumpers attach to doorways for baby's entertainment, but carefully consider safety features before selecting this style option.

Playpens or Play Yards

- There are many styles and colors of play yards available on the market to provide a safe place for baby to play.

- Most are a standard rectangular size and feature a floor, mesh sides, and top and bottom rails.

- Top and bottom rails that lock and unlock allow the unit to fold up for easy transport and storage. Some styles include carrying cases.

- Options may include a canopy, changing station, wheels, and storage pockets.

Other items on a parent's wish list may include a portable playpen (sometimes called a play yard), an interactive toy station that baby can play with while safely seated on the ground, a new car seat if you had initially purchased an infant carrier and baby is approaching weight limits, or a high chair. Attachable toy trays can be added to strollers or car seats. Look for storage pockets to offer convenience while taking baby with you.

Car Seat

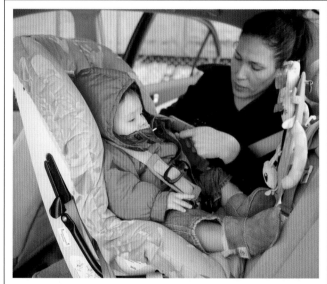

- If you selected an infant carrier for your newborn (a car seat with a carrying handle to avoid disturbing your newborn when transporting her), you may now be considering a step-up car seat.

- Most infant carriers safely carry infants weighing up to 20 or 30 pounds, but you may find a growing and active infant difficult to carry in this fashion.

- Infants will still need rear-facing car seats.

- Choose a model with a five-point adjustable safety harness.

Baby Chairs

- Baby chairs can provide more than just feeding convenience. There are many types available to let baby securely sit up.

- Chairs that adjust to table height can be used for feeding or just providing baby a safe place while joining the family.

- Portable chairs with built-in harnesses let baby sit safely while attending sports games and other events where a stroller isn't practical.

- Be sure the chair can't topple over when baby lunges or moves.

BATHING

Most babies and their parents find bath time a pleasurable, fun, and interactive experience

As your baby becomes more active, gets dirty more through exploration and play, and starts to eat solid food, you'll probably increase how often you give him a bath. You may still be bathing your infant using a baby bathtub or might have transitioned to a bath seat or ring, which allows baby to safely sit up in a secured fashion in an adult bathtub. Regardless of the

technique you use for giving a bath, hopefully you and baby alike enjoy the bath experience, and have some fun at the same time!

Baths at this stage can be more leisurely, and many babies will show their enthusiasm over taking a bath by kicking, cooing, or even squealing. They will relate the sound of running

Preparation

- Let baby be part of the bath preparation ritual. Have your infant listen and watch as you get supplies together and run the water.

- As you undress baby, tell him that it's time for a bath, and describe how much fun you will have together. Your

enthusiastic words will help to excite baby about what is to come.

- Share bath duties with family members as much as possible.

- Siblings can be bath-time helpers.

Bath Play

- Your baby is ready for bath-time fun.

- Introduce toys such as plastic cups and bowls or sponges cut into fun shapes, or more intricate toys that can float, paddle, make noises, or sink and encourage baby to interact with them.

- Coordinate bath-time to occur when baby is alert and happy if you want to play, or near nighttime to encourage relaxation.

- Now's the time for silly shampoo hair shapes using baby shampoo. Have your camera ready!

water and their bathtub (or seat) to the bath experience and respond accordingly. You may want to introduce more bath toys at this stage to add to the fun, and entertain baby with suds, silly bubble shapes or hairdos, or experiments (such as what happens when you hold an object under the water and then let it go).

Your baby may be better at not spontaneously urinating when taking a bath due to the sensation of warm water against her bare skin, but be prepared to start all over in case an accident does happen. Baths can help soothe bottoms that may have additional irritation from the changing bowel movements that result from solid foods being added to baby's diet. Since your infant has become more lively and strong, be sure you secure the position of baby's bathtub or ring so that it doesn't tilt or tip over from lively kicks, splashes, and strong body movements. If possible, give baths inside an adult tub instead of on a countertop or sink as a precaution. And never leave a baby unsupervised during bath time.

All Clean

- Make sure you don't let baby get too cold during or after a bath to keep the experience a positive one.

- Quickly diaper your baby to prevent accidents, and then snuggle with him while draped in a warm towel.

- Massage your infant and use baby lotion on dry skin, while maintaining loving eye contact and tone.

- Show baby how he looks in the mirror after a bath and all wet.

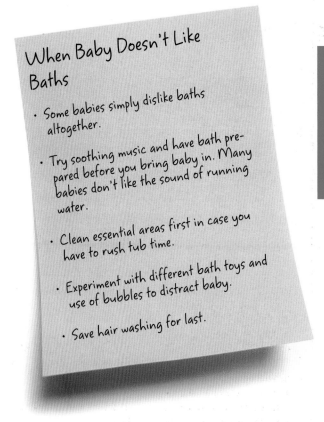

When Baby Doesn't Like Baths

- Some babies simply dislike baths altogether.

- Try soothing music and have bath prepared before you bring baby in. Many babies don't like the sound of running water.

- Clean essential areas first in case you have to rush tub time.

- Experiment with different bath toys and use of bubbles to distract baby.

- Save hair washing for last.

DRESSING

Layering clothes and adding in clothing extras like hats, socks, and jackets provides comfort, convenience

Dressing your six- to nine-month-old infant can be fun at this stage, as your baby's enhanced alertness and body control make clothes fit and look better. Parents should continue to closely examine clothes for safety and comfort, since babies will still spend much of their time sleeping. Look for styles that are easily taken on and off or that

have access to diaper areas, and fabrics that wash and wear easily.

Since a baby's routine may be more complex than before, parents should consider dressing their infant in layers to easily add warmth when needed and remove a layer when baby gets hot (which often occurs when traveling in a snug car

Undergarments

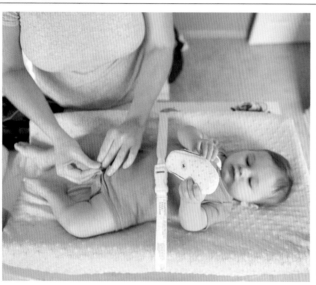

- Start with a stretchy body suit ("onesie") or a T-shirt top made in a cotton material for comfort and coolness.

- Make sure that all clothing that touches baby's skin is comfortable, lightweight, and absorbent.

- Stretch out the neckline of undergarments to avoid having to pull and tug them over baby's head. Be careful of clothes getting caught on tender ears.

- Snap or tie features are available for babies who hate clothes going over their heads.

Clothes for Crawlers

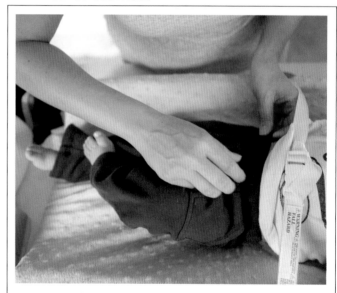

- Once your baby starts to crawl, look for durable pants that won't show dirt that your baby will pick up from the floor.

- Make sure baby outfits don't restrict movement. Avoid fussy dresses or loose pieces that can get caught under baby's knees.

- Look for pants with padded knees for protection, especially on hard surfaces such as tile or wood flooring.

- Make sure you allow ample room to accommodate a diaper when choosing clothing.

seat). Most babies are still fairly compliant about wearing hats and hair accessories, although some have already discovered how to grab and throw anything that is on their heads.

Your baby may now be able to sit up or even stand with support while getting dressed, making clothing changes easier. Make sure you keep a hand on baby at all times when getting her dressed or undressed, and form a "distract and dress" plan so that baby doesn't start complaining.

Outer Layers

Do Babies Need Shoes?

- According to the American Association of Pediatrics, babies don't need shoes until they begin to walk.

- Shoes are simply meant to protect baby's feet, and don't help them learn to walk faster.

- While parents may dress their infant in decorative shoes as part of an outfit, socks or soft-soled slippers are all that your baby needs at this stage.

- Forget about putting baby in gloves or mittens unless absolutely necessary. Some baby jackets feature built-in hand coverings that are more practical.

- Hoods allow you to keep baby comfortable and dry when outside.

- Hats, bonnets, and even baby sunglasses can help provide sun protection regardless of the weather—if your baby will keep them on.

- Don't use a scarf on a baby; it can become a strangulation hazard if baby gets tangled up in it.

DIAPERING

Active babies make changing diapers a greater challenge for parents

Diapering has taken an ugly turn for most parents, as an intake of solid foods results in smellier and more frequent bowel movements. The introduction of new foods also means an increased risk of diaper rashes. Plus, babies wanting to roll over and move around while getting their diapers changed means parents face an increased challenge.

Diapers that fit and worked well on your baby previously may suddenly be leaking. As baby changes and grows, the preferred style of diaper may need to change as well. Remain flexible about diapering preferences and "go with the flow" as much as you can!

While food is often the culprit behind irritating diaper

Diaper Changing Tips

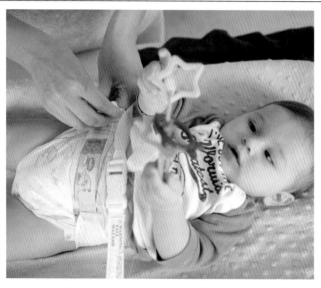

- Your nose knows. Don't wait to change soiled diapers, as feces will quickly irritate skin.

- Diaper-change frequency may vary broadly from about 6 to 10 changes daily, regardless of whether you use cloth or disposables.

- Carefully wipe in all skin folds, and be sure to lift baby up and clean his back-side as well.

- Give your baby a toy to hold and look at during a diaper change to minimize fidgets.

Diaper Fit

- Check the fit of diapers around baby's legs and waist. Red marks mean the diaper is too tight.

- Your son's penis should face down to avoid urine shooting out past the top of his diaper.

- If you are folding a cloth diaper, consider adding extra material up front for a boy and in back for a girl.

- Leaks may indicate that you should go up a size in disposable diapers or add a diaper cover if using cloth.

rashes, yeast can also be a cause. Most food-related rashes can be treated through diet and barrier creams, but yeast requires treatment with a topical antifungal cream. Changing your baby's diaper frequently, letting her go without for periods whenever possible, using unscented wipes or switching from wipes to a warm washcloth and baby wash, or minimizing the amount of wiping or scrubbing may also help to reduce irritation. Take time when changing baby's diaper to make sure the area is dry before putting a fresh diaper on.

Diaper Rash

- Certain foods, especially ones that are acidic, can cause diaper rashes in some babies.

- Most babies will get a diaper rash at least once, if not several times, before they are potty trained.

- If frequent rashes occur, consider changing the type of diaper you are using (brand used or disposable versus cloth, for example).

- Apply rash cream after each diaper change and maintain a careful log of foods to see if you can track down the source.

YELLOW LIGHT

Constipation can occur at any age. Bowel movements may be large, hard, or claylike. They may be infrequent and painful. Constipation is usually caused by not drinking enough fluids or by having a diet too high in constipating foods (like rice cereal and bananas). If you suspect constipation, first give a few extra ounces of water or juice. If symptoms continue, check with your pediatrician for advice about dietary changes and using a stool softener.

Baby's BMs

- The consistency and color of bowel movements change when solid food is introduced.

- You'll see much of what he eats again in his diaper (corn, for example).

- Movements may be irregular as baby's body learns to digest new foods.

- Don't worry about color changes in baby's stools. Baby's diet, digestive tract, and normal bacteria can affect color.

SLEEPING

Babies should begin sleeping through the night and adhering to fairly established sleep routine

By the age of six months, most babies can make it through the night (typically eight to nine hours) without needing to feed. But that does not mean all babies do so successfully. Other factors affect a baby's nighttime sleep, which in turn affects you! Babies may wake up in the middle of the night and desire comfort or be unable to put themselves back to sleep. Your baby may awaken and seek reassurance from a loved one, want to nuzzle at the breast out of habit, may have been woken up by a sound, is uncomfortable or hot, or needs a diaper changed. The reasons vary and are many, but the bottom line is that you want to help your baby solve her sleep problems so you can get the rest you deserve as well!

Setting the Stage

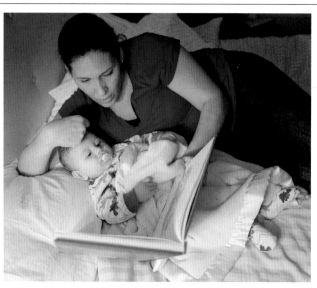

- Keep baby's room as dark and quiet as possible.

- Use a nightlight so you don't have to turn on a light if you need to tend to your infant in the night.

- Lay your baby down without turning it into a production. Some parents may overemphasize a routine to the point where it is hard for a baby to go to sleep without it.

- Avoid stimulating or playing with your baby when putting him down for sleep.

Self-Soothing Techniques

- Maturity is a key factor in your baby's ability to self-soothe.

- If you always rock your baby, walk around, or hold him until he falls asleep before putting him into bed, you're doing the soothing.

- Your baby may fuss or cry a little when laid down, which can be a sign of tiredness. Give him a chance to settle down on his own.

- If a noise awakens baby, you may need to soothe him back to sleep.

If your baby is able to mostly sleep through the night and re-settle himself after waking up, consider yourself lucky. But sleep studies of babies show that one-third to one-half of all infants age six months to one year still have problems sleeping through the night, according to their parents. If you feel you are sleep-deprived, most likely you may find it harder to concentrate or to play with your baby, and may feel angry, helpless, or just flat-out exhausted. That's why getting baby to sleep helps everyone in the family!

By now, you should have a fairly established routine and know when it's time for baby to sleep. You'll want to establish differences between daytime sleep (naps) and nighttime sleep, help your baby to learn to soothe himself (instead of you always doing it for him), and put your baby down while drowsy yet still awake to help him establish his own sleep association. Make sure his sleep environment is conducive to relaxation.

Back-to-Sleep Tactics

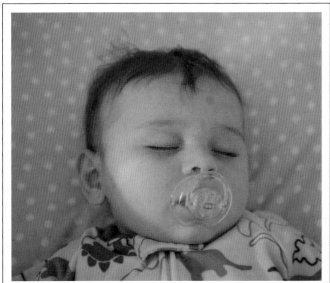

- Consider responding to cries quickly, and settle or feed baby quietly at this stage.

- Resist picking your baby up if you sense comfort is all that she needs.

- Try patting or rubbing her rhythmically, giving her a pacifier (and removing it after she falls asleep), or encouraging her to return to sleep while remaining in her bed.

- A diaper change can provide enough stimulation for baby to awaken fully, so avoid changing her unless necessary.

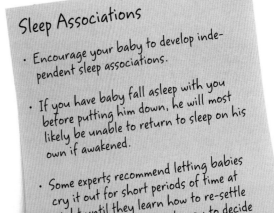

Sleep Associations

- Encourage your baby to develop independent sleep associations.

- If you have baby fall asleep with you before putting him down, he will most likely be unable to return to sleep on his own if awakened.

- Some experts recommend letting babies cry it out for short periods of time at night until they learn how to re-settle themselves, but it is up to you to decide whether you are comfortable with this method.

TEETHING

New bottom teeth may begin to appear; proper tooth and gum care is a must

Your baby may suddenly start drooling and eagerly chewing or biting toys or even his own hand. His usually good-natured temperament may change to irritability and he starts acting restless and fussy. Often, the behavioral changes are with good reason: Your baby is teething.

There is no "magic age" when baby's first tooth will emerge.

The two lower front teeth are usually the first to make their debut, and on average appear between 6 and 10 months. Some infants start early and cut their first teeth at three months, however, while others don't get their first teeth until close to their first birthday. Following the two bottom teeth, the top four incisors are next, and baby may get some or all of

Teething Basics

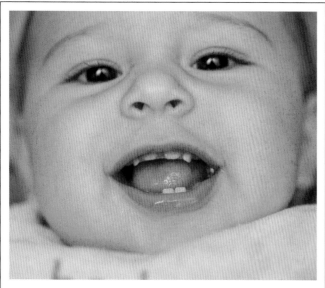

- Help relieve baby's discomfort by offering something cold and firm to chew on, such as a refrigerated water-filled teether or cold washcloth.

- Acetaminophen can relieve persistent discomfort, but check with your doctor before giving.

- Over-the-counter teething gels, which contain a topical painkiller, can provide pain relief but should be used sparingly.

- Massaging baby's gums where teeth are about to emerge can help teeth cut through, although your baby may resist you doing this.

Chewing

- Baby's first teeth are meant for biting, not for chewing.

- Your baby will start chewing with his gums long before he gets teeth at the back of his mouth to help him.

- Most infants will chew their hands, toys, blankets or teethers.

- Chewing is good for baby's developing jaw, but be careful about baby chewing off a small piece of food or object and then choking on it.

them between 8 and 13 months on average. For most babies, teeth arrive in a predictable order, although for infants with certain conditions such as Down syndrome, teeth may arrive later and erratically.

While some babies may whine due to tenderness and soreness resulting from teeth coming in, the truth is that most babies cut their first teeth with very little fuss. A pale bump under the gum is the most physical telltale sign a tooth is about to appear. Since the first two bottom and the two top teeth are flat and sharp, they typically don't cause much discomfort compared to a more irritating molar that arrives later.

Teething does not cause vomiting, diarrhea, fever, or more serious issues like seizures, so if your infant is displaying any of these symptoms while teeth are coming in, look beyond the gums for the cause . . . and call your doctor.

Parents can help teething babies by giving them a washcloth or something soft they can chomp on safely to help those first teeth break through.

Tooth Care

- Wipe new teeth with a washcloth, finger-cot style gum stimulator or with soft toothbrush made for babies twice daily.

- Establish a tooth routine now that can transition into regular toothbrushing later.

- Avoid toothpaste with fluoride. Instead, use infant tooth and gum cleaner.

- Schedule a visit with a pediatric dentist around the age of baby's first birthday. This first visit establishes a baseline and lets your child meet the dentist before there is a problem.

Fluoride

- Babies now need some—but not too much—fluoride for healthy teeth.

- Most can get fluoride from water they drink, as long as your water is fluoridated.

- Parents should limit the amount of fluoridated water until age one to about 16 ounces daily, and use fluoride-free for mixing formula or drinking water after that.

- Vitamin drops are another option.

153

ON THE GO

Traveling with baby in the car, on the plane, or out and about gets easier with proper planning

Traveling doesn't need to halt simply because you've added a baby to the family, although how you travel will never be the same. Gone are periods of mindless staring out the window or catching up on much-needed sleep. Your task is keeping baby safe and happy as much as possible. Preparedness is key for traveling on a plane, train, cruise, or an extended car trip.

If your journey involves going to a relative's home for the holidays, and it's too far to drive, your options will be limited. Choosing a flight time that is in conjunction with baby's routine may help. Some families choose late-night times for the very reason that they hope baby will sleep throughout the journey. Others prefer alert or "happy"

Bring-Along Health Basics

- Keep baby's health your priority when on the go.

- Prepare a take-along first-aid kit so you'll have everything you might need for minor medical problems.

- Carry an emergency card with contact information, and bring a copy of baby's immunizations. If your baby takes any medications, make sure you keep those with you.

- Carry a changing pad and plastic baggies for soiled diapers.

Travel Tips

- If flying, consider buying a seat for baby and securing her in her own car seat. Many babies won't want to be held for the duration of a flight.

- Keep pacifiers, blankets, and quiet cuddle toys easily accessible. If using formula, mix a bottle prior to board-

ing a plane for when baby becomes hungry.

- Offer a pacifier or bottle when plane takes off or ascends to help with pressure in the ears.

- If driving, provide frequent rest stops.

times. These are great plans if the flight is on time.

If you're planning a vacation, opt for a child-friendly destination. A snow-skiing outing may not be a best bet for a young family, while a casual weekend at the beach may provide ultimate rest and relaxation.

You may find baby's needs now fill the suitcases, but proper planning and having the right food, gear, and clothes for baby helps to ensure an enjoyable trip for everyone.

MAKE IT EASY

If you're flying with baby, keep gear in a carry-on bag and include extra clothes, bibs, diapers, footwear, blankets, and food. (You don't want to hunt down baby food or formula if your flight is delayed or cancelled.) Water cannot be brought through a security check, but you can bring empty bottles and then fill them at a fountain prior to boarding the plane.

On-the-Go Gear

- Review carry-on and checked-luggage requirements and fees before deciding what baby gear to bring with you on a flight.

- Some baby gear can be rented. Many hotels offer cribs, and car rental companies will loan car seats by reservation.

- Portable cribs and play yards often fold to a convenient travel size.

- Portable strollers or high chairs can often be purchased inexpensively at your destination.

Away from Home

- Know that your baby's routine will be disrupted and that your infant may awaken in the night for comfort.

- Keep plans simple and expectations low when traveling with a baby. If you set high goals, you may feel disappointed in your time away from home.

- Carefully check out surroundings for safety, and remove objects and tempting extension cords. Closely supervise your baby at all times.

- If possible, provide a darkened and quiet area for baby to sleep.

SOLID FOOD

Vegetables, fruits, and meats get introduced into baby's diet, often with mixed reactions

Once your baby has successfully mastered swallowing food and has learned to enjoy cereal, it's time to begin introducing vegetables and fruits in earnest. Once primary single-ingredient foods have been successfully introduced, you can start adding blends (mixed cereal with bananas, for example) and later begin meats.

It's important to keep in mind that breast milk or baby formula will continue to provide essential nutritional needs for babies, and that mealtimes should start or end with breast milk or formula.

Many nutritionists recommend that you "strive for five," meaning that baby gets five or more servings of fruits and

Safeguarding Baby's Food

Keep these safety tips in mind:

- Set your refrigerator at 40 degrees Fahrenheit or lower and the freezer at 0 degrees Fahrenheit or lower.

- Serve opened or prepared food immediately or store in the refrigerator promptly.

- Foods that have been sitting out for one or two hours should not be reserved.

- Always label baby's frozen food by date.

Pureed First Foods

- Most commercial baby foods are labeled according to baby's age and readiness. Stage 1 denotes food that has the texture of a milkshake.

- Stick with simple pureed varieties of single-ingredient and combination foods until baby shows signs of readiness for more complex tastes and textures.

- It is easy to prepare most homemade baby foods at this stage, and extras can be frozen for later.

- Many parents use both homemade and store-bought foods.

vegetables each day. For this stage, it can be simply a small sampling of a single ingredient amounting to as little as a tablespoon. You'll eventually build up to a quarter cup.

Keep a log of foods you introduce, and limit selections to two or three weekly. Vary offerings by color families for greater variety, but respect your baby's personal preferences. It won't create a nutritional void if your baby refuses to eat carrots or peas, for example. At the same time, avoid having your baby only eat the sweeter fruits. Avoid chunky foods altogether at this stage.

ZOOM

Most babies don't need supplemental vitamins or minerals. Feeding your baby iron-fortified cereal or other foods rich in iron will usually meet dietary iron needs. Babies who are exclusively breastfed may need a vitamin D supplement, but formula is already supplemented with vitamin D. Always check with your pediatrician before routinely giving your baby vitamins.

Increasing Food Options

- Signs your baby is ready for more complex tastes and textures include tongue and lip control and basic ability to chew (with or without teeth).

- Baby should begin to show food likes and dislikes.

- Baby should be able to move food from front to back of mouth and then swallow.

- Stage 2 foods include ones that have stronger tastes and single-meat preparations.

First Finger Foods

- Once your baby has mastered the pincer grasp, sits up well, and can bring foods to his mouth, he can be introduced to finger foods.

- Good choices include crackers, dry cereals such as Cheerios, plain wafer cookies, small pieces of toast, cooked pasta, and small pieces of cheese.

- Avoid foods that are slippery or hard.

- Only put a few pieces on the tray at a time and supervise your infant as he eats them.

GEAR

High chair, small containers, plates and bowls, spoons, and bibs are faves for feeding time

A high chair is considered an essential for feeding time for most families who may no longer want to hold a squirming infant while she eats. Self-feeding, which will come at the end of this stage, is more convenient in a high chair, and high chairs free you up to dine alongside your infant. Plus, a high chair helps protect you against some of baby's food messes!

Safety should be a key criterion when selecting a chair. Babies at this stage are at risk of slipping under the feeding tray if not securely strapped in. Not all models are designed with a post between the legs and a harness, so you'll always need to supervise your baby closely. Make sure the high chair has a wide base to prevent accidental tips as well.

High Chair Considerations

- High chairs provide feeding convenience by keeping baby secure and at table height.

- Plastic high chair styles may include adjustable height and angle settings and cushioned seats. Traditional wooden styles are also offered.

- Some styles feature detachable feeding trays for ease of cleaning, while others are essentially raised chairs that scoot up to the table.

- Traditional high chair styles tend to take up a lot of room, but compact or fold-up models are also available.

Portable or Loaner High Chairs

- Many restaurants have high chairs for your use when eating out with baby.

- Loaner chairs may be fine, but you may have concerns about their sturdiness, cleanliness, or overall safety.

- Consider bringing your own portable high chair that fastens to the side of the table and allows you to keep baby in a familiar chair that you know is safe.

- Wipe down a borrowed high chair with a disinfectant wipe before placing baby in it.

Other gear you may wish to consider includes shatterproof plates and bowls and rubber-tipped spoons. Some infant plates come with suction cups on the bottom to prevent baby from picking up the food container and throwing it. (There's no guarantee they won't throw finger foods later, however!) You may wish to keep a plastic mat under baby's chair for easier cleanup. Organizers for baby jars, utensils, and bibs are handy for keeping feeding supplies together.

MAKE IT EASY

What do you do when your baby doesn't want to sit in his high chair at mealtime? If you're home, you can simply remove him from the table to avoid disturbing others. But what about when you're at a restaurant? Minimize meltdowns by setting consistent mealtime routines from the very beginning. Bring baby foods and soft toys that won't disturb other diners, and plan to tip well.

Dishes and Utensils

- Don't feed baby directly out of a jar, but place small amount on dish and use a clean spoon to avoid food contamination.

- Your baby may try to grab the spoon and attempt to feed herself, but her hand-eye coordination isn't yet developed enough.

- Expect baby to attempt to dip fingers in food to feel texture before tasting.

- Keep a few rubber-tipped baby spoons on hand and throw them away if they begin to split.

Miscellaneous

- Spin-style or stackable organizers let you store and then see at a glance different baby foods. Many styles have space for utensils, bowls or plates, and bibs.

- If you make your own baby food, a variety of freezable baby cube storage options add convenience.

- Food placemats help minimize the mess that baby makes. If on the go, simply roll up and place in a plastic baggie for cleaning later.

- Look for resealable and self-feeding finger food holders.

6–9 MO.: FEEDING

159

WHAT TO DRINK

Drinking from a cup is natural transition from a bottle, but don't expect instant success

Once your baby begins to eat solid foods successfully, it's time to go ahead and introduce a cup. A cup with a spill-proof lid and soft spout makes for a natural transition from breast or bottle. The cup should be easy for baby to grip, and there are many shapes, sizes, and designs with or without handles to choose from.

Juice can become a part of baby's balanced diet any time after the age of six months as long as it is served from a cup and not added to a bottle, according to the American Academy of Pediatrics (AAP). Although you can offer your child juice at this age, you may prefer to offer water in a cup instead, since many kids end up drinking too much juice.

Milk Still Rules

- Breast milk or baby formula will remain the primary nutrition for your baby, even after solid foods are first introduced.

- Since babies can quickly fill up on liquid, let baby finish a meal rather than begin it with breast milk or formula.

- Your baby may become disinterested in eating solids if he doesn't feel well, and may prefer a bottle or breast.

- Encourage baby to eat at family mealtimes (even in small quantities) by the end of this stage.

What's in a Cup?

- Juices for babies come in flavors such as apple and white grape.

- Many parents dilute the fruit juice they serve to baby with water in a 50/50 mix, or serve water with only a splash of juice.

- Consider vegetable juices as a nutritional alternative.

- Encourage baby to drink plain water. It may take a while for some babies to learn to like the taste; others will drink it from the very beginning.

Juices are not all created equal, and many of them contain added sugar that is not good for baby. Avoid any type of citrus juice (like orange juice or pineapple juice) during baby's first year, as babies don't always tolerate them as well as noncitrus juices. Instead, go for pasteurized 100 percent fruit juice without any added coloring or additives. Favorites include apple, grape, cherry, or a blend, but make sure to introduce the fruit to baby's diet first. The AAP further recommends that only four to six ounces of juice be given daily, and keep in mind that you should likely dilute the juice with water. Most pediatricians recommend that you are better off giving your infant fruit rather than fruit juice. Remember that fruit juice has no nutritional benefits over whole fruits, which also have fiber.

Drinking too much fruit juice can be associated with diarrhea, cavities, improper eating habits, and being overweight.

Sippy Cup Features

- Sippy cups come in assorted styles and colors. Baby's preference may change as he gets used to drinking from a cup and is better able to manage the drinking action.

- Look for cups with easy grips or handles for small hands.

- Sippy cups should be no-spill, so liquid won't come out when baby turns them upside down and shakes them.

- Consider cups with and without valves and determine how easily they can be taken apart and cleaned between uses.

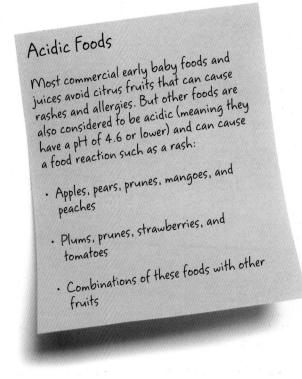

Acidic Foods

Most commercial early baby foods and juices avoid citrus fruits that can cause rashes and allergies. But other foods are also considered to be acidic (meaning they have a pH of 4.6 or lower) and can cause a food reaction such as a rash:

- Apples, pears, prunes, mangoes, and peaches

- Plums, prunes, strawberries, and tomatoes

- Combinations of these foods with other fruits

REFLEXES AND REACTIONS
Your baby uses senses to determine receptivity to foods and may still gag and sputter

Some food that goes in baby's mouth may very well come back out, as your baby is adjusting to new tastes, textures, and even the whole notion of chewing and swallowing. Your baby is still mastering how to move food from the front of his mouth to the back before swallowing, and is even learning the sensation of fullness so he doesn't overdo it.

Babies may react to certain foods based on how they look or the way they feel in their mouths, resulting in sputtering, choking, or gagging. That's why it is important for every single bite of food that baby takes to be carefully supervised at this time. The introduction of finger foods can bring with it new safety issues, and this is not the time

Pushing, Sputtering, or Spitting

- Your baby may enthusiastically open his mouth, only to spit food out upon tasting it. He has preferences too!

- The tongue extrusion reflex of pushing food back out is gone at this stage, but that doesn't mean babies won't do it willfully.

- Some babies "sputter" when tasting something they don't like. That's a habit you need to stop . . . unless you like the mess!

- Babies may let unwanted food sit in their mouths and not swallow.

Gagging and Choking

- Introducing textured foods before baby is ready can result in gagging.

- Choking is also a potential safety concern for babies just starting to eat.

- Finger foods should be cut very small (such as quarter-

ing a grape) to minimize safety concerns.

- Don't let baby stuff his mouth with foods. If there are more than a few items on the tray, baby may try to grasp them and put them all in his mouth at once.

to casually give a baby a bag of finger foods for snacking as desired.

As baby progresses from Stage 1 foods to Stage 2, the very textures he finds most edible and satisfying can cause the biggest problems. And while your baby is indeed learning how to chew foods, those early gummy chews aren't going to do much in the way of breaking up foods, so don't count on her taking a bite and breaking it down before swallowing.

Funny Faces

- Reactions can be funny to watch as baby's face may become quite animated when trying out new foods.

- Your baby may widen his eyes, squish up his nose, or have an expression of concern or uncertainty.

- Your baby may become visibly excited for food he likes and even vocalize for you to hurry with the next spoonful.

- Continue to reintroduce foods that baby initially rejects every now and then to see if he changes his mind.

Feeding Foods Baby Wants

- Once your baby is eating combination foods or several varieties at one sitting, the order doesn't really matter.

- If your baby initially refuses a vegetable and clamors for the fruit, go ahead and start with what he wants. Then, switch after a few mouthfuls.

- Don't worry about which meat goes with vegetable, or avoiding repetition. Your baby doesn't care.

SCHEDULE AND MENUS

Choose menus and work solids into feeding times when it fits with your family's schedule

Your goal is for your baby to begin eating three meals a day and perhaps a simple snack in between by the end of this stage. Afterward, five to six ounces of baby formula or breast milk should be given with each meal. Most babies will also have a bottle or will breastfeed right before going to bed. Ideally, that means five bottle or breastfeeding sessions are all that

baby needs each day, although variations can certainly work successfully for your baby and your family. Some parents give baby a small bottle or breastfeed in a limited amount when baby wakes up, and then save breakfast for a little later in the morning, for example. All in all, setting and then adhering to a simple schedule will make mealtimes easier for everyone!

Suggested Menus

There is no right or wrong when it comes to schedules. Here is one variation (don't forget a bottle or breastmilk with each feeding):

- Breakfast: ½ cup cereal and 2 ounces fruit

- Day: ½ ounce meat, 3 to 4 ounces vegetables and 1 to 2 ounces fruit

- Snack: Juice from a cup or 2 ounces fruit

- Evening: 3 to 4 ounces of meat and vegetable and 2 ounces of fruit

- Finish with breast or bottle

Foods First

- Try to begin meals with solids and then finish with breastfeeding or bottle. Otherwise, your baby can fill up on milk.

- If your baby is a reluctant eater, or continues to fuss if breast or bottle isn't initially offered, you can start with it and then quickly switch.

- Providing breast milk or infant formula first can take the edge off babies who become frantic when hungry.

- Try to burp your baby as a transition between food and milk or milk and food.

Don't worry too much about what you feed your baby other than trying to offer a variety of healthy foods. Since babies can't tell you why they like something and dislike something else, you have to take their cues about what's working for you both. Buy or make the smallest possible quantity until you know that baby likes something consistently. Sometimes, babies will like something one day and then refuse it from then on.

Your baby doesn't know that food can be served at different temperatures, so your actions now can set the stage for preferences or even pickiness later. If you only serve your baby refrigerated applesauce, don't be surprised if your infant later refuses to take it at room temperature. Babies don't require food to be heated, and microwaving food is not typically recommended because it can create "hot spots" that could scald your infant. Opt instead to place a food jar or thawing item under warm water until the right temperature is obtained. Be sure to follow food safety guidelines.

Infant Milk with Meals

- If you finish meals with the breast or bottle, use it as a special snuggle time and keep baby calm to minimize meal spit-ups.

- If you start baby's meal with milk, keep baby happy and awake for solids that come next.

- Have solid foods ready to feed so transition from milk to solids is almost immediate, or else baby will want more milk.

- Check with your pediatrician if you have concerns about your baby's eating at this stage.

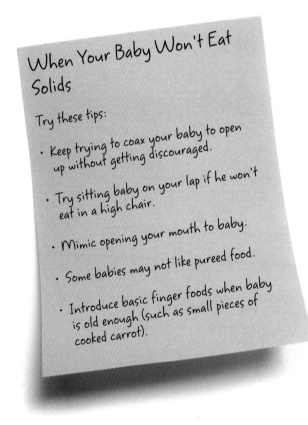

When Your Baby Won't Eat Solids

Try these tips:

- Keep trying to coax your baby to open up without getting discouraged.

- Try sitting baby on your lap if he won't eat in a high chair.

- Mimic opening your mouth to baby.

- Some babies may not like pureed food.

- Introduce basic finger foods when baby is old enough (such as small pieces of cooked carrot).

RECIPES

Make-ahead foods that can be frozen and stored in food cubes make easy meal options

Commercial baby foods make mealtimes as easy as pulling out a few jars based on infant's level of food readiness, the intended meal, and foods that are on the approved food list. Open the jars, ready baby in a high chair or feeding seat, put him in a bib, and then have him open wide. Homemade foods are easy to prepare as well, and making big batches provides you with the easy option of freezing extra for future meals.

Many parents prefer to make baby's foods, at least as often as possible, because it is simple, is less expensive, allows them to individualize any recipe preferences, and because they then know for certain no additional sugar, preservatives,

Preparing Fruits and Vegetables

- Peeling is recommended at this stage because it can decrease potential stomach upsets, decrease pesticide residue, and minimize chunks of peel that can cause choking or gagging. Peels can be served to older babies.

- Cut food into chunks.

- Boil, bake, or steam until food is tender.

- Use food processor or blender to puree to desired consistency, adding water if too thick.

Creative Fruit Combinations

- Be creative with combinations.

- Peel and mash an avocado (cooking is unnecessary) and add either applesauce or a mashed banana. (Note: You can use natural applesauce that is commercially prepared.)

- Skin and dice an apple, pear, and fresh peach and boil or steam until tender. Puree together and add mashed banana, if you like.

- Add prepared fruits to cereals.

or seasonings have been added. They can opt to use items that are organically grown or prepared in certain ways as well. There's no recipe to follow, and wash, peel, cook, and then puree or mash are the only steps you need! Homemade recipes also let parents tailor meals to baby's preferred texture (pureed or with small chunks, for example).

However, iron and vitamins that are added to certain commercial foods (which are labeled accordingly) reassure parents who may wonder if baby is receiving all the necessary nutrients. That's why many parents choose both options.

Vegetables

- You can use frozen peas, green beans, carrots, and other vegetables instead of fresh, if preferred.

- Consider baking certain vegetables, like squash or potatoes.

- If preparing fresh green beans, snap the ends and wash. Boil or steam until tender. Achieving a smooth consistency can be a challenge with a blender. Try pushing puree through a strainer or sieve to get rid of remaining skins.

MAKE IT EASY

Most daycare or family care providers will gladly feed your baby the food you have made at home, as long as it doesn't add time to their busy schedule. Simply thaw food items the night before and provide them to baby's caregiver. They can be stored in the refrigerator until it is time to eat. Make sure you label foods to be served and don't expect providers to wash your containers.

Meats

- Meats can be introduced at the latter part of this stage.

- Fully cook boneless beef, pork, veal, or chicken in small chunks.

- Puree or blend until a powdery mix forms.

- Add water (you can use juices in which you cooked meat or plain water).

- Blend until desired texture is created for your baby.

- Vegetables can be added.

6-9 MO.: FEEDING

167

PLAY

Life is one grand adventure as baby begins to understand objects and learn associations

Your baby seems to be everywhere and into everything, and there are some days when you aren't sure whether you should delight in newfound skills or collapse in exhaustion over never-ending actions needed to keep baby safe. Everything baby does at this stage involves grasping, grabbing, pushing, pulling, and attempting to put things into her mouth, and life is one grand adventure after another.

Exploration can be one of the most fun stages of baby's first year because while she is on the go, your baby isn't yet so independent and active that you struggle to keep up. Playtime is as fun for you as it is for baby, and silly games, simple

Associations

- Play peek-a-boo with a twist. Have baby peer through objects like tree branches or through clothes in the closet.

- Put something under an overturned bowl and ask baby where it is. Encourage him to lift up the bowl and find the object.

- Put a silly hat or a soft toy animal on baby's head and let him see himself in the mirror. Then, put it on your own head and watch baby's reaction.

- Encourage baby to point to familiar objects.

Baby Band

- Sounds can either be stimulating or soothing to babies; that's why there are so many sound products on the market.

- Identify sounds for your baby in day-to-day activities. Turn on the radio in the car, encourage her to listen as the car door shuts, and let her hear the microwave timer go off.

- Let baby make music by banging on parent-approved objects with a wooden spoon.

- Let baby explore and run her hands through a small wind chime.

explanation, and basic educational elements translate into a lot of laughter, smiles, and learning.

Your baby is now acutely aware of and interested in his body, and may use his senses to explore his fingers, toes, belly button, knees, and any other part as well. Support your infant's newfound focus and clearly identify names of various body parts, and encourage your baby to respond when you say, "Touch your toes," or, "Where's your nose?" That's how learning association begins!

Some of the most fascinating objects to baby aren't what you buy at a store, but what you already have available at home. Plasticware from the kitchen to play with; empty and washed plastic shampoo bottles in an array of colors, shapes, and designs to hold and examine; and an abundance of furniture textures to feel provide endless entertainment without you spending a dime. Your baby will now be more interested in looking at objects you point out during outings.

Your baby is less likely to become easily overstimulated, although too-loud sounds or bright lights can still put him into overload. Best playtimes are those spent with loved ones.

Touch and Go

- Babies like to "pat" objects, whether they are family pets, stuffed animals, or even soft blankets.

- Rub noses with your baby, give "butterfly" eyelash kisses by fluttering your eyes up and down on baby's cheek, while holding hands.

- Let baby explore your face with his fingers as you identify your eyes, nose, and so on. Be careful of getting poked!

- Hold up a pillow at baby's feet and encourage him to kick it.

Cup Play

- Plastic cups can provide endless fun.

- Show baby how to stack cups into a small pyramid and then knock them down with her hands.

- Roll a baby-friendly ball into stacked cups.

- Show baby a variation of the "shell game" using cups.

- Cut the bottom out of a cup and show baby how to amplify her voice.

COGNITIVE DEVELOPMENT

Exploration, curiosity, and experimentation are brain boosters for rapid learning and intelligence

Your baby is starting to grasp a basic understanding of your words and actions. You can see it in her eyes when she listens to what you're saying and in how she responds. She's also sorting out her world, and beginning to learn valuable lessons, such as that certain actions have effects, and that just because she can't see all of an object doesn't mean it doesn't exist.

Curiosity is a huge component of baby's learning at this stage. Doing something again and again—and then again some more—isn't meant to be irritating; each repetition drives home some important information. Your baby closely examines objects; wants to touch things; explores just about anything with her mouth by licking, biting, or attempting to

Actions

- Babies crave consistency, and reliable actions and routines help them learn.

- Your baby loves repeating an action over and over again. That's why she doesn't tire of games like peek-a-boo, or watching you drop a ball and catch it.

- Simple hide-and-find games provide endless entertainment. Hide part of an object, such as a favorite toy, under a blanket with a piece sticking out, and watch him delight in finding it.

- Babies may begin to anticipate upcoming actions.

Discipline

- Your baby is not yet old enough to understand the difference between right and wrong.

- Your baby cannot yet grasp the concept of discipline, but can understand the word *No*.

- Even if baby doesn't understand what you're saying, tell your baby simply why something may not be okay, use redirection, and substitute an acceptable object for something that isn't.

- Lavishing love on your infant will help with confidence and behavior later.

chew it; and capitalizes on her senses of smell and hearing as well.

You can almost see baby's mind a-whirling when you give her toys or objects to play with. Watch how baby may begin to use those items in more complex ways than previously, including playing with them in ways that may not have been intended. That shows emerging creativity and ingenuity! Your infant may begin to look at the correct picture when you name an image—another reason reading is so important!

ZOOM

Can you boost baby's intelligence? Most likely you already are, just by interacting through cuddling, play, and exploration. While certain educational products are touted as brain boosters, the truth is that providing your baby with attention and stimulation, along with encouraging curiosity and talking and reading to him regularly, are all the brain-stimulating activities he needs.

Memory

- Your baby has a short attention span at this stage.

- Babies can't remember what you've told them, so you may find that you are repeating yourself over and over again. That's how babies learn.

- Your infant will remember certain things, such as her name, names of loved ones, and certain familiar objects.

- Baby will start demonstrating the correct way of playing with something consistently, showing he remembers how to do it after being shown.

Preferences

- Babies may begin to show strong preferences. It's a healthy part of normal development.

- Parents sometimes get frustrated when they purchase an expensive developmental toy in which baby shows absolutely no interest.

- Babies may quickly change their minds about what they like and don't like.

- The simplest objects (such as an empty paper towel roll) often pique baby's interest the most.

SOCIAL DEVELOPMENT

Baby's emerging personality provides parents with a preview of what is to come

You'll get an insightful glimpse into baby's emerging personality at this stage, as she will begin more and more to express different moods, preferences, and feelings. Your baby loves being around you, and will literally grin from ear to ear when she sees a loved one or does something enjoyable. You'll find countless ways to make baby smile and laugh, and baby may have fits of giggles over things you find absolutely ordinary—such as a cat yawning or an older sibling racing around the house. Your baby now looks for ways to engage you in his life, although he may now be more wary of strangers. Let him warm up to new people, however, and he'll be entertaining and socializing with them in no time!

Personality Preview

- While it is by no means defined, you can identify essential elements of baby's emerging personality.

- Traits of being clingy or outgoing, easily adaptable or highly structured, calm or exuberant are beginning to become clearer.

- You are beginning to tailor your interactions and family's social activities to baby's temperament to make activities more successful.

- Baby's personality may still change dramatically over the coming year, so avoid typecasting baby's temperament just yet.

Socialization

- Play dates are actually parent connection opportunities, as babies don't yet socialize with other children.

- Same-age babies may engage in "parallel play" in which they may play side by side but not with one another.

- Your baby isn't intending to ignore another infant, it's just that he is often captivated by his own interests.

- If another child takes a toy away, baby may just seek out something else of interest.

172

But your life with baby isn't all fun and games. She may get bored, cranky, and seemingly inconsolable, and parents may find that they must be constant entertainers to make it through a trip to the store with baby in tow. Your baby may declare when "enough is enough," effectively ending many leisurely and carefree outings. This too will pass, but remember that your baby has no understanding of patience. It's also too early for discipline, although early parenting practices can set the stage for rules later.

Security

- Your baby may be more comfortable with social situations and meeting new people when he has a cherished toy, stuffed animal, or blanket that can serve as reassurance.

- You may find yourself bringing along baby's favorite "lovey" to new places and that baby clings to it, drool and all.

- Security blankets or objects help baby as she grows more independent from her parents.

- Don't worry if your baby doesn't have a need for a security object.

Separation Anxiety

- While your baby may become upset and look for you when you are away, true separation anxiety behavior occurs at an older age—typically between 12 and 18 months.

- Reduce anxiety by introducing baby to different people who may be caregivers in your absence, so he recognizes their faces when you're gone.

- Allow an adjustment period when leaving baby with someone new.

173

LANGUAGE

Baby talk, reading out loud, and early conversations help baby to communicate with you

Your baby's babbling and vocalizing will be increasing, and the stream of vowels and added consonants that form sounds and patterns may actually begin to sound like sentences. Of course, the adorable tones and pitches may not actually be words, but you can tell your baby is starting to mimic basic language. Your baby might even have a few random words in his vocabulary, such as the beloved "dada" and "mama" or even "bye-bye." You may not understand one another yet, but it's only a matter of time before you will!

Go ahead and talk baby talk with your infant, even in a high pitch with cutesy language, if that's what you like. Talking out loud to your baby whenever he is with you will help him to

Comprehension

- Your baby may begin to recognize his name and respond with smiles, coos, or babbles.

- Your baby may understand commonly used words such as "bottle" or "diaper" or "bath time."

- Expect babbles or responses to some simple requests, such as, "Do you want another bite of food?"

- He may look at the person when you ask, "Where's Daddy?" Prompt baby by saying, "There's Daddy. Can you say 'Daddy'?"

Baby Talk

- Baby talk isn't bad, especially when you use it to engage your infant in early language. Of course, you won't want to keep talking like that when baby is older.

- Sing silly songs to baby using exaggerated facial expressions and a great range of sounds. It doesn't matter whether you sing with actual words.

- Use high and low pitches and sound effects.

- Babble back to your baby. Try a sing-song rhyming pattern like, "Cutie poo, how are you?"

develop language proficiency more quickly. Of course, reading out loud from baby-friendly books is another way to help him begin to understand basic vocabulary, the way sentences are put together, and overall tone. When baby babbles, look him in the eye, listen to his sounds, and give a reassuring or interested response. When he stops, speak to him and watch him as he listens to you. Soon enough, he'll begin repeating back words you say.

Conversations

- Talking to your infant lays the groundwork for language later. Your baby will understand your words before using language.

- Narrate baby's activities. As you get him dressed, talk about his pants and shirt, for example. Say, "Let's get on your socks. See your socks?" Explain what he'll do next.

- Talk to baby about colors and objects, especially ones he seems most interested in.

- If baby seems unreceptive at times, it may be time for a conversation time-out.

Language Concerns

Early intervention is the key if you feel your baby may have a language delay or hearing problem. Check with your doctor if:

- Baby isn't attempting to make any sounds.

- Baby doesn't respond to your tone or speaking.

- Baby doesn't maintain eye contact.

- Baby babbled and cooed earlier but has stopped doing so by the end of this developmental stage.

MOTOR DEVELOPMENT

Better control of fine and large muscles means baby is now on the move

It's easy to begin comparing your baby's skills to those of other infants around the same age, but try to avoid doing so if you can resist. While some babies are already starting to figure out how to move and may be crawling, rolling, and transitioning from lying down to sitting up independently, others are perfectly content to have the world come to them. Your

doctor is keeping a close eye on your baby's development, so as long as overall milestones are being attained, relax and enjoy your baby at whatever particular stage he or she is in.

Regardless of whether your infant is a go-getter or a laid-back observer at this stage, you'll notice some significant strides in baby's motor development. Fine motor skills are

New Positions

- Your baby is learning to sit up without pillows or aids for support, although he can still topple over at times.

- Babies typically love to stand when you hold them up.

- Babies may jump up and down on your legs while

you're holding them. They're building up those leg muscles for walking later!

- Most babies can easily roll from back to front and from front to back, which may influence their sleeping position.

Gross Motor Skills

- Many babies will push themselves up off the floor and then rock back and forth on their hands and knees.

- Traditional crawling, slithering, scooting, dragging, and even frog hops are some of the techniques babies may use to move.

- Encourage your baby to move and change positions and to use those large muscles.

- Some babies will pull themselves up to standing while holding onto something and may even begin to move around an object with support.

increasing, along with the large muscles that baby will eventually use to walk. This is the stage when each day may bring new, and sometimes unexpected, achievements in baby's growth. Clumsy swipes at a desired object may now be replaced by successful grasping with baby's thumb and index finger. Without warning, your baby may awkwardly move to get an object previously out of reach. Without a doubt, this is the age when parents marvel at what a "big boy" (or girl) baby is becoming!

ZOOM

While baby exercise classes aren't necessary, they can be fun and beneficial. Babies get enough exercise doing what they do all day, and don't need exercise programs to help develop physically. But classes like these may help you to learn different ways to interact with your baby, provide special time together, and let you meet other parents who have babies the same age.

Fine Motor Skills

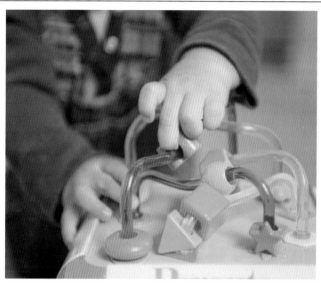

- Your baby will be paying more attention to the size and shape of objects.

- As baby reaches for things, he will begin to successfully grasp what he wants on the first or second try. He may be able to pick up tiny objects as well.

- Baby should be able to move a toy easily from one hand to another.

- Baby should be able to hold his own bottle while drinking.

Lefty or Righty?

- Your baby may seem to favor one hand and then switch to another. But you won't know whether she's left or right handed until she's a preschooler.

- Don't try to influence baby's hand choice.

- Baby's hand preference is determined before birth.

- Forcing a child to use a particular hand could lead to problems with hand-eye coordination and dexterity later on.

FOR DADS

Even as he works to help raise his baby, dad shouldn't forget to have fun

The first few months of a baby's life can be stressful for parents, especially first-time parents and first-time dads who don't have any experience taking care of a baby. For such a dad, even the thought of basic baby care tasks like bathing, washing hair, or even picking up his baby can make him anxious. Dad may want to be more helpful, but is scared of making a big mistake and so he doesn't take on a bigger role in his baby's life.

Fortunately, a lot of the new dad jitters quickly go away as dad starts to get some experience helping take care of baby. By now, dad may have even tackled things that he never thought he would, like giving baby a bath, getting

Why Play Matters

- Playing with your baby helps encourage the development of a strong bond, both for the baby and dad.

- Babies like to watch us do stuff, so almost any activity can turn into a fun game for them, from reading a book or playing peek-a-boo, to juggling balls.

- Make sure baby toys are age appropriate, haven't been recalled, and don't have loose parts from normal wear and tear.

- Watching TV or videos isn't considered playtime for baby.

Stay-at-Home Dads

- More dads are staying home with their babies as the primary caregiver, both out of necessity and as a personal choice.

- If you become a stay-at-home dad, find a support group or play group to meet other stay-at-home dads to talk to.

- Remember that a play group or class with stay-at-home moms isn't off-limits either.

- Staying at home with your baby usually doesn't mean just caring for baby, as you should share other household chores with your partner too.

her dressed, or taking her to the store on his own.

Being a dad isn't all changing diapers, waiting for burps, and staying up at night to help with feedings. It is a lot of fun, and hopefully as dad gets comfortable with day-to-day tasks, he will remember to enjoy his baby. As she gets older, baby will be awake more during the day, more aware of what is going on around her, and ready to play with her dad.

Be a Good Role Model

- Your baby will learn to look up to you if you are available, consistent, patient, and offer unconditional love to your family.

- Ask for help if you still aren't sure about your role as dad, either from other dads or your own father.

- A good dad knows his baby's feeding schedule, sleep schedule, who his pediatrician is, and so on.

Quality Time Matters

- In addition to spending quality time with your baby, be sure to spend quality time with your other children and your partner.

- Don't be jealous if your partner has less time for you these days because the baby requires a lot of her attention.

- Be flexible so that you and your partner can still do things together when you get a chance.

- Ask family and friends to help, or hire a babysitter, so you can spend some quality time with your partner.

HEALTH

Baby gets a pass on immunizations at nine-month checkup, but sickness may mean extra visits

As long as baby is up to date with immunizations and it isn't time for a flu shot, there are usually no vaccinations scheduled for baby's nine-month checkup! This is a welcome reprieve for shot-weary parents. Beyond taking routine measurements you've learned to expect, your doctor may spend additional time talking to you about your infant's adjustment to solid foods, sleeping, and interest in her world. Motor skill progress may also be checked. Most likely, your doctor will talk to you about the need for additional childproofing as your infant is about to enter the truly mobile stage.

As in any stage, you may also find yourself at the doctor's office if your infant becomes ill. Common colds top the list of

Providing Comfort

- Treat your baby to a warm bath if she likes it and is a little extra fussy.

- Natural aromatherapy or saline nose drops can help unblock stuffed air passageways. Consider baby bath products with natural ingredients.

- Encourage your baby to drink extra fluids, such as Pedialyte, as infants can become easily dehydrated. Don't be surprised if your baby doesn't want to eat solids when not feeling well.

- Your baby may crave extra cuddling and attention.

Treatments

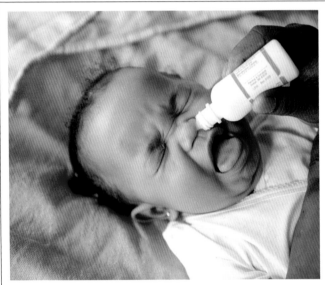

- Baby's nose may become crusty with mucus around the nostrils. Remove it gently with a washcloth or swab moistened with warm water, and then lubricate the outside of the nostril areas with petroleum jelly or hypoallergenic lotion.

- Keep eye areas free from crusts with a dampened washcloth.

- Use your baby's aspirator bulb to remove mucus from nostrils.

- Check with your pediatrician to see if saline nose spray is recommended.

reasons babies become sick, but their still-immature respiratory systems may mean that colds can turn into something more serious, like pneumonia. While a cold doesn't necessarily mean a sick child visit is needed, you'll need to keep a careful watch over baby's health, and if in doubt, call the doctor.

If your baby gets a cold, his whole routine, including eating and sleeping habits, and even overall temperament, may become out of sorts. A runny nose, cough, watery eyes, restlessness or sleepiness, crankiness, and a sore throat are classic symptoms.

RED ● LIGHT

Don't even think about giving your baby over-the-counter cold medicine. Doctors have raised concerns about the effectiveness and safety of cold remedies for infants and toddlers, saying that health risks outweigh any possible benefits. Instead, give your baby plenty of fluids, rest, and tender loving care to treat a cold. If you're unsure whether your baby has a cold or something more, or she has an illness that lingers, schedule a sick-child visit.

Vaporizer or Humidifier

- If baby is stuffy, you may wish to use a humidifier or vaporizer.

- A vaporizer heats water and emits a hot steam and a humidifier creates a cool mist. A cool air mist is generally recommended to prevent accidental burns from spilled hot water.

- Make sure you properly drain and clean products thoroughly after each use.

- If not properly maintained, bacteria can flourish and get emitted into air, ending up in baby's lungs, causing other problems.

Keeping Colds at Bay

- Did you know that the cold germ rhinovirus can linger on surfaces for days?

- Don't let baby play with toys in sick-child waiting rooms.

- Limit baby's touching of shopping cart handles, restroom fixtures, and public changing table stations as much as possible.

- Use a gentle hand sanitizer on baby's hands and then wash his hands carefully when out and about.

ILLNESSES AND AILMENTS

Common childhood ailments are usually harmless, but can cause discomfort and need for extra TLC

A cold is only one of the contagious ailments your child may pick up over the course of her first year. If your baby is around other children or attends any type of child care, the chances of picking up another type of the "ickies" are even greater. The good news is that many childhood illnesses are common and relatively harmless. Plus, exposure may help to build up

baby's immunity later on. The bad news is that your baby may feel discomfort or even feel downright awful, and often you may need to keep your infant out of child care and away from other kids until she is better. New parents may find that they often catch illnesses from their babies since they haven't been exposed (until now) to many of these common infections.

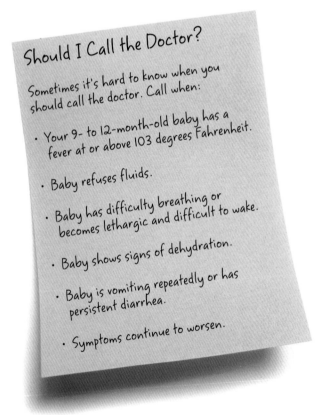

Should I Call the Doctor?

Sometimes it's hard to know when you should call the doctor. Call when:

- Your 9- to 12-month-old baby has a fever at or above 103 degrees Fahrenheit.

- Baby refuses fluids.

- Baby has difficulty breathing or becomes lethargic and difficult to wake.

- Baby shows signs of dehydration.

- Baby is vomiting repeatedly or has persistent diarrhea.

- Symptoms continue to worsen.

Respiratory Syncytial Virus (RSV)

- RSV is very common, and most children will have had exposure to it by age two.

- RSV causes many symptoms similar to a cold. Having it does not make a baby immune to it.

- For infants under age one, RSV is the most common cause of viral pneumonia or bronchiolitis. Infections typically last one to two weeks.

- Wheezing is a telltale sign of RSV, although not all babies will do it.

Stomach bugs, ears infections, skin rashes, low-grade fevers, croupy coughs, and runny noses are among the sicknesses that you might encounter during baby's first year. Other types of minor ailments may include conjunctivitis; fifth disease; RSV (respiratory syncytial virus); croup; hand, foot and mouth disease; pneumonia; and strep throat. These are harder to diagnose, and many start with common symptoms. A proper medical diagnosis and treatment will get your baby feeling better in no time.

Conjunctivitis (Pinkeye)

- Pinkeye is highly contagious, and appears as extreme redness of one or both eyes. But it looks worse than it actually is.

- Pinkeye can be spread by contact with something an infected person has touched or through coughing and sneezing.

- There are different types of pinkeye, with most being due to bacteria or viruses.

- Bacterial pinkeye usually requires antibiotic eye drops. Babies will need to be kept home until they have been on antibiotics for 24 hours.

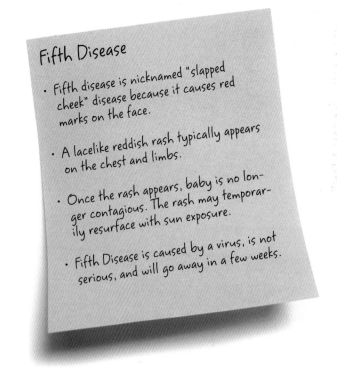

Fifth Disease

- Fifth disease is nicknamed "slapped cheek" disease because it causes red marks on the face.

- A lacelike reddish rash typically appears on the chest and limbs.

- Once the rash appears, baby is no longer contagious. The rash may temporarily resurface with sun exposure.

- Fifth Disease is caused by a virus, is not serious, and will go away in a few weeks.

GROWTH AND MOTOR SKILLS

Crawling and possibly walking will quickly change the pace of baby's newfound mobility

Your baby may now be actively crawling, pulling up to a stand, and perhaps beginning to stand for a few seconds independently—usually to quickly topple over. Often, a determined baby will sort out proper hand and leg placement to raise himself again (usually with support) and then try again. Your baby may begin walking by the end of this stage, or take another six months, but regardless of baby's timetable, one thing you know for sure: The days of your baby being content in a prone or sitting position are numbered, and your infant will begin to toddle before too long. After all, there is a reason that babies are renamed "toddlers" after they reach one year of age!

Motor Milestones

- Your baby may be actively crawling. There is no "correct" way to crawl, as positions vary by baby.

- Your baby may begin experimenting with favored mobility positions as motor skills improve and she gains confidence.

- Many babies may pull themselves up to standing and start to "cruise" along furniture, couches, and anything they can walk around with support.

- Your infant may stand with support and bounce on her legs, as if performing strength conditioning!

Preparing to Walk

- Your baby may demonstrate walking readiness, or show no interest whatsoever. Relax! Your baby will walk when she's ready.

- Some babies may begin to stand alone for a few seconds, usually to lose their balance quickly and topple over.

- Your baby may enjoy "walking" while you hold her up by the arms or around the waist.

- Placing one foot in front of the other is a complex skill and requires practice!

Learning to walk is a demanding and complex task. It first requires that your infant master control over his upper body, ability to turn at the waist, standing with support, and the ability to alternate his legs. Your baby has to then learn to bring all these motor skills together for the crowning achievement: taking his first independent steps.

You can help your baby start to master these skills by walking while you support her hands. She'll soon get the rhythm of putting one foot in front of another. If your baby doesn't seem receptive, however, relax! You can try again in a few weeks. You'll see signs of readiness when your baby determines it's time to give walking another try.

Once your baby takes those first steps, he'll have a funny posture that is distinctively typical of a young walker. His feet are wide apart with legs slightly bent, and often his tummy is protruding and arms held upward to provide extra stability. Babies may progress quickly to confident walking, or may maintain an unsteady gait and wobbly balance for quite some time.

First Steps

- Babies may test their balance by bending at the knees or clapping their hands while standing.

- Once your baby has mostly mastered maintaining her balance while standing upright, she may be ready to try a few steps on her own.

- Some babies may "toddle" with reservation for quite some time, while others seem to move quickly from toddling to independent walking at a faster pace.

- Be vigilant in keeping baby safe while she's learning to walk.

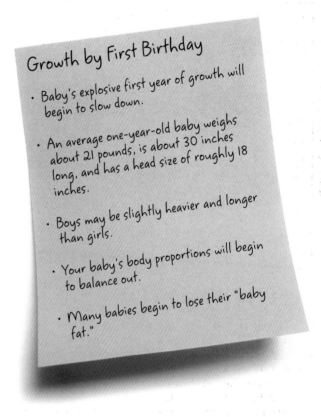

Growth by First Birthday

- Baby's explosive first year of growth will begin to slow down.

- An average one-year-old baby weighs about 21 pounds, is about 30 inches long, and has a head size of roughly 18 inches.

- Boys may be slightly heavier and longer than girls.

- Your baby's body proportions will begin to balance out.

- Many babies begin to lose their "baby fat."

185

EMOTIONS

Baby's easygoing nature may begin to change along with new emotions, fears, and self-confidence

Your baby's emotions are entering new highs—and lows—as she begins to experience more feelings and desires. Your baby is so much fun to be around at this stage; everything is a game, and she's quick to tell through facial expressions and moods the rules she wants to play by!

Your baby may be becoming the family clown, and finds pleasure in imitating gestures, smiling, blowing kisses, and grabbing you for hugs and snuggles. Show her a mirror, and she's apt to reach out to touch or kiss her own reflection. Your infant likes to be near you, and is less content to be away from the action whenever she is awake. She may demand to be held more, making it a challenge for parents to try to

Emotional Highs

- Your infant is beginning to develop self-esteem.

- Baby will likely respond to positive reinforcement and recognition, such as you clapping your hands in delight at something.

- Your baby may begin to notice other babies and watch what they do more, although she won't interact with them yet.

- Expect your baby to begin to seek your approval and avoid displeasing you. She is beginning truly to care what you think and how you feel!

Emotional Lows

- Baby may become more moody and quicker to demonstrate being sad or angry.

- There may be occasions when nothing seems to please your baby, but relax. She's just having a bad day!

- Your baby may not be receptive to strangers and begin demanding to have you by her side.

- Your baby may become uncooperative or stubborn at times as she gains a greater emotional understanding of her personal likes and dislikes.

get things done. Give her something to occupy her interest, however, and she's apt to be content as long as she can keep her eyes on you!

Your baby's moods are becoming more complex, and you'll soon have a better understanding of ways to keep your baby happy, as well as activities or periods that make her mad, upset, or even sad. You might even witness a temper, and perhaps a tantrum on occasion. Luckily, there are countless ways to keep your infant in the happy mode!

Your previously docile infant may suddenly demonstrate emotions more forcibly, especially frustration, fear, and anger. Why? These newfound emotions may be due to your infant constantly pushing herself to her limits and then becoming frustrated. Your baby doesn't grasp patience, yet she is growing more aware of things she can—and can't yet—do.

Emotional In-Betweens

- Your baby may become more cautious of heights and aware of potential dangers, although many babies are still fearless.

- Expect your baby to get overexcited or overstimulated easily, going from an emotional high to a low in a matter of seconds.

- You'll still need to help your infant to calm down, especially as she experiences newer emotions like anger or sadness.

- Your baby is developing a greater understanding of your reactions and what they mean.

Temper, Temper

- New parent controls may be needed to keep baby's emotions in check.

- Your baby may react forcibly to the word No.

- He may begin to test you to see if you really mean it. Be consistent so your baby will begin to understand rules.

- Your baby's emotions can get the best of him, so provide plenty of love and diversion!

LANGUAGE
Babies can understand a lot more than they can say, although simple words may debut

Did your baby just wave and say, "Bye-bye"? Or, say "Dada" or "Mama"? It could be. Or, maybe it is just what you want to hear. Listen closely to what your baby is saying, and regardless of whether your baby is saying actual words, you'll notice your baby is using language. Instead of the previously random inflections and babbles, your infant's

conversations are really beginning to take shape. Your tyke understands more words than he can express at this stage, and you may be surprised at how much he really does know. All of your talking and reading out loud has paid off, as baby is beginning to respond through simple language as well!

Practicing Language

- Your baby may begin to string together words, such as, "Go bye-bye."

- Your baby may like to mimic sound effects, such as clicking or popping. It's another way to encourage lip and tongue actions to form sounds.

- Baby may practice a certain word throughout the day, but eventually will use it to communicate its proper meaning.

- When your baby gestures at something, use words in response. "Do you want your bear?"

Encouraging Talk

- Give your baby plenty of opportunities to join in conversations, and maintain eye contact while she speaks as encouragement.

- Aid multilanguage development by teaching baby how to say "dog" in different languages at the same time.

- Your baby is understanding tone and interpreting words.

- Some baby talk is okay, and is a way to encourage early conversation, but don't go overboard. You want your infant to begin to mimic normal human inflection and tone.

Studies vary regarding how much a baby understands at this stage, but many findings support the belief that babies truly learn and remember certain words at around nine months of age. It is estimated that many infants may know the meaning of about 18 words before their first year. You will be able to see for yourself your baby's understanding of words by the way he reacts when you utter that you are going "bye-bye" or it's time "for a bath" or "bed." Expect to hear your baby babble a pattern of words more consistently; your baby may be trying to say something to you, but just doesn't quite have the vowel-consonant sequence down yet. With practice, he will in no time!

Babies speak repeating sounds (such as dada) first in many cultures, and recent studies of infant brain activities suggest that the ability to recognize these types of repetitive sounds more easily is hard-wired in the human brain. Essentially, it means that the brain areas that are responsible for language are specialized from the start, which is why babies more easily learn one or more languages than adults.

Reinforcing Language

- Help your baby's language development by providing simple sounds and words baby can imitate.

- Encourage your baby to say words back to you. "This is a cow. Can you say cow? The cow goes moo. Can you say moo?"

- Use simple words and short sentences when speaking to your baby.

- Give your baby your full attention when she begins to make sounds. Don't tune her out by speaking over her or turning away.

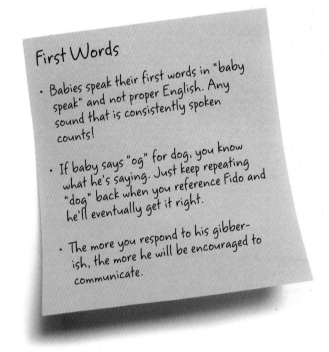

First Words

- Babies speak their first words in "baby speak" and not proper English. Any sound that is consistently spoken counts!

- If baby says "og" for dog, you know what he's saying. Just keep repeating "dog" back when you reference Fido and he'll eventually get it right.

- The more you respond to his gibberish, the more he will be encouraged to communicate.

GEAR

Toys and equipment need updating to keep up with the growing changes in your baby

An increasing ability to focus, enhanced motor skills, and a larger physical size mean baby's clothes aren't the only things that have been quickly outgrown. Gear and toys you only bought a few months ago suddenly seem, well, too "baby-ish" for your infant who is quickly approaching the one-year milestone!

Toys aimed at encouraging curiosity and exploration flood the market, and parents can become overwhelmed by a dizzying array of sound effects, bright colors, and whirling movements. While entertainment products are a personal choice, certain equipment may provide extra balance support to help your baby get a foothold on walking. Push toys,

Mobility Aids

- Push toys can be good confidence-boosters for emerging walkers.

- Make sure all stairs and level changes in the home are secured so your mobile baby cannot scale stairs or accidentally tumble down them.

- Be sure you carefully evaluate a toy for sturdiness so that baby can't topple it over while trying to use it to stand upright.

- Check with your child's pediatrician before considering a walker toy (which babies fit inside and scoot around).

First-Aid Essentials

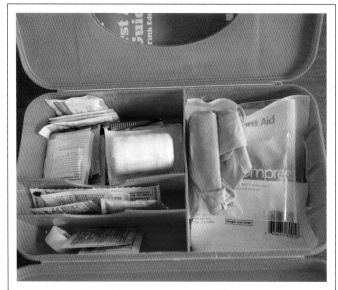

- Expect occasional boo-boos, especially when your baby is learning to walk.

- Stock a child-friendly first-aid kit and keep one with you at all times. Adhesive bandages, disinfectants and wipes, cotton balls, and gauze can help save the day.

- It is safe to use sunscreen on older infants. Choose one that is formulated for infants and has an SPF of at least 15 to 30.

- Do a skin patch test for an allergic reaction on your baby's back before applying.

which are crafted to look like a variety of common household items like lawn mowers or vacuum cleaners, provide your tot with something to hold onto while pulling up and taking those early steps.

Many parents are interested in gear that keeps their tyke safe and content at the same time—a balancing act that will continue to become more challenging. Look for backpack carriers that let baby have a bird's-eye view of his surroundings while on outings. Most likely, your baby will exceed recommended weight limits for front packs at this stage, so wearing your

baby is no longer safe or practical, especially due to baby's tendency to grab onto everything within reach.

Since you may enjoy taking your baby more places now, make sure you provide a safe place for naps out of the sun's harsh rays. Baby tents or nap canopies allow a growing infant to stretch out when a stroller suddenly doesn't seem as roomy as it did a few months ago. Another good idea is to keep a child's first-aid kit in your car or diaper bag. Bumps, scrapes, and falls will become more frequent, and you'll quickly learn the magical power of a Band-Aid!

On the Go

- Baby backpacks provide a safe way to transport your infant while keeping your hands free.

- Jogging strollers, child seats that attach to your bicycle, or separate units that attach to your bike's back wheel provide exercise options.

- Make sure your baby is properly fastened and secured tightly. Babies can easily wiggle out of loose-fitting harness straps and get hurt.

- Some babies are fearful of being carried using these methods.

Shade Tents

- Pop-up or foldable travel tents or canopies provide a safe way to let baby sleep or play when outdoors.

- Tents may offer screened openings to keep bugs away and padded flooring so that baby can take a nap right on the surface.

- Tents or canopies provide protection against the sun or wind, and keep toys and baby items in a secure location.

- Portable playpens often come with canopy tops that provide a similar protection and convenience.

BATHING

Getting clean is just one of the benefits of baby's bath time experience

Baths are now a time of fun and games for you and baby both! Your infant's better control of her body means that you now have more bathing options than ever before. While most parents still prefer to bathe their infant in a baby bathtub, tub seats or rings can also be used safely. Older siblings can take a bath with baby (with direct hands-on adult supervision at all times, of course), and some brave parents may even elect to take a bath with their baby to add some bonding time along with getting clean.

If you have multiples, baths are now easier, as you can bathe babies all at once. Expect to get wet, as most babies at this stage love to kick and splash, and may even protest

Safety

- Continue to use hypoallergenic and "no tears" baby bath shampoo and body wash products. Babies can play with bubbles and then, without warning, rub their eyes.

- Keep all baby supplies within arm's reach so you can safely keep a hand on your active infant at all times.

- Consider using a rubber mat to avoid any slips in soapy water.

- Keep all electrical appliances out of baby's reach, unplugged and put away.

Hygiene

- Be prepared for impromptu peeing when baby is placed in warm water. Keep a washcloth over a boy's genitals to avoid getting sprayed.

- Babies at this age need more thorough cleaning of their bottoms and in their skin folds from messier diapers that come with the introduction of solid foods.

- Infant-formulated body wash keeps your baby smelling clean without harsh chemicals or heavy scents.

- Pay special attention to cleaning under baby's fingernails.

when bath time is over. Keep in mind that your water heater still needs to be set at a safe 120 degrees Fahrenheit, and consider using a faucet cover to avoid scrapes or too-hot metal surfaces. You'll need to be even more vigilant than ever before with water safety. Infants can drown in as little as a few inches of water, so never turn away from them or leave the room. The phone or doorbell can simply wait.

MAKE IT EASY

Despite a parent's patience and clever tactics, some babies absolutely will continue to hate baths. If your infant screams every time you start the water, there are other ways to keep your infant clean. It's better to use a warm washcloth with soap for a quick suds of hair while on a safe surface at this stage than to force the issue. In a few weeks, try a bath again.

Tub Time Tips

- Your baby may feel as slippery as a fish. Maintain a firm grip on your baby with one hand grasping her underarm furthest away from you and the other supporting her bottom when lifting baby out of the tub.

- If you're kneeling over a bathtub, always follow proper ergonomic practices and avoid hurting your back with improper bending and standing.

- Avoid toys made of hard plastic that baby can whack against your tub surface or faucet.

Water Fun

- Apply a small amount of baby body wash on a wet sponge and let baby squish it with her hands to generate suds.

- Pour-and-dump bath toys are fun at this stage. Make sure baby doesn't pour water over his face.

- Silly shampoo shapes and bubble clothes can entertain and clean at the same time.

DRESSING

If your baby is beginning to take those first steps, it's time for shoes

Your baby will truly be stylin' now, as clothes seem to fit and look better. You may be discovering that all cute baby clothing isn't created in a one-style-fits-all fashion, as onesies may be too short in the crotch, arms or legs are too short or long, or tighter pants styles don't work well with your cherub's rolls of fat, still commonly found around thigh areas of many babies. Your baby's increased movement may mean that snap crotches are harder to fasten, and you'll need to provide extra care not to pinch baby's delicate skin while trying to refasten those pants after a diaper change. Be sure to pick styles that work well with your baby's mobility, and even begin to look for outfits that lend themselves to safe toddling and early walking.

When It's Time for Shoes

- Once your tyke begins taking those important first steps, he's ready for his first pair of shoes.

- When it's safe and practical to do so, let baby continue to go barefoot for overall coordination and so he can feel various surfaces.

- Shoes should be worn outdoors when it is cold or to protect delicate feet from splinters or rough or sharp surfaces.

Baby's First Shoes

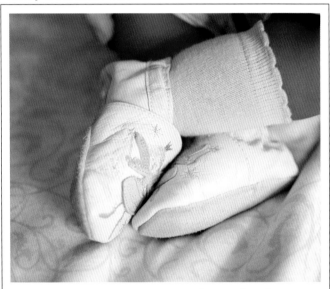

- Select a sneaker or similar breathable shoe made from soft leather, canvas, or cloth and not the stiff leather shoes worn by babies a generation ago.

- Avoid synthetic materials on the uppers that can cause feet to sweat.

- Make sure the soles are flexible, not stiff or hard. A nonskid rubber sole works well.

- Ridges on soles offer good traction and are preferred. Scuff smooth soles before baby wears them to minimize the chance of slips.

Dressing your baby may actually be easier than it has been in earlier months. Your baby knows the routine, and may even extend an arm, lift a leg, or grab a sock or shoe for you to put on. (Just don't be surprised if she immediately attempts to take any type of footwear right back off.) Ask your baby to help you with getting dressed ("Can you put your arm in this jacket?").

YELLOW LIGHT

Your infant may appear to be flat-footed (usually due to fat padding under the arches). He may even show a tendency to turn his toes in when taking steps, have a foot that turns in more than the other or one that rolls in at the ankle, or even prefer to walk on his tip-toes. Most likely there's no cause for concern, but you should check with your pediatrician just to be sure.

Trying on Shoes

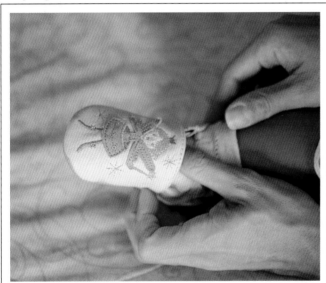

- Bring your baby with you to try on shoes rather than guessing proper shoe size.

- Shop later in the day when baby's feet have expanded, so you'll provide a better fit.

- Make sure there is enough room to place your small finger between baby's heel and the shoe, and a thumb's width between the end of his toe and tip of the shoe.

- Check that the shoe isn't too tight at the ball of the foot.

Keeping Shoes On

- High-top designs may be harder to put on but stay on better.

- Make sure laces are long enough to double knot (so you're not constantly re-tying).

- Velcro provides ease in putting on and taking off shoes. But babies quickly figure out how to undo the Velcro, and may elect to remove and throw their shoes at inopportune times.

- Buckle shoe designs typically stay on well and allow width to be adjusted as needed.

195

DIAPERING

Cruising and toddling bring new diapering challenges for avoiding leaks and droops

Basic baby care has become an interactive experience that often includes squirming, grabbing, and even protesting because your infant is too busy to be laid down for cleanup or a clothes change. Your baby's increased attention span, energy, and alertness mean you'll have to become adept at distraction and speed.

Changing baby's diaper is now a familiar part of your day, as by now you've changed your infant's diapers hundreds of times. While the routine is automatic, the solid food baby is now eating means messier and smellier diaper changes. Since you're likely on the go more with your baby, preparedness can make all the difference between a quick change at a

Quick-Change Magic

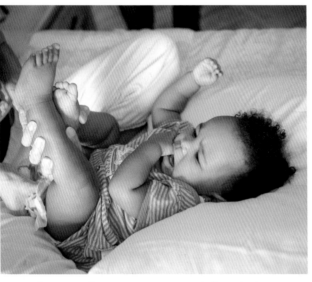

- Save fancier outfits requiring more time for special occasions.

- Look for snaps that extend all the way to the bottom so you don't have to push feet with shoes on through leg openings or remove shoes each time.

- Keep baby-safe objects near the diaper-changing area to give baby something to look at and hold during diaper changes.

- Maintain eye contact and sing or talk while changing a diaper.

Diaper Fit

- Different brands and types definitely fit babies differently. You may want to switch types to coincide with baby's growth and body changes.

- Many parents discover that diapers put on while baby is lying down gap at the waist when baby stands up.

- Tighten diapers more than you previously have (but not too tight) and adjust if needed when baby is upright.

- If leaks or gaps continue to be a problem, consider using a diaper cover.

changing station at a store and having a mess on your hands (with a howling baby as well).

Just as babies at this age may quickly discover how to remove shoes with Velcro, the same holds true for the tab fasteners on disposable diapers. More than one parent has been caught by surprise by a newly naked baby crawling across the floor. Since toilet training doesn't come until later, a baby's quick mastery of unfastening and removal of Velcro-style disposable diapers and certain cloth diaper designs means more clothes are now in order! Extra care should now be used when it comes to fasteners, as babies will explore anything they find of interest. Removing a diaper and checking out what is inside doesn't mean they are ready for potty training—they are just curious!

Parents may also find that the diaper style and fit that has worked so well with their tyke in previous months is now causing leaks or even droops. As babies begin to stand upright and even toddle, the way diapers hug their bodies may need adjusting. Explore different diaper styles—especially around the leg openings—to minimize accidents.

Diaper Stations

- When changing your baby out in public, you want to be able to get the deed done in record time.

- Have wipes out of container and fresh diaper ready before laying your baby down.

- If the changing table seems unstable, look for a counter area. In a pinch, you can have your baby stand while you provide a quick change.

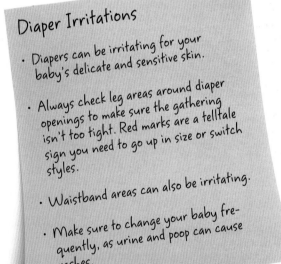

Diaper Irritations

- Diapers can be irritating for your baby's delicate and sensitive skin.

- Always check leg areas around diaper openings to make sure the gathering isn't too tight. Red marks are a telltale sign you need to go up in size or switch styles.

- Waistband areas can also be irritating.

- Make sure to change your baby frequently, as urine and poop can cause rashes.

SLEEPING

Baby's self-settling and the end of night feedings may mean more rest for you!

Your baby is most likely sleeping from 10 to 12 hours a night—sometimes even longer—and napping twice daily for an hour of two at a time. It's all that sleep that is enabling your baby to grow and thrive during waking hours, and your baby's seemingly endless energy is what leaves you so tired that you might be ready to hit the sack when baby does!

If your baby now sleeps at night without waking, then congratulations are in order. Your infant has successfully learned how to settle back to sleep on her own. If your baby hasn't yet established a regular sleep schedule that works for your family, then you might need to make it a priority now to get one started. Babies at this age don't need feedings at night,

Sleep Practices

- A positive bedtime routine will help your baby transition through sleep challenges that may develop.

- Most babies typically take one nap in the morning and one in the afternoon. Quality naps keep them from becoming overly tired

- or too crabby to sleep well at night.

- If your baby cries for you in the night, remember to provide quick reassurance and then a quick exit.

- Provide a favorite small toy or baby blanket in the crib for comfort.

Anxiety

- Babies may become acutely aware of "separateness" at this stage and not want to be left alone for sleep.

- Many parents become surprised when their previously easy-to-sleep baby begins to demonstrate tears and even tantrums at bedtime.

- Your baby may wake up and immediately look for loved ones instead of trying to resettle.

- Consistency is key as your actions now will influence future bedtime habits for the entire family.

so if you are still providing a middle-of-the-night meal, it's time to get that stopped.

Babies who wake up in the night haven't yet mastered putting themselves back to sleep, or awaken and want comfort from a loved one. It is normal to wake up very briefly several times every night—we all do it—but putting yourself back to sleep easily and quickly may be something your baby hasn't yet been able to do. So that you aren't exhausted all the time, this is a good stage to get a sleep routine well established.

Don't be surprised if your baby suddenly changes her sleeping habits at this stage. Your infant may have previously slept through the night or put herself to sleep without fuss, but is now awakening. Sleep disturbances such as waking up, being unable to settle back down, or becoming a night owl or an early riser are all part of normal growth and development. You may have to provide sleep training reinforcement or late-night comfort until baby once again establishes an acceptable sleep routine.

Comfort

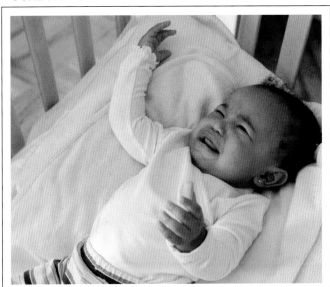

- Trying to establish a routine for future nights of uninterrupted sleep is often a balancing act.

- "Giving in" by providing a bottle, rocking your baby back to sleep, or holding her until she falls asleep in your arms may not set the stage for improved sleep habits, but it's not the end of the world either.

- Try to comfort baby while she remains in her bed.

- Parents should do what they are most comfortable with and what works with their routine.

Night Terrors
- Night terrors are different than bad dreams.

- They occur during the transition between deep sleep and another level of sleep.

- Children don't remember them and will eventually outgrow them.

- Provide plenty of love and reassurance if your baby wakes up screaming and scared (you will know the difference between normal crying and outright screaming with true fear).

SAFETY

Keeping a curious baby out of harm's way requires close attention at all times

It's impossible to provide a guaranteed safe environment for your increasingly mobile and curious infant. Potential dangers lurk everywhere—from objects left on the floor to normal-use items that can be choking or accident hazards to infants. The best any caregiver can do is to be on alert at all times for possible dangers, and to be particularly vigilant in supervision. While that may seem like a lot of pressure for parents, the truth is that proper attention, carefully selected toys, and a thorough safety inspection of your home and baby equipment will keep baby safe.

The biggest challenge at this age is with mobility. Once your baby begins to pull up on objects, you'll find yourself

Stair and Step Dangers

- Homes with stairs or raised or sunken levels can result in dangerous falls for a curious baby. Install baby gates or keep areas off-limits and secured.

- Many babies try to climb objects, such as chairs or couches, often tumbling over in the process. Keep a close eye on your baby at all times.

- Step stools (including ones for older siblings) are often an irresistible temptation for babies.

- Rolling furniture should be temporarily put away.

Once Baby Pulls Up

- Tablecloths and dangling accessories can be dangerous temptations.

- Move or secure any flimsy objects that baby may try to use to pull up, and topple over in the process.

- Once your baby pulls up using the sides of the crib, it's time to remove any bumper pads that baby can use to get a "leg up" over the side.

- Remove any decorations or mobiles that baby can now reach from a standing position in the crib.

200

scampering around and providing encouragement and protection at the same time. Everything is a potential pull-up opportunity, and baby's growing strength means that drawers, cabinets, and anything that is not nailed down and sealed shut is of possible interest to your baby.

Expect occasional ouchies when your baby unexpectedly lurches one way or pulls up, only to fall. Your baby will also continue to pick up small objects (now with her pincer grasp) and often still want to place them in her mouth. Once her balance becomes better and her eye-hand-mouth

experimentation lessens, you'll be able to relax a little, but for now, the saying that parents need eyes on the backs of their heads couldn't be truer.

A visit to the park or similar outdoor fun should also be balanced with safety precautions. Babies at this age may love the feel of grass on their toes, crunching leaves, or being pushed in an infant swing, but be sure to check for exposed nails or splinters, safe equipment, and sharp objects first.

Kitchen Dangers

- Since parents spend much of their time in the kitchen, it's only natural that babies will too.

- Kitchens hold particular dangers. Range-top oven doors are within baby's reach, knives and sharp objects are present, and surfaces that are used for food preparation may be unsanitary.

- Make sure your dishwasher is kept locked; the pull-down door can pinch fingers or hit baby's head.

- Cook on back surfaces only, or keep handles turned away from the edge.

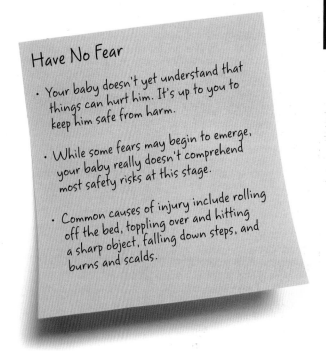

Have No Fear

- Your baby doesn't yet understand that things can hurt him. It's up to you to keep him safe from harm.

- While some fears may begin to emerge, your baby really doesn't comprehend most safety risks at this stage.

- Common causes of injury include rolling off the bed, toppling over and hitting a sharp object, falling down steps, and burns and scalds.

CHILD-CARE ENVIRONMENT

Consider green factor, allergens, outdoor outings, and food allergies when choosing child care

Your baby's safety and well-being, cost, and convenience are all valid reasons for choosing child care. So is the type of child-care setting. It's okay as well to change types of care (in-home care to daycare, for example) to coincide with your baby's stages. Child care that worked well for your newborn may not be your preferred type when your infant becomes more mobile and begins to walk.

A growing number of parents are paying particular attention to and asking detailed questions about child-care facilities' "green factor," in terms of the use of chemicals for cleaning and pesticide treatments. Since babies in child care can spend about 40 hours there every week, these concerns

Green Factor

- Schools and institutional daycare centers follow carefully restricted pesticide treatment programs. Those rules don't apply to family caregivers, however, so ask what the provider does to keep pests away.

- Many professional-grade cleaners aren't green.

- Some providers now use eco-friendly cleaners like baking soda, white distilled vinegar, and hydrogen peroxide.

- If your baby is showing signs of asthma or allergies, ask detailed questions about cleaning processes used.

Outdoor Play

- Ozone and particulates can cause respiratory problems for babies with weakened immune systems.

- Ask your child's caregiver how she determines it is safe for outdoor play.

- If a family caregiver plans an outdoor outing and you don't want your baby to participate, you'll need to provide backup child care, as in-home providers don't have additional staff available.

- Many communities publicize ozone action alert days and air quality indexes.

are certainly valid. While most babies are fine around common chemicals, certain infants with weaker immune systems may get overloaded by toxins in their environments.

You'll also want to be sure you are comfortable with mealtime practices and how your baby is fed, and whether your infant is taken along with other children on field trips or outside to play. Some caregivers strictly leave babies indoors the first year, while others have the attitude of "family fun" and take all kids in their care to the park and special events—regardless of age.

Eating

- Most daycare centers require that parents bring food until baby is able to eat food choices that they serve.

- Provide easy-to-understand written directions to increase the likelihood that they will be followed.

- Talk with your caregiver about food dos and don'ts for your baby. Just because you know that babies are not to eat eggs, peanut butter, or honey, for example, doesn't mean your provider does.

- Make sure that baby formula or breast milk is given at most meals.

Don't be afraid to ask how toys and shared surfaces at child-care centers are cleaned and how often. While smaller home-based centers may sterilize toys and use alcohol-based wipes daily, larger centers may find that task impractical and opt for disinfectants. Ask how often play, sleeping, and eating areas are cleaned and what solvents are used, and make sure you are comfortable with the answers provided.

Baby's Health at Child Care

- One study showed that kids who attend daycare or participate in play groups have a 30 percent lower chance of developing a life-threatening cancer.

- Youngsters in regular contact with their peers are exposed to a multitude of infections, so they typically develop a stronger immune system. This later helps kids' bodies fight off childhood diseases.

- If your baby exhibits a chronic runny nose or other classic allergy symptoms while at day care, allergies might be the culprit. Common triggers include dust mites, pollen, molds, and animal dander. Check with the daycare to see if your child has been exposed to any of these allergens.

TRANSITIONING TO A CUP

Giving up the beloved and familiar bottle marks a big change from baby to toddler

You've most likely already introduced baby to a cup for water or juice, but until now have continued to provide infant formula or pumped breast milk in a bottle. Your baby, after all, associates the bottle and its familiar contents with both food and cuddle time. As baby's first birthday approaches, however, it's time to begin the gradual process of leaving bottles behind altogether. Often, total weaning from a bottle may span several months with the final feeding of the evening traditionally being the last bottle to go.

If your baby has already started drinking other fluids from a cup, the transition may not be as challenging as if baby doesn't yet use a cup at all. Expect the process to take time;

Cups to Consider

- Sippy cups with easy grips and soft silicone spouts may provide an easier transition option for some babies because the design is similar to a bottle.

- Look for varieties that are BPA-free and have replacement spouts or valves (which are easier to replace

than buying a whole new cup).

- Avoid sippy cups with pop-up straws at this stage.

- If your baby seems to be sucking too hard and becoming frustrated, find another style.

Trainer Cups

- Trainer cups are marketed as first cups for babies and are most likely smaller in size and easier to grip than ones meant for toddlers.

- Slot-style sippy cups are generally not recommended for this stage, as liquid can flow too quickly and cause choking.

- Consider ease of cleaning before purchasing.

- Some cups have small crevices where liquids can dry up and collect mold or gunk. Keep cups clean and dry between uses.

initially, even a baby who is receptive to drinking from a cup won't be able to drink enough milk from the cup at mealtimes. You will still need to finish up the meal with a bottle to ensure proper nutrition. Many families opt to begin the transition process by only offering cups at meals and bottles during other times. Once your baby drinks around four ounces from the cup at each meal, you're truly ready to begin replacing bottles with cup feedings at other times as well. Keep in mind that your baby will need practice drinking fluids this way.

A cup style is only a good design if your baby will willingly drink from it, so try different types until you find one that baby seems to be most receptive to using. Some cups offer stages of spouts designed to make the transition easier for infants who are hesitant to drink from a cup. Most parents prefer to use a cup that won't leak or drip when turned upside down or shaken and that is shatterproof.

Training Tips

- You can start holding the cup yourself and let baby sip from it.

- Model drinking from a cup to show baby how to do it.

- Some parents prefer to have babies learn to drink from a cup without a lid, although lots of spills should be expected.

- Avoid becoming impatient or upset. Your baby will pick up on those emotions and may become more hesitant in learning how to drink from a cup.

Why Age One?

- Babies are usually ready to be weaned from the bottle by 12 to 15 months of age.

- The longer you wait, the more difficult it can become to get baby to give up drinking from a bottle.

- Your baby may become more willful or demanding about keeping a bottle the older he gets.

- Drinking from a bottle increases the likelihood of tooth decay because of the way the liquid sometimes pools around emerging teeth from not being immediately swallowed.

WEANING FROM BREASTFEEDING

Gradual weaning by reducing one feeding at a time works better than stopping at once

Deciding when to wean your baby is up to the mom and her family. It could be based on lifestyle decisions, a mother's desire to feel less restricted with her schedule, medical reasons, or because it just feels right. Sometimes, a baby becomes less interested in breastfeeding, easing the transition for both mom and infant alike. For many breastfeeding mothers, weaning occurs around baby's first birthday, in part because it seems a natural time to begin drinking from a cup. After their one-year checkup, most babies are also able to begin drinking cow's milk. (Note: The American Academy of Pediatrics recommends that babies drink only breast milk or infant formula for the first year.)

Must I Wean?

- Breastfeeding can continue as long as mom and baby desire to do so.

- The World Health Organization recommends breastfeeding for a minimum of two full years and the AAP recommends breastfeeding for a minimum of one year.

- Baby's cutting of teeth doesn't require breastfeeding to stop, although you might offer baby a teether before nursing or use a different nursing position.

Gradual Weaning

- Substitute a cup for breast-feeding at your baby's least favorite feeding. If possible, let someone other than mom try this.

- La Leche League suggests "don't offer, don't refuse" weaning by simply not offering the breast.

- Begin using a cup (with expressed milk, water, or juice) and then end with a short breastfeeding session.

- Avoid nursing in a baby's favorite nursing chair that he has long associated with breastfeeding.

Once you decide it's time to wean your baby from breast-feeding, knowing how to do it is altogether a different matter. La Leche League International recommends that you "do it gradually, and with love." Common advice is to drop a single feeding at a time, starting with when baby is least likely to miss a breastfeeding session. Dropping a feeding or two may be all that a mom wants to do for a while longer, and her body will adjust to a lower milk production that still meets the nutritional needs of her infant. Removing a single feeding at a time will also help mom's body to adjust more

easily, and lessens the likelihood of breast engorgement and possible infections.

Breastfeeding moms may find that their baby will take a bottle or cup from someone else rather than from them. That's because baby knows a mom's smell, and knows that where there is mom there are breasts for milk. Once a baby takes a bottle or cup from someone else successfully, it may become easier for mom to use that alternative method of feeding as well.

Sudden Weaning

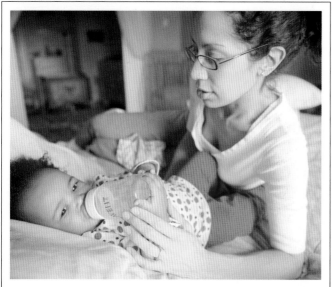

- Be sure to check with your doctor before nursing while sick or on medications.

- Nursing moms sometimes have to wean suddenly for medical reasons, making the gradual process impractical.

- If possible, express milk for the adjustment period to provide comfort and allow your baby to get used to a bottle or cup.

- Even if you can't give your infant the breast milk, you'll need to express milk until your breasts lessen production to avoid engorgement.

Holiday Weaning

- The term "holiday weaning" refers to a baby weaning due to a special event, such as vacation, celebration, or holiday.

- Excitement, distractions, and visitors may keep baby and mom apart more than normal and make baby less interested in breastfeeding.

- Busy families may be quick to offer cups or bottles instead of breastfeeding.

- This a good time to wean if the mom chooses; otherwise, special efforts need to be made to keep the routine of breastfeeding intact.

FINGER FOODS

Baby's pincer grasp, increasing appetite, and greater interest in food encourage eating independence

What are finger foods? Just about anything that is bite-size, approved for baby to eat at this stage, and can be picked up counts as a finger food. Encouraging your infant to feed himself works best with finger foods such as pieces of banana, cooked carrots, crackers, or O-shaped cereal. Finger food is fun for babies because it allows them to choose which item

to eat and take an important step toward independent eating. And while the experience may sometimes be messy, it allows them to continue to fine-tune motor skills and coordination.

Some babies may exert their desire to feed themselves by grabbing at the spoon or food container. They may also grab

Favorite Finger Foods

- Finger food fruits may include chunks of banana or peeled fruits like pears, peaches, cantaloupe, honeydew, plum, or watermelon.

- Very small chunks of cheese or well-cooked pasta in finger-friendly shapes are typically well received.

- Small chunks of well-cooked vegetables like carrots, potato or sweet potato, or peas are popular with babies.

- Try giving your baby saltine crackers, melba toast, or rice cakes that dissolve easily in the mouth.

Best Time to Introduce

- Finger foods can be added to mealtimes anytime after you have checked the particular food for allergic reactions.

- Your baby should be successfully eating pureed foods without choking or spitting food back out.

- Don't wait for teeth; best finger foods can be gummed or dissolved in the mouth before being swallowed.

- Mealtimes can have a variety of food choices. Some parents start with finger foods first and then finish by feeding baby pureed food.

food off your plate or pretend to feed themselves (as if practicing) during play sessions. You get the hint—go ahead and let them try!

The key to successful finger food offerings is to limit it to a few pieces at a time, so you don't end up picking up hurled or smashed food off the floor. If your baby begins to play with food that is laid out, firmly say "No," remove the finger food offering, and resume feeding your baby. She'll quickly learn that food is not a toy. At the same time, some experimentation with food is to be expected, such as mashing a banana chunk and then slurping it off the fingers. Just keep wipes—and your camera—ready for those "learning moments" as baby begins to eat on her own.

Always feed your baby where you will want him to eat later (such as at the kitchen table). Establishing proper family routines by placing him in his high chair to eat and not in a chair in the living room helps your baby to understand where he is expected to eat.

Dos and Don'ts

- Do offer a few pieces or selections on a high chair tray or a secured dish.

- Don't offer too many pieces at once. Continue to add a few pieces after baby eats what is offered.

- Do put a stop to food throwing at once and tell baby "No" while removing food. If you laugh or react, your baby may want to make food throwing or dropping part of mealtime entertainment.

- Don't let mealtimes become food battles.

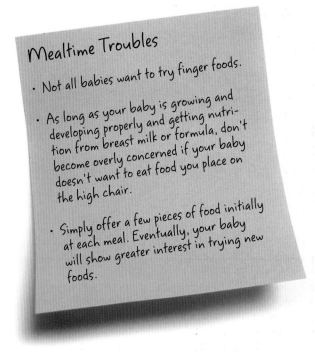

Mealtime Troubles

- Not all babies want to try finger foods.

- As long as your baby is growing and developing properly and getting nutrition from breast milk or formula, don't become overly concerned if your baby doesn't want to eat food you place on the high chair.

- Simply offer a few pieces of food initially at each meal. Eventually, your baby will show greater interest in trying new foods.

SCHEDULE

Your baby is learning to expect certain times to eat and places where meals will be served

Your family should now be operating on a fairly consistent and effective routine. Establishing a schedule for when baby eats that works with parent work schedules, older sibling activities, morning and afternoon naptimes, and special events or occasions can be trickier, but it is still very doable. Essentially, you'll serve your baby solid foods at breakfast, lunch, and dinner, with breast milk or infant formula provided at in-between times, along with snacks. Parents may find that they now can often actually sit down and enjoy eating their own meal while feeding their baby, who hopefully is showing an increased interest in eating and participating in mealtimes.

Breakfast Rush

- Baby's breakfast may present a challenge for parents who face morning madness trying to get everyone ready and where they need to be on time.

- Child-care providers usually have set times for breakfast, so make sure baby doesn't miss out if he eats there.

- Stay-at-home parents may opt to start the morning with breast milk or infant formula to stave off the hungries.

- Babies can eat breakfast after the morning chaos is over.

Leisurely Lunches

- If your baby attends day-care, she'll most likely eat lunch with other peers in a dining-room setting and will learn to eat on schedule.

- Lunchtime is often the most social meal of the day for babies, who are typically active and hungry after a morning nap.

- Stay-at-home parents may choose to make lunchtime a leisurely and fun time with baby since there is less stress for mealtime preparation.

- Eating out may be less stressful at lunch than at dinner.

Of course, there's no set rule that baby has to sit down for breakfast as you're trying to get ready for work or scramble to get kids off to school. The nice thing about schedules is that they can be built around what works best for your family—and baby will adapt to times and places that become a familiar part of his routine. If your baby attends full-time child care, breakfast and lunch during weekdays may be served up by the child-care provider, and your baby will quickly learn that dinnertime and weekend meals will be at home with mom and dad.

Some babies will adapt to "loose" feeding times while others prefer to adhere to a preset tummy clock. If your baby is used to eating breakfast at 7 a.m. on weekdays, for example, don't be surprised if she insists on her morning meal around the same time on weekends, even if you wanted to sleep in. Others won't care. It's all about your baby's personal preferences and how you work your schedule.

Cranky Eaters

- There will be occasions when baby wants nothing to do with food.

- Your baby may resist being put in a high chair, crush or throw food, bat the spoon away, or refuse to open his mouth.

- Avoid trying to "force" your baby to eat; it is a battle you won't win.

- Unless you feel your baby is not receiving proper nutrition, don't worry about it and simply offer food again at the next meal.

When Baby is Picky

- Despite your best efforts, some babies are simply picky when it comes to food choices.

- There is no cause for concern if your baby is still drinking infant milk and is starting to eat some solids.

- Don't worry that your infant refuses bananas or spits out peas. Simply reintroduce the food later, or mix it with another food he does like.

MEALTIME IDEAS

Think simple, nutritious, and delicious when offering your baby foods for meals and snacks

Just because you think baby's food is bland doesn't mean it needs seasoning. Plain and simple is the key to appropriate food offerings at this stage. Your baby doesn't yet have a taste for anything beyond what is grown or produced straight from nature. Most so-called tasty adult foods have a lot of sugar, preservatives, and spices—and calories—so carefully

consider what's in the food on your plate before sharing it with your baby. Otherwise, your infant may develop a preference for spicier, sweeter, or salty foods and no longer want what he has previously eaten enthusiastically.

Don't worry about repetition in food choices. Your baby is tasting new foods and developing likes and dislikes already,

Breakfast

- Whether it's homemade, boxed, or from a jar, baby cereal is the most common food served for breakfast. After foods are introduced, you can add more variety.

- Add ¼ cup of diced fruit such as a banana. You can also stir in applesauce.

- Mashed cooked egg yolk can be given to babies, but not egg whites until after age one.

- Give baby ¼ cup plain yogurt with fruit mixed in.

- Finish with four to six ounces of breast milk or formula.

Lunch Ideas

- Meat isn't necessary for lunch and dinner, but when you do serve it, it is recommended that you start with white meat like chicken before moving to other meats.

- Offer ¼ cup diced or shredded cheese and/or white meat.

- Try ¼ cup green vegetables (such as peas or green beans).

- Give baby ¼ cup plain yogurt with fruit mixed in.

- Finish with four to six ounces of breast milk or formula.

so don't be surprised if he refuses a food that he devoured only days earlier. In spite of clever marketing and the multitude of choices available on grocery shelves in the baby food sections, your infant doesn't need dessert either. Rather than buying a jar of "peach cobbler" baby food, for example, opt instead to serve diced peaches served as finger food or mixed in with plain yogurt.

Starting healthy eating habits now will help lay the foundation for healthier food choices when your child is older.

Dinner Ideas

- Your baby may be able to start eating selections of what everyone else eats at the table.

- Try ¼ cup diced meat or tofu (which can be mixed in with rice or vegetable to provide some variation).

- Feed ¼ cup cooked and diced yellow or orange vegetables (such as squash or carrots).

- Offer ¼ cup of diced and cooked russet or sweet potato or rice.

- Finish with four to six ounces of breast milk or formula.

Simple Snacks

- Teething biscuit, small pieces of soft bread, or crackers (avoid heavily salted commercial foods)

- Diced cheese or cut-up pasta

- Quartered grapes or other diced fruit

- Natural smoothie (plain yogurt mixed with fruit, blended, and then spoon-fed to baby)

- Cottage cheese

- Four to six ounces of breast milk or formula, water, or heavily diluted juice

213

DINING OUT

Eating outside the home becomes easier, but choking hazards and interruptions remain high

Busy families are constantly on the go, and mealtimes can sometimes occur at less-than-desirable places or during the middle of an activity. A hungry baby can also make travel in the car stressful for all. While parents may want to give their baby finger foods like cereal or crackers to eat while out and about, it is not recommended from a health or safety standpoint.

Why shouldn't you give your baby a quick morsel to eat when driving? After all, many parents and older kids eat in the car more frequently than we'd all like to admit. The main reason is safety, as choking is still a likely concern with babies at this stage. Your full attention and focus need to remain on your baby when he eats. The reclining position of a car seat

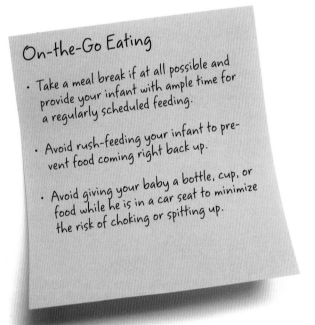

On-the-Go Eating

- Take a meal break if at all possible and provide your infant with ample time for a regularly scheduled feeding.

- Avoid rush-feeding your infant to prevent food coming right back up.

- Avoid giving your baby a bottle, cup, or food while he is in a car seat to minimize the risk of choking or spitting up.

Keeping Food Safe

- While commercially prepared food that isn't opened can be transported safely, make sure you keep home-prepared foods and finger foods stored properly until mealtime.

- Ice packs and insulated bags help to keep food at correct temperatures.

- Look for plasticware with freezer-pack lids that keep items like cheese or yogurt cool.

- Remember that babies may not mind that water or juices are served at room temperature and not chilled.

doesn't lend itself to safe eating, and baby may also try to put too much food in his mouth at once, causing himself to choke. Another reason to resist the urge to offer convenient finger foods is that unless you are right there to supervise every single bite, you may find that food gets smeared all over the car seat and thrown in the car, creating a huge mess that offsets any convenience.

YELLOW ● LIGHT

Inattentive parents who let their rambunctious youngsters play with salt and pepper shakers, tear open sugar packets, and knock over drinks, and who seem oblivious to the disruption when a baby starts to scream, are among top complaints of restaurant customers and staff alike. Seek out kid-friendly restaurants and avoid peak serving times until your infant is old enough to bring only smiles to fellow diners and the servers who will be waiting on your family.

Tricks to Try

- Place food items in resealable plastic baggies.

- Premeasure water into a bottle or cup, and measure the proper amount of formula powder in a baggie so all you need to do is combine and shake when needed.

- Keeping food and diaper essentials separate helps avoid odors, spills, or contamination.

- Freeze grapes overnight to take with you. By baby's mealtime, they will be thawed and ready to eat. (Remember to cut into quarters.)

Surviving Eating Out

- Eating out with your baby is possible at this age with proper planning.

- Bring your own finger foods or meals (don't rely on a restaurant having crackers or baby-friendly foods).

- Bring objects that will keep baby entertained.

- Call the restaurant ahead of time to make sure high chairs are available.

- Don't bring toys that are noisy or annoying to other diners.

- Don't overstay your welcome.

COGNITIVE DEVELOPMENT

Baby's first 12 months are an explosion of endless learning and brain growth

Your baby continues to learn and amaze you practically every day! Newfound skills or even words seem to come out of nowhere, and it's becoming obvious that your infant won't be a baby for much longer. Toddler-like behavior, which may come in varying forms of independence, communication, motor development, tantrums, and will, is being

demonstrated by your cherub every day, especially as the first birthday draws nearer.

Your baby's brain is developing at a rapid rate, and all these emotions and skills are normal and to be expected at this age and stage. Everything your baby does is done to learn—and not to annoy you or give you a fright. Your baby's incessant

Brain Gain

- Your baby's interactions with loved ones are crucial to cognitive development in the first year.

- Baby's personal experiences influence baby's abilities.

- If you haven't previously, consider reading daily to

your baby to help with associations, thinking, and language.

- Your baby may now be able to follow the attention of another person or share her interests with you by pointing out things she wants you to look at.

Thinking

- Your baby is starting to understand that other people think, know, and do things, and have emotions that may differ from hers.

- Babies may begin to understand intentions, when others behave a certain way to achieve something.

- She may understand a difference between interactions with people and those with pets or objects.

- Baby may begin to differentiate different types of communications (verbal versus nonverbal).

curiosity and seemingly endless energy enable him to process information and learn new skills. While he's still easily distracted, your baby's memory capacity will continue to grow. The old "distract and forget" tricks that worked just a month or two ago may no longer work, as baby may now remember what he wanted and may try to find a sought-after object or activity, even after you've removed him from the situation.

Your baby has now acquired a stronger sense of self, and is increasingly aware of cause and effect reactions and where the parts of her body are in relation to other parts of her body.

When you ask your baby to point to her nose or her toes, she may very well be able to do that—if she's in the mood.

A greater understanding of intentionality means that your baby may respond based on whether she thinks you are doing something intentionally (such as teasing her by taking away a toy) or accidentally (such as dropping the toy). Your baby may even begin to demonstrate patience while waiting for you to retrieve a forgotten item.

Emotions

- Your baby is exhibiting newer emotions such as anxiety, fear, or sadness, but may not understand "why" she feels a certain way.

- Allow your baby to maintain a sense of control over a chosen activity, as long as it is safe and not disruptive or destructive.

- Baby's emotions typically reflect that she feels a certain way, and are not targeted "at" someone at this stage, although this will soon change.

- Provide plenty of comfort and reassurance to your baby.

Problem Solving

- Your baby is learning to solve problems by himself.

- Allow your baby to find solutions through trial and error without you always fixing the problem for him. That's how he learns.

- Encourage your baby to keep trying and experimenting until he can do something for himself.

- Your baby can now remember past experiences to solve new problems—a major milestone!

PLAYING

Baby's life is all about fun and activity, so let the games begin!

All your careful nurturing and childproofing efforts have paid off, and this stage is all about play. Your baby has enhanced body control, is becoming more aware of abilities, and finds just about everything amusing—at least for a few seconds—before going on to something else. Let the games begin, as play is how your baby will best interact with you and others, and he will learn some important life lessons at the same time.

The world still revolves around baby (to him, anyway), but your tot is becoming more aware of other babies and adults beyond his or her close-knit circle. While your infant won't truly grasp manners or socialization concepts at this stage,

Interacting with Baby

- Use your baby's cues as learning opportunities. Your baby may point at something of interest, or try to swipe or shove something else out of the way. Comment on objects of interest to further her curiosity.

- Follow baby's pace of play. Sometimes babies may want to do one thing over and over again.

- Don't become impatient because you're tired of an object.

Baby in Charge

- Respect your baby's play choices and don't try to force your baby to explore something in which he shows no interest.

- Don't judge the way baby chooses to play with something, and don't intervene unless there is a safety or health concern.

- An object that is ignored today may become his favorite toy tomorrow.

- Rotate play objects. Giving baby too many things to look at and explore can be overwhelming, and baby's attention span is quite limited.

this is a good time to begin introducing concepts of sharing and waiting for a turn. As patience becomes more possible, you may be surprised to learn that your baby will actually start to do just that!

Let your baby lead the way with initiating various games. Respect her interests, and don't try to redirect your baby if she'd rather play with the ribbons and paper rather than the present inside the wrappings. She'll get to it soon enough. By taking the role of an observer and supporter of your baby's focus, you'll be encouraging her to learn and explore items at her own pace. Some babies may spend significant time on a seemingly boring object like a spatula, while others disregard it entirely and move toward noisy and interactive activities. By responding to his cues or following his lead, you'll gain better insight into your baby's emerging interests and overall personality.

When playing with baby, get to the same level and demonstrate how things work or introduce a new activity, but don't force it if baby ignores you. Your baby will let you know if he's interested in knowing more.

Fun and Games

- Play "pick-up sticks" with Popsicle sticks, blocks, or other items.

- Sort toys with your baby by color or shape, or however your baby prefers.

- Explore new places together and let your baby point out items you describe ("See that pink flower?").

- Place stickers or colored dots on yourself or your baby, and ask for help ("Can you find the green dot? Where should we stick it?").

Play Groups

- Play groups can provide age-appropriate entertainment and allow parents to socialize.

- One-hour play dates are about all the fun a baby needs at this time.

- Don't overplan activities; babies may watch others but probably won't interact much.

- Babies might stack blocks or try "team" activities together for a short time.

- Make sure all bottles and similar items are labeled to avoid mix-ups.

SEPARATION ANXIETY

Stranger anxiety will activate baby's system of attachment, but the behavior is a healthy sign

Although stranger anxiety and fear of being separated from a loved one can be both endearing and frustrating for a parent, these are actually healthy signs of your baby's social and emotional attachment to loved ones.

Separation anxiety and stranger anxiety, while similar, are actually two different emotions. Separation anxiety is when

baby doesn't want to let you out of his or her sight for even a minute, and cries inconsolably when a favored loved one leaves. Babies may now begin to experience separation anxiety when being put down to sleep (or when they awaken in the middle of the night)—causing parents to feel all their bedtime habits have taken a backslide for a while. Babies

Helping Baby Adjust

- Help an anxious baby adjust to your leaving his sight by singing, humming, or talking out loud as you go from one room to another.

- Offer reassurance that you are nearby and won't leave.

- Determine ground rules for privacy, and establish those expectations early. If baby is not to come in your bedroom, don't make exceptions now.

- Set limits. You really don't need baby clinging to you while you use the bathroom, for example.

Meeting New People

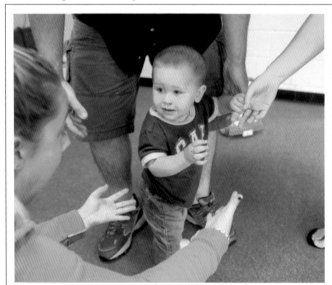

- If using a new babysitter or daycare, or introducing your infant to a stranger, it's reasonable to expect that your baby will protest.

- Realize that baby's cries are not a tactic, but reflect a genuine fear or feeling of anxiety or shyness.

- Don't try to force baby to socialize with a stranger. He'll interact once he's comfortable.

- Don't sneak away from baby; you may feel better but your baby may cling more next time you try to leave.

may want to stay physically close to you or a preferred loved one, especially when she needs comfort and is not easily consoled by other people.

Stranger anxiety occurs when your baby doesn't want others to hold him—or sometimes even to look at him. He can tell the difference between people he knows and loves and those he doesn't. Your baby has strong preferences for being around people he knows well, and has developed a fear that carries over to people he views as strangers. Since it is most likely you will someday need to leave your baby with someone he doesn't know, plan to allow ample time to get used to the person, and let your baby see that you are comfortable with the other person.

Baby may initially rebuff grandparents and others who visit your baby on an occasional basis when they try to hold him or interact, but their patience and understanding will be rewarded. Once baby adjusts to the presence of another person, feels comfortable and safe, and knows you feel the same way, he will be won over.

Separation from Baby

- In spite of your best efforts, your baby may still howl when you leave.

- Most babies adjust to the new situation and caregiver within a short period of time after you depart.

- Don't make matters worse for the caregiver by reappearing after you've left to "check" on baby, hanging out, or calling and wanting baby to hear your voice.

- Ask the caregiver to contact you if your baby is truly inconsolable after a reasonable length of time.

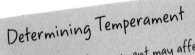

Determining Temperament

- Your baby's temperament may affect his actions.

- Babies with easy temperaments easily adapt to new situations, react calmly and mildly, and are typically positive.

- Babies with difficult temperaments may have intense reactions and irregular routines, and may have negative moods.

- Babies who are slow to warm up may withdraw, don't like to be pushed into situations, and are thought of as shy or sensitive.

221

LANGUAGE

Your baby is actively conversing, but knowing what baby is saying may be a challenge

Depending on your baby's overall temperament, you may be hearing babble and utterances of conversation from the moment your tyke awakens until it's time for bed. Baby babbling may become more frequent and is punctuated with short and fully inflected nonsensical sentences. The truth is, your baby is practicing for the verbal language that will start soon.

While your baby may now be able to utter words such as *dada, mama, bye-bye, more, milk,* or other short single-syllable or rhyming words, most babies don't yet have a handle on speech. But while you may not be able to understand his words, he can understand yours, and is now able to respond to many simple questions and commands. The understanding

Language Builders

- Playing "talking on the phone" or chatting with the family pet are ways to boost language development.

- As you read to your baby, begin to ask questions about the pictures that encourage a dialogue ("What animal is that? A cat? What does a cat say? Meow? Can you say 'meow'?").

- Ask for actions and reward with words. ("Where are your shoes? Can you bring me your shoes? Can you say 'shoes'?")

- Don't overcorrect emerging language.

Encouraging Talk

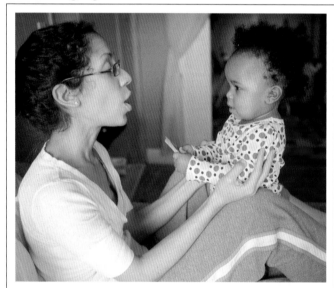

- Use a rich variety of words while talking. Baby may not understand everything you're saying, but will learn from your speech tones and patterns.

- Repeat things over and over. Repetition helps babies to remember and learn, so it's okay to sing that same song baby loves over and over . . . and over again.

- Echo what your baby says as words begin to evolve. That lets your baby know you are listening and that you understand.

- Narrate activities out loud.

may increase if you provide clues with hand gestures such as pointing, signing, facial expressions, and body language. Some babies may begin to answer you through words, gestures, or head-shaking.

You can help encourage early language by talking with your baby out loud and encouraging choices and simple responses ("Which socks do you want? Blue or red?").

If your baby is not babbling or saying any words by 12 months, talk with your pediatrician at your child's one-year checkup.

ZOOM

After babies have a vocabulary of about 50 single words, they may begin to string together two-word phrases with an action, such as "more milk" or "up please." While you may understand what your infant is trying to say, don't expect others to be able to do the same. Most babies at this age make the minimum sounds needed, as they don't yet have the mouth coordination for proper pronunciation.

Acquiring Language

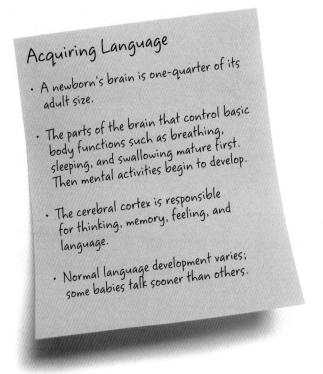

- A newborn's brain is one-quarter of its adult size.

- The parts of the brain that control basic body functions such as breathing, sleeping, and swallowing mature first. Then mental activities begin to develop.

- The cerebral cortex is responsible for thinking, memory, feeling, and language.

- Normal language development varies; some babies talk sooner than others.

A Growing Vocabulary

- In almost every language, first words are typically *dada* and *mama*.

- Next words are ones frequently repeated throughout the day, such as *bye-bye, milk* (often sounding like "ilk"), *hi, up, and me.*

- If your tot points to an object, animal, or person and labels it the same way consistently, it's a word even if it doesn't sound right!

SIGN LANGUAGE

ASL gestures may help bridge communication gap until baby is able to use words

American Sign Language (ASL) is sometimes taught to infants to enhance communication before babies can clearly express their needs and wants. The gap that exists between baby's desire to communicate and the ability to do so can sometimes result in frustration and even tantrums. That's because an infant's cognitive abilities are ahead of spoken language.

Proponents of teaching normally developing babies sign language say that being able to use simple gestures for common words—such as *mom, dad, milk, more, sleep, food, thank you,* and *play*—enhances an infant's self-esteem and overall happiness. Some believe that infant signing also increases a baby's intelligence, although this is sometimes debated.

Teaching Signing

- Always speak the word while using the sign so your baby doesn't rely on signing alone to communicate.

- Choose commonly used terms that bridge communication essentials until your baby is able to communicate verbally.

- Teach family members signs so that they will be able to communicate with and understand your baby's needs and wants.

- Don't overdo the number of words you are trying to teach your baby or family members.

Signing Basics

"milk"

- If you choose to teach signing to your baby, start by incorporating signs into daily situations.

- Signing is most effective when the word is signed and spoken, and appropriate facial expressions are used to help relay the meaning.

- Don't push signing on babies or show disappointment if your child doesn't always sign.

- Most parents already informally teach signing to their baby by showing how to wave bye-bye or blow a kiss. It's the same teaching concept.

Opponents to teaching infants sign language say that using nonverbal signs may cause a delay in a baby learning to speak, as basic communication is already being accomplished. But it appears that the majority of research has found otherwise. Another argument against teaching sign language is that unless siblings, friends, and caregivers all know the signs, early communication may become limited to only a particular parent rather than encouraging baby to make his desires known to others.

If you want to teach your baby simple signing before her language skills catch up to her cognitive abilities, a host of books, workshops, and instructional videos are available. Parents can also take classes with their infant in tow and learn signs together. If you use consistent signing gestures, your baby will first understand and then begin to use them back.

Signing is sometimes recommended in cases of language or developmental delays, such as with premature babies or infants with Down syndrome or hearing impairment. But it is also considered an effective way to begin communicating with babies with no risk factors.

No Show and Tell

- Signing is not a performance, and parents should not show off a baby's signing ability to others.

- Avoid making comparisons to other signing babies.

- The overall focus is to enhance communication, and while ASL is recommended for consistency, it is okay if you create some signs that work for your family.

- Signing should be taught as part of daily life and not as a lesson. Instructors recommend that parents "don't teach, just sign."

Is Signing Necessary?

- Normally developing babies do not have to be taught sign language in order to learn to communicate.

- Signing is a personal preference, and choosing not to sign won't make you a bad parent or cause communication difficulties with your infant.

- Some parents find that teaching their baby only key words helps bridge the communication gap.

- Others teach babies a full vocabulary of signing words.

FOR DADS
The end of the first year is the beginning of a world of baby firsts

You may be breathing a sigh of relief that you have made it through your baby's first year. It's over now, right? No more diaper changes, waking up at night, or trying to comfort a crying baby? Unfortunately, while many things do get easier, as your baby is likely now sleeping all night, has outgrown the weeks or months of colic, and is more easily comforted when he or she is upset, the years ahead will bring new challenges.

The toddler years also bring plenty of new things to get excited about, though, especially considering the fact that your baby will soon be taking her first steps and speaking her first words. Playtime gets more fun too, as your older infant

What Dad Can Do

- Although dad often gets the role of disciplinarian in the house, there's no reason that responsibility can't be shared.

- One good role for dad is to be a strong supporter for his partner when family and friends question the way she does things.

- Be quick to praise and slow to criticize your partner when it comes to childrearing. Remember that being a new parent is stressful.

- Dad can also encourage a strong relationship with baby's grandparents.

More Firsts for Baby

- In addition to fun stuff, like your baby's first steps and first words, you can expect her first temper tantrum too.

- Although babies can usually start whole milk at 12 months, be supportive if your partner wants to keep breastfeeding your toddler.

- Even babies who have been sleeping through the night will occasionally go through days or weeks when they start to wake up at night again.

- Watching the first reactions to new experiences is fun too.

or toddler participates and gets more involved in the games you play with her.

It isn't all fun and games, though. The appearance of your baby's first words will likely mean he will learn to say "No" soon. And his first steps probably mean he will start climbing and running, and no matter how careful you are, he will have his first fall too. Of course, all of these challenges are just part of the joy of fatherhood.

Feeding Your Older Baby

- Offer baby a wide variety of foods, including fruits and vegetables of different colors, to encourage healthy eating habits.

- Limit juice, sugary snacks, and "kid" foods, like hot dogs, pizza, and French fries.

- Avoid foods that are a choking hazard, such as popcorn, peanuts, chewing gum, and foods that can't be cut up into small, half-inch pieces.

Your Growing Family

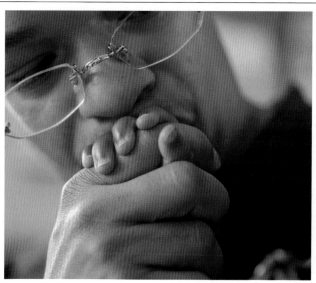

- As your baby gets older and begins to seem less like a baby, you may start to think about having another one.

- In addition to financial considerations, there are many factors to consider about the best spacing between siblings.

- Short spacing may mean two kids in diapers, dealing with jealousy, and two kids in day care.

- Longer spacing may mean siblings who don't share the same interests and parents who have to get used to all of the baby stuff again.

RESOURCES

A wealth of information about your baby's health, essential care, breastfeeding, nutrition, and general parenting can be found on the Internet. By no means is this an exhaustive list. Some Web sites provide basic information to help guide you throughout baby's first year, while others are dedicated to specific issues or safety. Keep in mind that child-rearing approaches may vary. Ultimately, it is up to parents, along with advice from their chosen pediatrician, to determine how best to raise their baby over the course of this first important and memorable year.

Your New Baby

About Twins and Multiples http://multiples.about.com
American Academy of Pediatrics www.aap.org
APGAR Scoring www.childbirth.org/articles/apgar.html
Babyzone www.babyzone.com
Circumcision Resource Center www.circumcision.org
Mayo Clinic www.mayoclinic.com
Moms of Multiples www.momsofmultiples.org
Preemies www.preemies.org

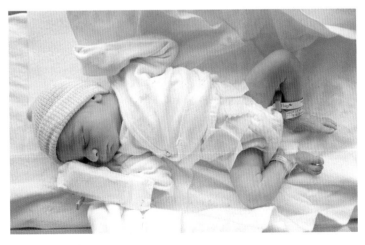

Umbilical Cord Blood Banking www.umbilicalbloodbanking.com
WebMD www.webmd.com

Baby Comes Home

AAP Car Safety Seat Guidelines
   www.aap.org/family/carseatguide.htm
American SIDS Institute www.sids.org
Baby Center www.babycenter.com
Dr. Greene www.drgreene.com
National Sudden and Unexpected Infant/Child Death Center
   www.sidscenter.org
Juvenile Products Manufacturers Association www.jpma.org
Parenting Preemies www.parentingpreemies.com
Seat Check www.seatcheck.org

Newborn: Milestones

About Babies and Toddlers http://babyparenting.about.com
About Pediatrics http://pediatrics.about.com
Adopting a Child with Special Needs
   www.special-needs.adoption.com
About Special Needs Children http://specialchildren.about.com
FirstAidWeb www.firstaidweb.com
Kids Health www.kidshealth.org
Pediatric GERD www.gerd.cdhnf.org
Special Needs Answers www.specialneedsanswers.com
U.S. Consumer Product Safety Commission www.cpsc.gov

Newborn: Care

Babies 'R' Us www.babiesrus.com
BabyCenter www.babycenter.com
Children's Digestive Health and Nutrition Foundation
   www.cdhnf.org
Cloth Diaper News www.clothdiapernews.com

Keepkidshealthy www.keepkidshealthy.com
Kids Health www.kidshealth.org
National Institute of Child Health and Human Development
   www.nichd.nih.gov/
One Step Ahead www.onestepahead.com
Wonder Time www.wondertime.go.com

Newborn: Feeding

About Breastfeeding http://breastfeeding.about.com
Adoption.com www.breast-feeding.adoption.com
American Heart Association www.americanheart.org
AskDr.Sears www.askdrsears.com/
Bisphenol-A www.bisphenol-a.org
Breastfeeding.com www.breastfeeding.com
Kids Health www.kidshealth.org
La Leche League International www.llli.org
March of Dimes
   www.marchofdimes.com/pnhec/28699_19954.asp
U.S. Food and Drug Administration www.fda.gov

Newborn: Dads

About Fatherhood http://fatherhood.about.com
About Pregnancy and Childbirth http://pregnancy.about.com
About Stay-at-Home Dads http://stayathomedads.about.com
Brand New Dad www.brandnewdad.com
iparenting www.dadstoday.com
Parents.com www.parents.com
Parenting.com www.parenting.com
The Brand New Dad www.thebrandnewdad.com

Newborn: My World

Babies Online www.babiesonline.com
Baby Development News www.babydevelopmentnews.com
Baby Weekly www.parentingweekly.com
Baby.com www.baby.com
Discovery Health www.health.discovery.com
iParenting www.babiestoday.com
iVillage www.parenting.ivillage.com
March of Dimes www.marchofdimes.com
Newborn Channel www.newborn.com
Zero to Three www.zerotothree.org

3–6 Months: Milestones

About Pediatrics http://pediatrics.about.com
Childproofing Our Communities www.childproofing.org
Childproofing Products www.childproofingproducts.com
DrGreene www.drgreene.com
Family Education www.familyeducation.com
Kids Health www.kidshealth.org
Mayo Clinic www.mayoclinic.com
Tender Baby Care www.tenderbabycare.com
U.S. Consumer Product Safety Commission www.cpsc.gov

3–6 Months: Care

American Dental Association www.ada.org
American Dental Hygienists' Association www.adha.org
Baby Care Advice www.babycareadvice.com
BabyCenter www.babycenter.com
Babyzone www.babyzone.com
Discovery Health www.health.discovery.com
Keepkidshealthy www.keepkidshealthy.com
Pediatrics www.pediatrics.com
Robyn's Nest www.robynsnest.com
The Baby Channel www.babychanneltv.com
WebMD www.webmd.com
Wondertime www.wondertime.go.com

3–6 Months: Feeding

About Baby Parenting http://babyparenting.about.com
About Kids Health www.aboutkidshealth.ca
About Nutrition http://nutrition.about.com
Breastfeeding www.breastfeeding.com
Global Pediatrics www.globalpediatrics.com
La Leche League International www.llli.org
ParentTime www.parenttime.com
SheKnows Pregnancy and Baby www.pregnancyandbaby.com

3–6 Months: Dads

American Academy of Pediatrics www.aap.org
About Child Care http://childcare.about.com
About Stay-at-Home Dads http://stayathomedads.about.com
Baby Development News www.babydevelopmentnews.com
Brand New Dad www.brandnewdad.com
iparenting www.dadstoday.com

Newborn Channel www.newborn.com
Tender Baby Care www.tenderbabycare.com/

6–9 Months: Milestones

About Pediatrics http://pediatrics.about.com
Child Proofing Our Communities www.childproofing.org
Childproofing Products www.childproofingproducts.com/
How Kids Develop www.howkidsdevelop.com
Kids Health www.kidshealth.org
Mamasource www.mamasource.com/advice/childproofing
MedicineNet www.medicinenet.com
Mommy Club www.mommyclub.ca

6–9 Months: Care

About Baby Parenting http://babyparenting.about.com
Baby Zone www.babyzone.com
Baby Center www.babycenter.com
Baby Earth www.babyearth.com
Discovery Health www.health.discovery.com

Family Parenting www.family.go.com
Just Multiples www.justmultiples.com
Keepkidshealthy www.keepkidshealthy.com
The Baby Channel www.babychanneltv.com
WebMD www.webmd.com
Wondertime www.wondertime.go.com

6–9 Months: Feeding

Act Against Allergy www.actagainstallergy.com
Allergies, Intolerances, Food www.babyandkidallergies.com
Carolina Pediatric Dysphagia www.feeding.com
Food Allergy Help www.helpfoodallergy.com
Keepkidshealthy www.keepkidshealthy.com
My Healthy Baby www.mybetterbabyfood.com
She Knows Pregnancy and Baby www.pregnancyandbaby.com
Wholesome Baby Food www.wholesomebabyfood.com

6–9 Months: My World

About Baby Products http://babyproducts.about.com
About Child Care http://childcare.about.com
About Stay-at-Home Dads http://stayathomedads.about.com
Baby Care Help www.babycarehelp.com
Baby Development News www.babydevelopmentnews.com
Baby Zone www.babyzone.com
Brand New Dad www.brandnewdad.com
It's a Mom's World www.itsamomsworld.com
Dads Today www.dadstoday.com
Tender Baby Care www.tenderbabycare.com/

9–12 Months: Milestones

American Academy of Pediatrics www.aap.org
About Pediatrics http://pediatrics.about.com
Childproofing Products www.childproofingproducts.com
Kids Health www.kidshealth.org
Mamasource www.mamasource.com/advice/childproofing
Mommy Club www.mommyclub.ca
Baby Medical Questions and Answers
   www.baby-medical-questions-and-answers.com

9–12 Months: Care

BabyCenter www.babycenter.com
Baby Zone www.babyzone.com
Discovery Health www.health.discovery.com
Family Parenting www.family.go.com
iParenting www.babiestoday.com
Keepkidshealthy www.keepkidshealthy.com
The Baby Channel www.babychanneltv.com
WebMD www.webmd.com
Wondertime www.wondertime.go.com

9–12 Months: Feeding

A Place of Our Own www.aplaceofourown.org
Act Against Allergy www.actagainstallergy.com
Allergies, Intolerances, Food www.babyandkidallergies.com
Baby Care Help www.babycarehelp.com
Just for Multiples www.justmultiples.com
La Leche League International www.llli.org
My Healthy Baby www.mybetterbabyfood.com
She Knows Pregnancy and Baby www.pregnancyandbaby.com

9–12 Months: My World

About Baby Products http://babyproducts.about.com
About Kids Health www.aboutkidshealth.ca
About Stay-at-Home Dads http://stayathomedads.about.com
Brand New Dad www.brandnewdad.com
Father's First Year www.fathersfirstyear.com
Dads Today www.dadstoday.com
It's a Mom's World www.itsamomsworld.com
Mayo Clinic www.mayoclinic.com
Parentpedia www.family.go.com/parentpedia
Twinslist www.twinslist.org
TwinsTalk www.twinstalk.com

GLOSSARY

APGAR Scoring
APGAR stands for activity, pulse, grimace (reflex irritability), appearance, and respiration. A score is given for each sign, typically at one minute and then again at five minutes, after birth. A low score in no way means that your newborn won't become a healthy infant.

ASL
ASL is an acronym for American Sign Language, which is the dominant sign language of the deaf community in the United States. It is also the language style most generally recommended for use in signing with babies for consistency purposes.

Bilirubin
Bilirubin is excreted in bile. It is responsible for the yellow coloring of bruises and for baby's yellowish skin in the case of jaundice.

Blocked Tear Ducts
Blocked tear ducts are fairly common in infants, and may result in excessive tearing or intermittent crusting. In the case of an infection, the eyelid may become red and swollen and mucus may be present. In most cases, the blockage will open on its own, but you should consult with your pediatrician.

BPA
The chemical bisphenol A is commonly used in the making of plastic water and baby bottles as well as food and beverage can linings. Its hazard is debated, but many infant products are now being made without the chemical and have a label that says BPA-FREE.

Circumcision
Circumcision is the removal of the foreskin, which is the skin that covers the tip of the penis. There are medical benefits and risks to circumcision.

Cognitive Development
Cognitive development relates to thinking or thought processes and how babies learn and solve problems.

Conjunctivitis
Conjunctivitis, commonly called *pinkeye,* is a common eye infection. It can either be bacterial or viral in nature and is highly contagious. See your pediatrician if you suspect your infant has conjunctivitis, as treatment may be necessary.

Cradle Cap
Cradle cap is common and is essentially an extra layer of crusty skin that appears as patchy or red scales. It is often prominent around the ears or the eyebrows and may appear cracked or greasy, and it may even weep. Treatment is generally not needed except in extreme cases or if baby has itching or discomfort. Frequent gentle shampooing or treating with baby oil and then rubbing off can help.

Croup
Croup is a common respiratory problem characterized by a harsh, barking cough.

Developmental Hip Dysplasia

This is a childhood condition caused by abnormal development of the hip joint. Your baby will be checked for normal hip development at well-child visits.

Developmental Milestones

This is a term commonly used to indicate certain skills that many babies will achieve within a given timeframe, such as smiling, holding up the head, or crawling. While ranges are typically listed for many stages of development, parents need to keep in mind that all babies develop at their own pace. Red flags may also be noted to help parents to determine whether additional testing or medical evaluations may be recommended.

Emotional Development

Babies will quickly expand their emotions from basics of wanting comfort or love, being hungry, or feeling tired to learning fear, sadness, happiness, and frustration over the course of the first 12 months of life.

Fifth Disease

Fifth disease is a common childhood viral infection that causes a distinctive rash, often referred to as "slapped cheeks." Following the appearance of a rash on their cheeks, babies get a red or pink lace-like rash on their arms, legs, trunk, and buttocks. The rash may recur especially when baby becomes overheated.

Fine Motor Skills

Fine motor skills use small muscles for grasping and basic hand-eye coordination such as reaching for and holding an object.

Flu

The flu is a contagious disease that can cause symptoms such as high fever, sore throat, coughing, extreme tiredness, runny or stuffy nose, and even nausea and diarrhea in children. It spreads easily from person to person. Yearly flu vaccinations should begin once a baby is at least six months of age and as soon as vaccine is available (typically around October and throughout the flu season, which extends into December, January and beyond).

Fluoride

Fluoride is a naturally occurring mineral that is present in all water, but is often removed from bottled water. It is an effective and safe way to prevent tooth decay. Fluoride can be best obtained by drinking fluoridated water (such as what may be used to mix infant formula). Babies may also benefit from supplements. Always check with your pediatrician first before giving an infant any type of supplement or vitamin.

Fontanels

Fontanels are soft spots found on your newborn's skull where skull bones have not yet fused. There are six fontanels on your newborn's skull, but only two are evident. The larger, diamond-shaped fontanel is on the top front of the head while the smaller fontanel is at the base of the skull.

Formula

Commercially prepared infant formula is regulated by the Food and Drug Administration and provides appropriate nutrition for babies whose mothers opt not to breastfeed.

GERD

GERD is an acronym for gastroesophageal reflux disease, a condition in which stomach acid or even bile flows back into the esophagus and causes symptoms such as poor weight gain, choking, or pain.

Gross Motor Skills

Gross motor skills involve the large muscles that baby will need to develop in order to sit, roll, crawl, and eventually walk.

Heimlich Maneuver

The Heimlich maneuver is a series of under-the-diaphragm abdominal thrusts. They're recommended for helping a person who's choking on a foreign object (foreign-body airway obstruction) but should not be performed on infants younger than one year of age.

Humidifier

A room humidifier may help to alleviate symptoms of a cold or allergy. A humidifier is an electric device that releases a cool mist into the air. It is considered safer than a vaporizer, which heats and then releases warm mist in the air, because it eliminates the risk of being scalded by heated water.

Infant Attachment

This generally describes a bond between an infant and primary caregiver. A healthy attachment is formed within the context of a family and allows an infant to feel secure and loved.

Jaundice

Jaundice is a condition that makes a newborn's skin and the white part of the eyes look yellow. It occurs when there is too much bilirubin in the baby's blood. Bilirubin is a substance that is made when the body breaks down old red blood cells. It usually gets better or goes away on its own within a week or two without causing problems, but a newborn who looks yellowish should be checked by a doctor.

Language Development

This skill refers to a baby's ability to understand and use language. Babies will understand many more words and phrases than they will be able to say during their first year.

Meconium

Meconium is the earliest stools of an infant. It is a dark greenish-black, thick, sticky substance and is comprised of materials ingested during the time an infant spent in utero.

Milia

Milia is common to newborns and appears as tiny white bumps or small cysts usually found around the nose and eyelids. No treatment is needed.

Pincer Grasp

This grasp uses the thumb and index finger. Baby usually masters this grasp between 7 and 10 months of age.

Positional Plagiocephaly

This is a disorder in which the back or side of an infant's head is flattened. It most often occurs as the result of babies spending a lot of time on their backs or in a position where their head is against a flat surface (such as a stroller or swing). A flattened or asymmetrical head shape can usually be corrected easily with different positioning, a home exercise program, or by having the baby wear a custom-fitted helmet or head band.

Reflux

Gastroesophageal reflux in babies is when stomach acids are regurgitated into the esophagus. Check with your doctor if your infant has painful blasts of crying, writhes as if in pain, is fussy, and spits up frequently, as these could be symptoms of a more serious ailment.

Rooting

Newborns "root" as a way to find the breast. Rooting is triggered when your newborn's cheek is touched or stroked alongside her mouth. She will then turn her head and open her mouth toward the touched side in search of something to suck.

Roseola

This is a contagious viral illness in young children, most commonly affecting those between the ages of six months and two years. It is often marked by several days of high fever and swollen lymph nodes in the neck, with a distinctive rash appearing just as the fever breaks. The red rash may last from a few hours to a few days.

Rotavirus

Rotavirus is a common cause of viral gastroenteritis in babies, causing vomiting, diarrhea, and fever. Babies can now receive a rotavirus vaccine to help decrease the likelihood of contracting the virus.

RSV

Respiratory syncytial virus (RSV) may cause just a cold in older children, but can affect an infant's lungs, causing symptoms of bronchiolitis or viral pneumonia.

Separation Anxiety

Toward the end of their first year, many babies develop a strong attachment toward a particular parent or loved one and feel tremendous anxiety or even fear when apart from the person. This is a perfectly normal stage of development.

SIDS

Sudden infant death syndrome (SIDS), for which risk begins at about one month of age, is rare. The risk factors increase until a baby is about three months of age. Laying a baby down to sleep on his back greatly reduces the chance of SIDS.

Social Development

This child development skill relates to a baby's ability to interact with others, such as by smiling, waving, or reaching out to a loved one.

Startle (Moro) Reflex

This primitive reflex occurs in newborns. You can see it when a baby arches her back, flings out her arms, and throws back her head, and then pulls her arms and legs in close and cries. The reflex is usually in response to a loud noise, a sudden change in position or temperature, or movement.

Stranger Anxiety

This anxiety occurs in infants who suddenly become shy or withdrawn around people they do not know. Once they have a chance to feel comfortable around the person, the anxiety will usually disappear.

Swaddling

Swaddling a baby by wrapping him up tightly in a blanket is an age-old practice. A baby properly wrapped in a blanket typically feels warm and secure, and the wrap can help prevent a baby from throwing his arms up and startling himself.

Symbiosis

The word *symbiosis* refers to interdependence or mutual cooperation, as in a parent-child relationship.

Tongue Extrusion Reflex

An infant's thrusting of the tongue assists feeding from the breast or bottle. If solid foods are offered while the reflex is still active it may seem like your baby is pushing the food out of her mouth with her tongue. The reflex may mean your baby is not yet ready for solid foods.

Tummy Time

This is the practice of putting baby on her tummy for short periods of time while awake. Since babies are laid to sleep on their backs, they may begin to prefer lying on their backs if they aren't placed on their tummies. Tummy time can encourage babies to learn to roll over, sit up, lift their heads, and crawl.

Vaporizer
See *Humidifier.*

Weaning
Weaning is when babies make the transition from breast milk to other sources of nourishment.

Whooping Cough
Pertussis (whooping cough) is a serious infection that can be avoided with a vaccine, yet continues to be a problem. While many kids with whooping cough have coughing spells followed by a "whooping" sound, not all kids have the distinctive cough. Antibiotics may be given, but babies may need to be hospitalized.

INDEX

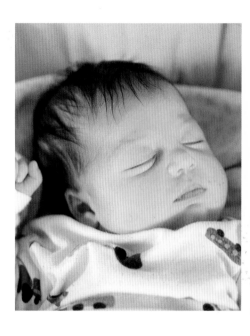

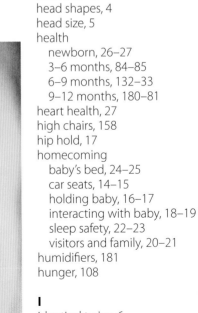

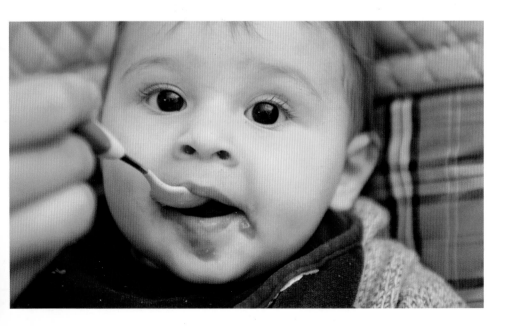

ACKNOWLEDGMENTS

Robin: Any mom or dad can tell you that the act of having children (by birth or adoption) doesn't make you a great parent. It takes lots of love, hands-on care, sleepless nights, adjustments to your routine, and constant trial and error. I remember watching my first diapering job literally fall off my newborn . . . but I sure got it right after a few more attempts! In spite of my initial inexperience and nervousness, my children have thrived through the nurturing and support of family and friends.

Looking back, I want to acknowledge the contributions of my children's grandparents, as well as my friends and co-workers, who were always present to say, "Good job!" My heartfelt thanks and appreciation also go to early educators who have positively touched the lives of my family, and provided me with sound advice and support from the arrival of my firstborn and continuing today. Child-care providers everywhere deserve a hug for their wisdom and love of children. Their savvy insights from their vast experiences are reflected in many of the tips and suggestions found in this book.

Finally, I would like to thank my agent, Barb Doyen, for her belief in me and my writing; Vince Iannelli for his assistance; Susana Bates for her astounding photographs that have truly captured the beauty and magic of babies; and Globe's editors, Imee and Maureen, for their hard work and vision in making this book happen.

Susana: I would like to thank Jon Naso, without whom this project would not have happened for me. Also, my gratitude to editor-in-chief Maureen Graney and author Robin McClure. Thank you to Odalys Montpeirous and the doctors, nurses and staff at Queens Hospital Center; to Dorothy Wagner and the staff at Christ the King Community Day Care/Pre-school; and to Lora Heller at Baby Fingers LLC. I would also like to thank the families of the beautiful babies, especially those who invited me into their homes. The main babies photographed are: Charlotte, Colin, and Lily Moonlight (newborns); Keerat, Lucas, and Zoey (3–6 months); Max (6–9 months); and Amaris, Madison, and Morgan (9–12 months). Other babies included in the book are newborns Alina, Cormac, Declan, Denslea, Densley, Jordan, Kevin, Liam, Raphael, Riley, Sebastian, and Tristen. The Snugglies II group, some of whom did not appear in the book, includes AJ, Allen, Brianna, Conn, Kayla, Mila, Reiner, Ronan, Thomas, and Veronica. Ruby Sunrise, Lily Moonlight's older sister, and Luna were also featured.

Finally I would like to thank Warren, Thoth, Theresa, Julia, and Harpreet for their input.